Using Quality Benchmarks for Assessing and Developing Undergraduate Programs

Dana S. Dunn

Maureen A. McCarthy

Suzanne C. Baker

Jane S. Halonen

Published by Jossey-Bass
A Wiley Imprint
989 Market Street, San Francisco, CA 94103-1741—www.josseybass.com

Jossey-Bass books and products are available through most bookstores. To contact Jossey-Bass directly call our Customer Care Department within the U.S. at 800-956-7739, outside the U.S. at 317-572-3986, or fax 317-572-4002.

Jossey-Bass also publishes its books in a variety of electronic formats. Some content that appears in print may not be available in electronic books.

Library of Congress Cataloging-in-Publication Data
Using quality benchmarks for assessing and developing undergraduate programs /
Dana S. Dunn . . . [et al.].
p. cm.
Includes bibliographical references and index.
ISBN 978-0-470-40556-7 (hardback)
978-0-470-89245-9 (ebk)
978-0-4708-9246-6 (ebk)
978-0-4708-9247-3 (ebk)
1. Education, Higher–Evaluation. 2. Educational tests and measurements. I. Dunn, Dana.
LB2331.62.U85 2011
378.1'662–dc22 2010034707

Printed in the United States of America
FIRST EDITION
HB Printing 10 9 8 7 6 5 4 3 2 1

The Jossey-Bass Higher and Adult Education Series

Contents

For Virginia Andreoli Mathie and Rob McEntarffer,
old friends who helped us begin our work

Foreword

Peggy Maki

Surrounded by and bombarded with demands to demonstrate accountability, institutional effectiveness, fulfillment of quality indicators, and student achievement levels, colleges and universities rhythmically churn out form after form, day after day. Each day brings the possibility of a new form or a proposed new way of demonstrating accountability, as external or internal decision-making bodies mull over what they "really think" they want. Never before in the history of higher education have institutions been under so many microscopes at one time. Yet with all the documents and forms that institutions fill out, which ones really get at what matters?

Along come Dunn, McCarthy, Baker, and Halonen—four seasoned psychology educators whose combined professional experiences as faculty, administrators, program reviewers, and contributors to national education organizations have positioned them to cut to the chase to identify a model for undergraduate program review. These four authors identify eight domains that define quality undergraduate academic programs and departments in the arts, humanities, social sciences, and natural sciences:

- Program climate
- Assessment, accountability, and accreditation issues
- Student learning outcomes
- Student development
- Curriculum
- Faculty characteristics
- Program resources
- Administrative support

These domains immediately resonate with faculty and administrators; that is, they reflect the contemporary professional context within which faculty and administrators work and the issues that define their lives, such as the current focus on assessing student learning.

Laying out a rationale for a new model that assesses the quality of undergraduate programs and departments—our students' academic homes—the authors identify (1) benchmarks for programs and departments to assess themselves formatively, represented in performance scales; (2) guidelines for how to apply these scales; and (3) representative disciplinary case studies that demonstrate how to apply performance scales. By design and example, then, readers immediately understand the usefulness and relevance of the authors' proposed framework, not only for periodic program review but also for formative review as a chronological way to identify patterns of strength and weakness in departments or programs. That is, programs and departments can routinely explore for themselves across the eight domains and benchmarks to guide behaviors and decision making and to judge how well these behaviors, decisions, and practices are improving the quality of a program or department.

An irresistibly authentic model for periodic program review as well as ongoing review aimed at taking stock of how well a program or department is working, *Using Quality Benchmarks for Assessing and Developing Undergraduate Programs* represents a refreshing break from the world that educators typically inhabit in traditional program review. Provosts, deans, chairs, and faculty will find that this new model for program review grounds educators in what matters. The domains and benchmarking scales provide programs and departments with essential information and data that are unquestionably relevant to educational practices and the decisions that surround those practices.

PREFACE

Higher education is slow to change, but change it must. Social, economic, and accountability pressures are challenging college faculty members to rethink how they teach their courses; advise students; contribute to the intellectual lives of their departments or programs, as well as wider institutions; and advance the interests and knowledge of their disciplines. Academic leaders—department or area chairs, deans, provosts, even presidents—want the programs at their institutions to succeed by attracting, retaining, and educating students who will become supportive alumni and alumnae whose futures reflect well on their alma mater. And, of course, what about the students themselves—the key constituents of any institution—as well as their families? After decades in which energy has been largely focused elsewhere, undergraduate education is recognized as a core issue of concern. Teaching matters. How well students learn is as important as what they learn. The assessment movement is no longer a nascent concern or one that is going to disappear anytime soon.

With the energy and push of all these educational trends, we wrote this book to argue for quality benchmarks—selected performance criteria—for promoting how best to deliver a meaningful educational experience to undergraduate students in the arts, humanities, social sciences, and natural sciences. Such benchmarks provide a set of standard reference points for internal self-studies and external reviews. Benchmarks have been used in higher education as a way to improve the climate for learning within departments. The use of benchmarks is not only for assessing student learning; our goal is actually a more holistic one. We are interested in helping department faculty and their administrators think seriously about evaluating program quality broadly. By broadly, we mean examining student learning, creating meaningful faculty scholarship, promoting and rewarding quality teaching, and connecting vibrantly to the community where a college or university resides.

Our framework explores the attributes of undergraduate programs by focusing on educationally related activities in eight domains: *program climate*; *assessment, accountability*, and *accreditation issues*; *student learning outcomes*; *student development*; *curriculum*; *faculty characteristics*; *program resources*; and *administrative support*. We conceptualize a continuum of performance for each attribute in each of the domains to characterize *underdeveloped, developing, effective*, and *distinguished* achievement for undergraduate programs. Our goal is to encourage individual departments at various types of institutions to evaluate what they currently do formatively while identifying areas for refinement or future growth. We believe that our recommended benchmarks can improve program quality, encourage more effective program reviews, and help optimally functioning programs compete more successfully for resources as well as protect their resources in economically challenging times based on their distinguished achievements.

Our experiences as program reviewers, faculty members, and administrators inform us that departments, department heads, and deans all want reasonable, valid, and professionally respectable methods for evaluating the performance of undergraduate programs. We believe our developmental framework will satisfy all parties because we emphasize formative assessment (meaning that evaluation should be used to identify areas of existing quality and those for future growth—not for summative or punitive reasons, such as resource cuts, reduction in faculty lines, or the like). Furthermore, we designed our framework to help programs identify and tout what they already do well even in situations of seriously constrained resources. Finally, using performance benchmarks to identify areas of program strength can, in turn, be used to recruit and retain students, to seek funding via grants or alumni support, and to enhance the perceived rating of an institution. When benchmarks reveal that a program or areas within it are underdeveloped or developing, faculty and administrators can then plan for where they can best place subsequent efforts and resources to improve a program's performance and ability to serve students.

OUR AUDIENCE AND OUR GOAL FOR THIS BOOK

The primary audience for this book is department chairs and program heads (especially new ones) representing disciplines in the arts, natural sciences, humanities, and social sciences, as well as faculty members and administrators (chiefly deans and provosts) who want a convenient collection of formative tools for examining the quality of their programs and the educational experiences of undergraduates in those programs. This book can help leaders in college and university communities evaluate a current undergraduate program by identifying areas of existing strength (including distinguished qualities) and areas for growth and improvement. Thus this book is ideal for internal program reviews. Our work provides a vehicle for discussion within programs about where their strengths lie and which areas they would like to highlight for future growth and development. At the same time, the work will help external evaluators, including external review committees, effectively assess departments and programs during site visits.

We wrote this book's chapters with flexibility in mind. Although all institutions of higher education have some common features, each also has unique or local qualities. We crafted each chapter so that readers can shape general principles to fit their own circumstances, local conditions, and institutional folkways. We anticipate that some readers will be interested in our book so that they can do a targeted or focused review (e.g., a critical examination of student learning outcomes or the curriculum). Thus, one or two chapters will draw their attention. Other readers will want to evaluate an entire program, which means they will be drawing on the content of all the chapters in the book.

Each chapter concludes with a set of "guiding questions" designed to help readers think about the current strengths and challenges faced by an existing program. Whether a review is internal (a self-study) or external (routine scheduled review), these questions will be written to encourage reflective and constructive discussion at the program or department level.

OUR EXPERIENCE AND BACKGROUNDS

We four have extensive experience serving as external reviewers for psychology programs. Currently, Halonen is a dean of arts and sciences, McCarthy has served in the Education Directorate of the American Psychological Association, Dunn is the director of his college's general education curriculum, Dunn and Halonen have served as department chairs on repeated occasions, and Baker is an assistant head of a large department. All of us have been active in the assessment movement in our discipline; this is not the first book we have produced related to the topic (see Dunn, Mehrotra, & Halonen, 2004). Two of us (Baker and Halonen) have been active participants in Project Kaleidoscope, a national organization that explores curriculum reform in the sciences. Finally, all four of us are active members of the Society for the Teaching of Psychology (STP), the national organization devoted to advancing the teaching and learning of the discipline's knowledge base, and serve as regular speakers at national, international, and regional conferences. Three of us (Dunn, Halonen, and McCarthy) have served as president of STP.

We look forward to hearing reactions from users of our book—college and university leaders at all levels who care deeply about their institutions and higher education more generally. We believe that academic program review can be an exciting opportunity for all parties concerned. We look forward to learning about your experiences using quality benchmarks to improve the teaching and learning of your students.

ACKNOWLEDGMENTS

This book represents the completion of a long-harbored desire to work with Jossey-Bass, a publisher without peer in the study of trends in higher education. We were delighted to meet and work with our editor, David Brightman, on this project. We thank our good friend and editor, Chris Cardone, for introducing us to David. We owe a special debt of gratitude to our frequent coauthor and close friend, Bill Hill, who was unable to join us on this project. We believe he is still a contributor to the final result, as many of our ideas developed through our many discussions with him on matters of teaching, learning, assessment, and administrative issues. Finally, we thank Virginia Andreoli Mathie and Rob McEntarffer. Ten years ago, Ginnie's leadership on the Psychology Partnerships Project (P3) introduced us to one another; we cannot imagine what work we would each be doing if our own partnership had not resulted from that fateful week in June 1999. Happily, Rob accepted the leadership of the "Assessment All-Stars," and he helped us forge a scholarly bond that has been our scholarly wellspring for over a decade.

We are also grateful to the American Psychological Association (APA), which published our first ideas on quality benchmarks, and to the Society for the Teaching of Psychology (STP; APA Division 2), which has been a willing crucible for much of what we discuss in this book. Deans Gordon Weil and Carol Traupman-Carr of Moravian College provided helpful comments on an early draft of Chapter Seven.

We invited guest scholars to assist us with specific chapters. We thank Claudia Stanny, George Ellenberg, Eman El-Sheikh, and Greg Lanier from the University of West Florida for their contributions to this work. They particularly helped us move beyond our home discipline of psychology to see the implications of our work for other fields of study.

Dana is grateful to his wife, Sarah, and to his children, Jake and Hannah, who are unfailingly supportive of his writing and research efforts. He is also grateful to Moravian College, as portions of this work were written during Dana's sabbatical leave in spring 2009. He feels lucky to work with his talented teacher-scholar coauthors, Suzie, Maureen, and Jane.

Maureen is grateful to Brenda Karns and her family for their support of her writing efforts. She is particularly thankful to her parents, Dennis and MaryAnn McCarthy, for providing her with the foundation that made this book possible. She would also like to thank the American Psychological Association for providing the support for the genesis of this project.

Suzie would like to thank Marshall Graham for his unwavering encouragement, patience, and good humor as she spends hours staring at a computer screen working on various projects. She would also like to thank her wonderful colleagues in the Department of Psychology at James Madison University.

When she thinks about the characteristics of a distinguished program, she thinks of them.

Jane feels blessed to have had a teaching career that has involved so many assessment-friendly colleagues at University of West Florida, James Madison University, and Alverno College, and a devoted husband, Brian, who, with predictable good nature, tolerates partner deprivation so she can get her projects across the finish line.

We hope readers find this book to be helpful as they think about ways to assess, evaluate, and subsequently improve undergraduate education in their departments and programs. We welcome comments and suggestions for future editions of this work.

About the Authors

Dana S. Dunn is currently professor of psychology and director of the Learning in Common Curriculum at Moravian College in Bethlehem, Pennsylvania. He has chaired Moravian's psychology department as well as served as acting chair of its philosophy department. Dunn is the author or editor of eleven books and over one hundred articles, chapters, and book reviews. He frequently speaks on assessment matters, issues facing higher education, and psychological topics at professional conferences.

Maureen A. McCarthy is professor of psychology at Kennesaw State University. She formerly served as the Associate Executive Director of the Office of Precollege and Undergraduate Programs for the American Psychological Association. While serving at the American Psychological Association, McCarthy initiated efforts to identify profiles of undergraduate psychology programs and she served as the APA liaison for the American Council on Education project to Internationalize the Disciplines. McCarthy is the coauthor of numerous articles, and regularly speaks on the topics of assessment, pedagogy, and ethics in undergraduate psychology.

Suzanne C. Baker is professor of psychology at James Madison University in Harrisonburg, VA, where she also currently serves as assistant department head in psychology. Baker is the author of numerous articles and book chapters on topics related to teaching and curriculum. She frequently speaks at conferences on topics such as curriculum development in psychology, engaging undergraduate students in research, and the use of technology in teaching. She teaches a wide range of courses, including introductory psychology, animal behavior, and cyberpsychology.

Jane S. Halonen is professor of psychology and the dean of the College of Arts and Sciences at the University of West Florida in Pensacola, FL. She formerly served as the director of the School of Psychology at James Madison University and the chair of the behavioral sciences division and coordinator of psychology at Alverno College. Halonen has authored and collaborated on textbooks as well as articles and books on faculty development and curriculum. Halonen's work has been instrumental to benchmarking efforts in various curriculum initiatives of the American Psychological Association, which also honored her with the American Psychological Foundation Distinguished Teaching Award in 2000.

Using Quality Benchmarks for Assessing and Developing Undergraduate Programs

Chapter One

The Need for Quality Benchmarks in Undergraduate Programs

The hour for recognizing the singular importance of undergraduate education is here at last. Department chairs, faculty at all ranks, deans and provosts, and even college and university presidents finally realize that educating undergraduates is arguably the most important mission of higher education today. For those of us who have watched the focus shift from graduate and post-baccalaureate professional education to the education of traditional and nontraditional four-year students, the change is both powerful and palpable. Teaching undergraduates well is now a dominant focus in higher education. We are not suggesting that educators and administrators should not attend to the important and pressing concerns of graduate education; rather, we believe that the best support graduate and professional schools can receive is to send them well-prepared students.

As a result of the new emphasis on undergraduate education, colleges and universities aspire to provide the best educational experience for student majors that their resources will permit. Their common goal is to assess what and how well students have learned during their time at the institution. The issues involved, similar to the work itself, are challenging. Where should institutional self-reflection about undergraduate learning begin? Within the administration? Among the collective faculty? Or should alumni be tapped for their feedback on how their time at the institution shaped their futures? What about the opinions of other stakeholders, including the students themselves?

When institutions turn their focus to undergraduate education, we argue that the place to begin this important work is at the departmental or program level—the unit of analysis that has the most day-to-day as well as discipline-based impact on student learning. Assessment in undergraduate education is often aimed at general education; that is, the distribution requirements of liberal arts offerings that all students in a given college or university must complete. Evaluating student learning in general education courses is certainly important, but we believe that the breadth and depth of discipline-based knowledge acquired within department-based majors is the more appropriate forum to capture assessment activities that reflect the true accomplishments of the baccalaureate program. How well are chemistry majors learning foundational materials in basic and intermediate courses? Does this foundational material later help these student majors display the necessary critical thinking skills in the advanced courses in the major? As they near the end of their major courses, can chemistry students conceive and design experiments? Are they able to interpret and explain the results of their research using the discipline's vernacular? The same sorts of questions could be appropriately framed and examined for any other major area of study, whether it be architecture, urban planning, or Urdu.

One challenge is that there is little formal consensus about what constitutes program quality in undergraduate education in the arts and humanities, social sciences, and natural sciences. Ratings or rankings are either aimed at graduate programs (for example, the top twenty forestry programs in the United States, best graduate business schools on the West coast) or, as we will see, the placement of the institution as a whole on higher education's pantheon (for example, the list of best regional small universities in the southeast, the top one hundred national liberal arts colleges). Ratings and rankings have their place, but they tell a limited story regarding quality undergraduate education. We wrote this book to help educators at all sizes and types of four-year institutions, including teachers, researchers, scholars and administrators, to constructively evaluate and document the effectiveness of current programs aimed at educating undergraduates.

We realize that there is nothing new about conducting academic program reviews. As is well known, most colleges and universities have implemented a formal review cycle for individual departments or programs, typically every five years or so. The pursuit of "educational quality," for example, has been a key campus concern for a couple of decades now (see Berquist & Armstrong, 1986; Bogue & Saunders, 1992; Boyer, 1987; Haworth & Conrad, 1997). Following the groundbreaking work of Boyer (1990), debates about the nature of scholarship have become standard procedure as campuses define the implications for what faculty should do in and out of the classroom. What is *new*, however, is the availability of helpful assessment tools for evaluating the strengths, challenges, and unrealized opportunities within departments or other programs. Such tools—including discipline-based learning guidelines, curriculum evaluation guides, standardized student surveys, rubrics for teaching and evaluating writing and speaking demonstrations, and instructor-designed measures tailored to evaluate whether the learning goals of assignments are met—constitute some other possibilities.

We advocate the use of a particular assessment tool: *quality benchmarks*; that is, reasonable, reason-based, and peer-sanctioned criteria that can be used to assess the performance of academic programs and departments. Benchmarks provide a guiding standard for comparing what *is* with what *could be* achieved with redirected effort, energy, attention, or resources (see, for example, Astin, 1993a; Banta, Lund, Black, & Oblander, 1996). Formative rather than summative, quality benchmarks allow constituents—department chairs, program directors, faculty, deans, and students—to review progress, identify problems, establish or revisit goals, and reflect on student learning outcomes or establish new ones.

The term "benchmarks" has a particular meaning that differs somewhat from terms such as "criteria" or "rubrics" and the like. Benchmarking is the process of assessing a program's qualities by comparing them with—and trying to shape them to conform to—what are considered to be the best practices or ideal program features. In essence, benchmarking provides a snapshot of program performance that helps the relevant constituents understand how particular educational activities within key domains compare with acknowledged standards. The upshot of such benchmarking is that a program will undertake changes in order to improve teaching and learning. The aim of benchmarking is to improve some particular aspect of program performance (such as student research skills, faculty scholarly output), but it is part of a larger continuous process in which departments and the colleagues who teach and administrate within them continually seek to challenge their practices.

We argue that benchmarks provide a set of standard reference points for internal self-studies and external reviews. Of course, benchmarking processes also are routinely invoked when comparing one program to another or when sizing up whether a program has achieved the standards set forth by an accrediting agency. Regardless of whether the focus involves internal or external standards, the process of comparing achievement to an identified standard can serve multiple purposes: benchmarking can assess institutional reputation locally or nationally, verify goal achievements, and measure whether outcome targets have been realized, among other objectives.

The emphasis of the benchmarks we propose is internal. We suggest using these selected quality benchmarks to assist undergraduate programs in establishing quality objectives, monitoring progress toward their achievement, and ultimately achieving a level commensurate with department talent, energy, and resources. In the process, working with developmental standards can further define their program missions and document their effectiveness.

We also want to be clear that benchmarks are not national standards for accrediting departments or programs. We are not proposing that the quality benchmarks presented in this book should be used to compare a given institution with its peer or aspirant counterparts. Again, we propose that departments and other academic programs establish appropriate internal benchmarks for measuring their own progress on various dimensions. By doing so, we advocate that departments concentrate on their own goal setting and progress. Further, accreditation standards are generally all-or-nothing propositions, whereas quality benchmarks are designed to be developmental measures for assessing a program. We urge readers to keep these points in mind as they read this book and subsequently reflect on, evaluate, and improve their departments or programs.

AN EXAMPLE: USING BENCHMARKS FOR PROGRAM ADVOCACY

Consider a familiar example on many campuses. A department chair wants to search for and hire a new faculty member to offer courses in a key topical area that currently receives little or no coverage in the program's curriculum. The dean or the vice president for academic affairs (VPAA) reviews the request and suggests that a self-study is in order before any additional faculty line can be considered. The dean also points out that several other departments are simultaneously claiming an equally pressing need for new hires but the projected budget for the next academic year cannot possibly accommodate all requests. To make things interesting, let's imagine that enrollment in the department is solid and steady, but some of the competing departments have seen moderate growth in the numbers of students they serve.

How can this department chair hope to convince the dean that the requested hire is truly needed and worthy of support? How can the chair convince herself that her request is justified, given the needs of her colleagues who are leading other departments? We'll present two possible scenarios.

Scenario one. The chair dutifully undertakes the writing of a self-study, the first in several years. Department colleagues are supportive but expect her to carry the burden of gathering information, drafting arguments for the position, and writing the actual proposal. The majority of department members agree that the hire is justified, but aside from drawing up a list of reasons for the hire from the department's own perspective and perceived immediate needs (for example, enrollment crunch, recent retirements, most recent new line was five years ago), little attention is paid to how the hire could fit into the larger constellation of department issues, including curricular changes, wider institutional service, and enhancing undergraduate education. In other words, the department operates in an academic "business as usual" model, coupled with the oft-heard claim of "too many students to serve, not enough resources."

Although the final proposal was compelling in many respects, the dean received equally cogent arguments from other departments. In the end, the dean gave the hire to another department, one with fewer full-time faculty members than the others and, up to that point, larger class sizes. After spending considerable time and effort on the proposal, the department chair is somewhat demoralized; her colleagues are frustrated, disappointed, and somewhat aggrieved. What little collaborative spirit existed in the department disappears for quite some time.

Scenario two. Imagine that the perceived need to hire a new colleague spurs the interest and involvement of the entire department. They agree to an approach based on benchmarking. Instead of expecting the chairperson to do all the work, the faculty members divide up the tasks related to the potential hire. For example, some colleagues identify both new and established courses that the new person would teach (curriculum), others examine the hire's advising responsibilities (student development), and so on. With the help of colleagues, the chair drafts a proposal that documents the department's current mission and goals, highlighting particular areas that are *distinguished* (for example, a recently revised curriculum that meets national disciplinary standards, an outreach program to the local community) as well as those that are *effective* (such as undergraduate research presentations delivered at regional and national conferences), or still *developing* (for example, the department now requires that students give formal, oral presentations in upper-level courses), or that need attention because they are *undeveloped* (for example, faculty publishing has declined precipitously in recent years). (We define and explain the italicized terms in the next section of this chapter.)

The proposal specifically explains how a new hire with a desired specialty can contribute to the areas of strength while also supporting the developing and underdeveloped areas of the department. In the course of the self-study, members of the department streamlined a few procedural issues that ended up helping the department's budget. The comprehensive nature of the proposal clearly documented the need for the new hire. The department chair was gratified by the level of enthusiasm, camaraderie, and participation of her colleagues. The colleagues, in turn, realized that while there were some areas of concern, the department was clearly moving in the right direction. The dean concurred, impressed by the amount of effort, goodwill, and careful, thoughtful planning. The proposal was much more focused and reason-based than the competing proposals from the other departments.

Scenario one is all too familiar on most campuses. Scenario two is less familiar. Let's imagine that the dean in scenario two is convinced by the evidence and grants the new faculty line. Everyone in the department is overjoyed, especially the chair. But consider this: even if such benchmarking does not always succeed—there are usually any number of legitimate reasons to postpone valid hires—the act of comparing the current state against quality performance benchmarks still provides department members, the chair, and the dean with a sense of which aspects of the program are working well (often very well) and where some improvements could be made. Most important, not all improvements require an outlay of capital or an expanded budget; some are procedural, others organizational, and some rely on a combination of good will and common sense. The point is that something beneficial grew from the program review that embraced the benchmarking approach.

What are some of the concrete advantages of using performance benchmarks? These include:

- Engagement of faculty and students in crafting and revising the mission statement of a department or program
- Formative evaluation of teaching and learning outcomes
- Curricular review, refinement, and revision
- Recruitment and retention of quality faculty and students
- Assessment of resource needs
- Long-range academic program planning
- Evaluation and demonstration of program quality

Benchmarking and Program Assessment for Educational Renewal

Benchmarks are used in higher education as a way to improve the climate for learning within departments (see, for example, Umbach & Porter, 2002; Umbach & Wawrynski, 2005). We recently proposed performance benchmarks to assist undergraduate psychology programs in defining their missions and goals as well as in documenting their effectiveness (Dunn, McCarthy, Baker, Halonen, & Hill, 2007). The developmental framework we proposed garnered considerable interest among communities of teachers and administrators within the discipline of psychology. The interest we received led us to think more broadly about how quality benchmarks could be used to evaluate virtually any academic department or program. Indeed, our experiences as program reviewers, faculty members, and part- or full-time administrators informs us that departments, department heads, and deans all want reasonable, reliable, and professionally respectable methods for evaluating the performance of undergraduate programs.

We believe the developmental framework presented in this book will satisfy all parties because we emphasize formative assessment. We do not advocate the use of summative assessment—here defined as the use of benchmarks to reward (for example, add faculty lines, build new facilities) or punish (for example, eliminate faculty, trim the budget) a program for its standing. Furthermore, we designed our framework to help programs identify and tout what they already do well even in situations involving seriously constrained resources. Finally, the performance benchmarks used to identify areas of program strength can, in turn, be used to recruit and retain students, to seek funding via grants or alumni support, and to enhance the perceived rating of an institution. When benchmarks reveal that a program or areas within it are undeveloped or developing, faculty and administrators can then plan where subsequent efforts and resources are best placed to raise a program's standing.

Our framework explores the attributes of undergraduate programs by focusing on educationally related activities in eight domains: *program climate*; *assessment, accountability, and accreditation issues*; *student learning outcomes*; *student development*; *curriculum; faculty characteristics; program resources;* and *administrative support.* We conceptualize a continuum of performance for each attribute in each of the domains to characterize undeveloped, developing, effective, and distinguished achievement for undergraduate programs. We will discuss this continuum of performance in more detail shortly. Our goal is to encourage individual departments at various types of institutions to evaluate what they currently do formatively while identifying areas for refinement or future growth. We believe that our recommended benchmarks can improve program quality, encourage more effective program reviews, and help optimally functioning programs compete more successfully for resources based on their distinguished achievements.

CHARACTERIZING PROGRAM PERFORMANCE

Within any of the eight educational domains, we construed a program's performance attributes as characterized along a fourfold continuum from undeveloped to distinguished. Exhibit 1.1 lists and defines the continuum's characteristics. An undeveloped characteristic is one that is interfering with a department or program's ability to pursue its educational mission. The problem may be, for example, resource-based (such as insufficient lab space) or personnel-based (such as too many part-time adjunct faculty relative to full-time tenure-track colleagues), or it can be the result of political turmoil (such as loss of faculty lines following colleague retirements, personal conflicts between colleagues, rivalries between faculty camps) or the absence of leadership or organizational skills displayed by the chairperson or director. Whatever its source, an undeveloped quality (or qualities) adversely affects students' educational experiences.

EXHIBIT 1.1 CHARACTERIZING DEPARTMENT OR PROGRAM ATTRIBUTES: FOUR PROGRESSIVE, CHARACTERISTIC DESCRIPTIONS

Undeveloped—makes no contribution to undergraduate learning or is even counterproductive

Developing—makes a marginal, limited contribution to undergraduate learning

Effective—makes a suitable, satisfactory, and favorable contribution to undergraduate learning

Distinguished—makes an outstanding contribution to undergraduate learning in the department or program and discipline

When a characteristic is labeled as developing, the outlook is a mixed one. Consider a program's attempt to provide adequate curricular exposure to issues of diversity for students. Where an undeveloped curriculum would ignore or overlook the relevance of diversity matters, a developing one would create one opportunity, perhaps within a common course that all majors must complete. Ignoring the dearth of female physicists versus openly discussing why relatively few women pursue graduate education and active research in the discipline would be an example. On the one hand, recognition that sociocultural differences among people exist is in itself a favorable outcome; on the other, however, limiting the discussion to one part of one course obscures the importance of the issue and dilutes its impact on student learning. Hence we consider developing qualities to offer marginal benefits to students, so that the areas for improvement are relatively obvious.

An effective characteristic for benchmarking is one that offers a minimal or adequate, yet still positive, influence on undergraduate education and student learning in a program or department. An example of an effective characteristic is found in the place of service learning in a department's curriculum. Service learning involves teaching, learning, and thinking where discipline-based knowledge is used to tackle some problem or need faced by an entire community or a group (such as teenagers or seniors) within a community. An undeveloped curriculum would not present information on service learning, whereas a developing one would discuss common community-based contexts and review book-based examples. In contrast, an effective curriculum would actually offer students the opportunity to engage in learning about a local community's concrete and real needs through a disciplinary lens.

The fourth and highest level on our continuum is labeled distinguished in that such benchmarks appear to offer an extraordinary opportunity for students to become immersed in the challenges of a particular topic. If we continue with the service learning example, a distinguished departmental curriculum might be one in which students actively designed and executed a project (or, better still, projects) that helpfully addressed a community's problem. The educational benefit is increased substantially because the outcome uses a department or program's expertise, improves town-and-gown relations, and benefits students who directly witness the constructive impact of discipline-based insights.

We developed this continuum to reflect the reality that departments and programs in humanities and the arts, the natural sciences, and the social sciences come in various forms. Some are large—numerous faculty members, large enrollments, significant resources—whereas others are small, housing few faculty, students, and resources. In some programs, scholarly activities (research, publication, performance, exhibitions) represent the hallmark, whereas teaching in all its forms, from lecture to discussion to online communities, is the *raison d'etre* of other departments. Obviously, many departments fall between these extremes.

We do want to be clear about one thing: receiving a rating of undeveloped or developing on some quality within a domain is not meant to be pejorative or probationary; again, benchmarking is for developmental, not accrediting, purposes. Neither a department nor its members—nor its head or chair, for that matter—should be criticized for one or more of these two ratings among the eight academic domains. Again, we view our benchmarking approach as developmental, which means that forward progress is always a possibility—a department can move ahead, say, from developing to effective, on one quality within one domain with a bit of reflection and more helpful assessment strategies. Similarly, the presence of an undeveloped or developing rating should never be used for summative assessment, only for formative assessment aimed at improving the educational experience for undergraduate students—which, once change is implemented, will provide other benefits to the department or program and its members and constituents.

Finally, the benchmarking examples we offer throughout this book are just that—examples. There is no attempt to establish "one size fits all" departments or programs. We offer a variety of detailed examples that can be exported, revised, and rewritten by readers and their colleagues to fit local needs, traditions, and circumstances. Arguably, the conversation that involves such retrofitting of the benchmarks is an equally important part of the process of program evaluation as is doing the actual benchmarking.

Considering Institution Type

Institutions of higher education vary a great deal from one another. There are well over three thousand educational institutions of various types in the United States. Some are research-oriented universities that are known around the world, others are small liberal arts colleges that draw students from all over the country. Still others are regional colleges and universities whose student bodies tend to be filled by individuals from the local area. Selectivity ratings for admission differ; some schools admit few applicants, others admit virtually everyone who applies. Many schools are public; that is, they are supported by a state or local tax base. Other schools are private, dependent on fundraising through alumni donations, foundation or other grants, gifts, and income generated from their endowments.

As we wrote this book, we were conscious that we could not create an institutional profile or model for benchmarking that would fit every institution. Instead, we have tried to focus on the general sort of parameters for benchmarking that should be found at most institutions. Before you begin the process of benchmarking your department or program, be sure to consider whether the nature of the larger institution is at all relevant to the process. If your school has some unusual qualities that bear on your department—the type of faculty it attracts, the nature of the courses or the students who take them—then you may want to factor such issues into the benchmarking process.

Although we wrote primarily with four-year colleges and universities in mind, we believe that, with some slight modifications, our system is readily applicable to most two-year institutions. Indeed, we imagine that all readers will use this book with an eye to adjusting our evaluative dimensions, benchmarking descriptions, and other materials to fit their local customs and relatively unique circumstances. When a dimension or description does not "fit" or seem otherwise germane, just move on to the next one. Similarly, the benchmarking conversation may inspire other dimensions that uniquely capture the program that have not been identified in the current proposal.

(Recent) Past as Prologue to the Emerging Focus on Undergraduate Education

Why are colleges and universities suddenly so concerned with improving and evaluating what and how well undergraduates learn? Chiefly for three related reasons: accountability pressures, the assessment movement, and the desire to advance the recognition some programs or departments receive in the wider world. As we discuss the influence of these reasons within higher education, we consider how benchmarking can ameliorate their impact within departments or programs.

Accountability

As having an undergraduate degree is no longer perceived to be a luxury but, rather, seen as more or less a necessity for those who wish to pursue a professional career in many fields, the ivory tower is no longer a refuge from public scrutiny. As the cost of education has risen dramatically, the public and often their elected representatives want proof that there are true educational benefits associated with the cost of higher education. Public institutions have always faced accountability pressures. Private institutions are now increasingly under the public microscope as well. Various prestigious universities have announced tuition waivers and scholarships for low income and middle class families (see, for example, Crimson Staff, 2006; Damast, 2008). Some politicians have called for wealthy schools to spend more of their endowments instead of seeking to increase their worth still more through fundraising activities. Although no college or university community likes the idea of outside regulation, claiming academic freedom, educational expertise, or entitled tradition does not garner much support beyond the campus gates—colleges are being held accountable. To engage rather than combat such public scrutiny, institutions would do well to explain their strengths and weaknesses while justifying the quality of the education they are able to provide to undergraduate students.

Concern over the power of public opinion, coupled with the realization that higher education's cost should be justified, has refocused campus energies toward demonstrating that educating undergraduate students is the primary mission of four-year institutions. The upshot is that faculty and administrators want to be able to demonstrate to various constituencies—families, trustees or regents, local or national government, and granting agencies, among other stakeholders—that their programs are effective, that there is a true synergy between teaching and learning. In the final analysis, the best measure or demonstration of accountability is the whole experience of students as they take their educational journey through an academic department. (We invite readers to pause for a moment and to think back to their own undergraduate experiences, paying special attention to the impact of their "home" departments on what they learned and, perhaps, who they have become in the intervening years. We suspect that those readers who had a positive experience in the department or program housing their undergraduate major will agree with us about its importance.)

No department or program is apt to be immune from accountability pressures; however, their specific nature may vary according to local customs, traditions, resources, the type of institution, and so on. Accountability pressures have led to the establishment and growth of assessment practices.

Assessment

Simply defined, *assessment* refers to the measurement and evaluation of how well students are learning the material being taught to them (Mentkowski et al., 2000). Besides the aforementioned accountability pressures, most teachers and program directors harbor the authentic belief that they should be able to show that students are benefiting from their studies, justifying the bulk of educational claims. As a result, educators are shifting their focus from traditional outcome measures, like grades, to a broader focus on the processes involved in teaching and learning. Part of the assessment movement has focused on finding, adapting, or creating assessment instruments that tap into how faculty members actually teach and how students really learn (see, for example, Maki, 2001; Zubizarreta, 2004).

We believe that when it comes to the importance of assessment, the focus should be a bit broader than on just what happens in the classroom. We are interested in this fundamental question: Is a department or program doing a good job of educating its undergraduate students? By the term "students," we mean both majors and nonmajors, and typical or average learners as well as those who are considered gifted or talented. Can the program's effectiveness be characterized and demonstrated? The proper focus is captured by Halpern (2004, p. 11), who notes that each department or program "has a list of outstanding alumni of whom they are rightfully proud, but few consider that their most outstanding alumni are hardly representative of the vast majority of current or former students." Thus assessment is aimed at everyone who passes through a program, not simply high performers or other outliers. Much can be learned from focusing on and evaluating the experiences of most students.

What is the assessment philosophy and practice advocated in this book? Like many educators, we believe that there is no single or "best" assessment indicator. Thus one of the main reasons we rely on performance benchmarks is that they can characterize the various facets of a department or program. We also believe that the assessment of a program or department is best carried out by all its members. Ideally, the faculty and administrators within a unit must coöperate and do the work together; beyond organizational and record-keeping functions, subcommittees are usually suboptimal. Finally, there is no reason to assess the benchmarks of a department unless the faculty use the information wisely and constructively. Where collecting undergraduate student performance data is concerned, for example, the findings should never be used to evaluate faculty performance (that is, for purposes of retention, tenure, promotion, salary adjustment). Assessment, then, should not be used to mete out rewards or punishments but rather to continually improve the education offered within a program or department.

ADVANCEMENT

After accountability and assessment, the third driver of the need to focus on undergraduate education is institutional advancement. Whether they are willing to play or not, colleges and universities are now very much a part of a nation-wide ratings game. Although a few have opted out (see, for example, Finder, 2007), most are willing to use whatever means available to get the word out about the strengths of what they have to offer. Attracting the best and the brightest students is now a matter of marketing—a term that is distasteful, if not upsetting, to the ears of many academics. Nonetheless, the advent of the ratings and ranking system of *U.S. News & World Report,* coupled with a small industry that routinely publishes ''insider'' guides to the ''best'' institutions in the country, has led to pressure to advance institutions publicly at all levels. As a result, departments and programs want to distinguish themselves from each other while making students, their parents, alumni, administrators, trustees, and often state legislators aware of what makes them especially distinguished.

Although we do not want to sanction, let alone take part in, the quasi-arms race of comparing competing institutions with one another with a winner-gets-more-and-better-students mentality, we think there is a point worth exploring here. Namely, that each and every department is apt to have some clear strengths or qualities that make it stand out from peer departments. These strengths might be related to the curriculum, characteristics of the faculty, program resources, or some other important dimension. Identifying such strengths by using performance benchmarks will allow a department to publicize these qualities both internally (to other departments or programs or even colleges within a university or university system) and externally (to other programs at peer colleges or universities).

Within the context of accountability, the other side of benchmarking is equally important: those areas within a program that need improvement can be recognized and then addressed. Benchmarking thus can be an impetus for planning for the future, a task with which many departments struggle. Our own experiences as program reviewers and department members remind us that resource constraints often preclude quick action where areas for improvement are concerned. Nonetheless, we maintain that doing benchmarking and sharing the results with administrative units allows a department or program to justify specific needs in order to move to the next level of performance. If nothing else, advancing a department or program's agenda via benchmarking can lead to frank discussions among faculty, department or program administrators, and upper-level administration (such as deans, VPAAs, provosts) about how best to use available resources to achieve shared ends. The value of the resulting collegiality should not be underestimated.

Looking Ahead: Using Quality Benchmarks for Your Undergraduate Program Needs

Readers who want to take a broad perspective on using quality benchmarks for evaluating the educational experiences of undergraduates are apt to read this book from cover to cover. Individuals who want to address a more specific issue, such as program climate, will want to turn to a particular chapter (in this case, Chapter Two). To accommodate both sorts of readers, we wrote the chapters in this book so that they could stand alone as much as possible. Thus although it might be desirable to complete the whole book before writing a self-study of your own academic department (see Chapter Twelve), you could nonetheless turn to Chapter Four now if you needed to immediately begin to think about student learning outcomes. To brief both types of readers, we provide a chapter-by-chapter overview and then offer concrete advice about how to most effectively use the guidelines offered in this book.

Chapter-by-Chapter Overview

The topic of Chapter Two is evaluation of program leadership. What kinds of behavior help department chairs and program directors realize the greatest success in working with faculty? Some programs connect well with the wider institution while others languish in isolation, which is often a direct result of skilled leadership or its absence. Some programs thrive even when resources do not appear to be adequate because of the commitment of the faculty, whereas programs rich in resources may not take full advantage of their riches. We offer a developmental framework to capture a continuum of leadership quality across several dimensions of program climate.

Chapter Three establishes the importance of assessment, accountability, and accreditation to any undergraduate program. A brief history of the assessment movement in higher education is presented. In the course of discussing our assessment framework, we identify what kinds of information departments should routinely collect and consult in the course of program evaluation. We also consider the useful role of assessment data for program accountability and promotion. The chapter concludes with a discussion of the impact of accreditation on quality processes.

As already noted, student learning outcomes are the focus of Chapter Four. This chapter proposes how faculty and administrators can evaluate students' writing, speaking, research, collaboration, and information literacy and technology skills through the lens of a given discipline.

Chapter Five concerns curriculum evaluation. Relying on our benchmarks framework, this chapter presents the key factors that should be addressed by any undergraduate program's curricula. We also discuss how programs can tailor our standard framework to evaluate unique qualities present in their programs.

Student development is not only the concern of student services offices. Chapter Six examines student development through the lens of a sponsoring program or department. What happens to students in the course of their education within a program? How and to what degree are they changed and challenged? Do students feel a part of the program and the larger discipline? Programs often neglect concrete activities that can enhance the experiences of their undergraduate students. This chapter presents ways to determine and enhance current student involvement in the life of a program.

The assessment movement has not overlooked faculty evaluation, which can be a thorny issue for many institutions. Chapter Seven offers guidance on how to constructively evaluate faculty characteristics within a given department or program. Admittedly, faculty members are wary of having their teaching or professional activities assessed, yet evaluation is very much a part of academic life. We reiterate the importance of formative rather than summative assessment in the constructive evaluation of faculty efforts in and outside of the classroom. Using our developmental framework, we discuss ways to assess teaching, scholarship, resource generation, service, professional involvement in the discipline, community participation, availability to students, and ethical conduct. We also discuss the importance of faculty development.

Higher education is increasingly expensive. Thus Chapter Eight will be of great interest to many readers, especially program directors, department chairs, and deans, because it deals with how to review program resources. Some programs are equipment intensive, others can seek external funding, and still others need relatively few resources save for a requisite number of faculty members. This chapter explains how our developmental framework can be used to characterize available educational resources. Special attention is given to using the results of the benchmarking exercise to seek additional resources, including faculty lines and equipment.

Aside from the availability of resources, one of the most practical concerns for any academic program is administrative support, the subject of Chapter Nine. The truth of the matter is that programs respond to support and encouragement from their academic administrations. Programs cannot excel if they do not receive quality support from administrations. This chapter presents a framework for characterizing administrative support for

- Carrying out a program's mission
- Following university bylaws and procedures
- Adhering to appropriate and fair evaluation systems
- Making teaching assignments
- Advancing scholarly work
- Recognizing a program's efforts

All programs can benefit from a candid assessment of program climate and leadership, student learning outcomes and the curriculum designed to meet those outcomes, resources both administrative and fiscal, and issues of student development. These dimensions are sometimes specifically influenced by the nature of the discipline. Many books dealing with nascent issues in higher education adopt the tools, techniques, and approaches of the social sciences. Indeed, the authors of this book are all psychologists by training. Yet we are keenly aware that faculty members who teach in programs in the arts and the humanities often face special considerations and challenges. We wrote Chapter Ten to tackle some of these considerations, including the different perspectives on scholarship, such as performance or exhibition, different teaching approaches, and, of course, distinct resource needs. We also examine the special challenges of crafting meaningful assessments in specialized programs, such as interdisciplinary majors.

Following that, in Chapter Eleven we offer suggestions for evaluating support for the natural sciences. We address factors that are unique to development of student learning outcomes, assessment, and curriculum within the natural sciences.

We are mindful that readers will have different reasons for consulting this book. Some will want to prepare a benchmark-based self-study in anticipation of an internal or an external review; others may want to develop skills before serving as an invited external reviewer for a program or department. Chapter Twelve offers advice on how to conduct an undergraduate program review using quality benchmarks. The chapter ties together the frameworks presented in the earlier chapters by providing concrete guidance on effectively conducting an internal program review (self-study). To aid would-be external reviewers, we wrote Appendix A, a guide for how best to use benchmarking while serving as an outside reviewer of another institution. In Chapter Twelve and Appendix A, we provide recommended timelines and suggest what information should appear in evaluation reports.

Finally, we close the book in Chapter Thirteen by considering how we can better serve our students and our institutions by using formative tools like quality benchmarks. This brief concluding chapter discusses how quality benchmarks and the various developmental frameworks presented in the earlier chapters can benefit the experience of students and improve the quality of our colleges and universities. We sincerely believe our approach can refocus and invigorate the work being done within academic programs.

HOW TO USE THIS BOOK

Now that you have an overview of the book, how should you plan and prepare to use it for benchmarking purposes once you are done reading? First, no serious program review, especially a self-study, can occur without the active, engaged, and interested participation of the faculty who teach within it. Second, these teacher-scholars need to agree with one another about the department's or program's mission. Thus, before undertaking any program review, the department's mission statement must be revisited and then renewed or revised. Once the mission is agreed upon and shared by the faculty, only then should a benchmarking review begin in earnest. When the review does begin, all colleagues within the program or department should have a role. Without a collective sense of purpose and commitment, the practice of benchmarking to identify strengths as well as areas requiring attention will not be taken seriously.

As noted earlier, some readers may want to focus on a particular issue, such as assessing the quality of a departmental curriculum. Others may want to assess the entire program. In the latter instance, a team approach may work best, one in which teams of two or three colleagues read a relevant chapter of the book and then focus their attention on using the quality benchmarks (and gathering appropriate data) linked with the domain of interest. Each chapter contains a matrix of relevant dimensions plotted along the four possible program attributes just described.

As we will emphasize throughout the book, no program should expect (or even aspire) to be distinguished in each and every area. Our framework is designed to help programs identify and tout what they already do well even in situations of seriously constrained resources. Finally, using performance benchmarks to identify areas of program strength can, in turn, be used to recruit and retain students, to seek funding via grants or alumni support, and to enhance the perceived rating of an institution. When benchmarks reveal that a program or areas within it are undeveloped or developing, faculty and administrators can then plan for where subsequent efforts and resources would best be placed in order to raise a program's standing.

Each chapter ends with some Guiding Questions. These questions are designed to encourage readers to link a chapter's material to the current state of the relevant domain in their departments or programs. We believe that these questions—and others derived from them—are a good way for departments and programs to begin a self-study. Program chairs, administrators, and faculty member should join one another in trying to answer these questions as a starting point for a program review. Indeed, we want to reiterate the point that the most successful climate for promoting change and development within a program is achieved when all parties participate. Thus each chapter closes with a set of questions so that readers and their colleagues have a place to begin the process of benchmarking their department or program.

GUIDING QUESTIONS

1. Before doing any benchmarking, how would you describe the state of undergraduate education in your department or program? At your institution more broadly?
2. What qualities, if any, make your program stand out from other programs in your division (humanities and arts, social sciences, natural sciences) at your institution? Would colleagues in other departments in your division agree with your assessment? Why or why not? Do you believe your dean or provost would share your opinion?
3. What qualities, if any, make your department or program distinguishable from others at comparable institutions (that is, those comprising your formal or informal peer group)? Would disciplinary colleagues at these other schools agree with your assessment? Why or why not?
4. What are your goals for department or program evaluation? What do you hope to accomplish?

Part One

Benchmarking for Eight Key Program Domains

Chapter Two

The View from the Top: Checking the Climate and Leadership of a Program

The impetus for the original work (Dunn, McCarthy, Baker, Halonen, & Hill, 2007) that inspired this volume was a fateful conversation in a bar. All of us had developed substantial experience as external reviewers in academic program reviews. We were comparing experiences over wine when this claim emerged: "It only takes about fifteen minutes on site to know whether you have landed in a solid program or if you have landed in the 'program from hell.'" Although the statement was clearly an exaggeration, we began to compare stories about the particular examples from programs we had visited that made us all want to return and spend time individually thanking our newly appreciated colleagues in our home departments.

What observations gave fuel to the claim of fifteen-minute academic diagnoses? We had encountered a variety of indicators early in our visits that later proved to be bellwethers of programs in trouble. Some indicators were subtle; others were brutal. Problematic programs were rife with unhappy people: complaining students, whining faculty, disgruntled staff, defensive program leaders, and desperate deans. Individuals took pains to pull us aside to tell us "the real truth about what's going on." We each endured more than our fair share of whispered conversations behind closed doors, our informants casting frequent sidelong glances. Another telltale indicator of an adverse climate was the grungy appearance of the work environment: dirty kitchens, dramatically outdated materials on the bulletin boards, cluttered hallways, and an absence of signage. Walking into spaces such as these as a visitor was demoralizing, which gives only a hint of how challenging it would be to report to work in this sort of environment on a regular basis.

In contrast, "dream team" programs immediately felt different. People smiled. Students spontaneously made positive, even charming, comments about the dedication of their faculty. Campus colleagues knew about, accurately described, and expressed admiration for the accomplishments of the program in question. Bulletin boards displayed up-to-date, helpful information in hallways; well-designed workspaces invited interaction. Office doors were open, greetings were exchanged, and signs of activity and ongoing social interaction were rife. In these scenarios, we could imagine being happily transplanted and conducting satisfying academic careers among colleagues who had "gotten it right." Such characteristics reinforced the kinds of environments that provide a safe and responsive context that not only optimizes learning but can contribute to positive character development (Cohen, 2008).

We concluded our fateful conversation over wine with the observation that there would be enormous value in articulating indicators more comprehensively to help stakeholders monitor and fairly evaluate quality in undergraduate programs. The result was eight rubrics in separate domains of activity to differentiate programs that were languishing from neglect or other misbehavior, which we called *undeveloped*; programs that had pockets of positive activity within otherwise undistinguished performance, which we called *developing*; programs that provided a serviceable major, which we designated as *effective*; and programs that had truly created a special, vibrant track record, which we identified as *distinguished.*

In each of the rubrics, we identified the most salient dimensions that could shed light on program quality. In the case of program climate and leadership, we adopted the following dimensions that are summarized in Table 2.1 (adapted from Dunn et al., 2007): Pride Reflected in Environment, Campus Reputation, Collegiality, Respect for Individual and Cultural Differences, Equitable Problem-Solving, Program Leadership, Relationship with University Community, and Program Involvement in Local Community. Although other dimensions also affect program climate, we concluded that these dimensions were the most enlightening for purposes of assessing and facilitating program quality. We elaborate our observations on each dimension in the rest of this chapter.

Pride Reflected in Environment

Although it is rare for any program faculty to be satisfied with the space to which the program has been assigned, distinguished programs tend to exploit the spaces they have to full advantage. In such programs, faculty and students alike take pride in ensuring that workspaces are welcoming and upbeat. They may scavenge garage sales for items they can contribute to common spaces to make the environment homier; a related indicator is that the common spaces are frequently occupied. They may negotiate tax write-off contributions of furniture from local vendors. They share kitchen chores without being nagged. They designate specific individuals to monitor bulletin boards to remove outdated materials, and they use display spaces to show off high-quality student work. They may dedicate space to alumni business cards to display "life after graduation" pathways. When the entire unit conspires to make an environment pleasant, it seems self-perpetuating. For example, littering and graffiti are less likely to be found in such environments.

Effective programs demonstrate many of these features, but somehow the environmental effort does not produce such consistent, positive results. The work environment manages to be comfortable, but it is not vibrant as it is in distinguished programs. Common space may be available, but students and faculty tend to pass through it rather than use it. In fact, the environment found in an effective program is much like a well-cared-for but little visited gallery in a museum: people take a brief look before moving on.

TABLE 2.1 PROGRAM CLIMATE DOMAIN

	Undeveloped	*Developing*	*Effective*	*Distinguished*
Pride Reflected in Environment	Demonstrates little or no attention to environment	Shows minimal attention to environment	Maintains reasonable attention to environment	Actively addresses environmental needs
Campus Reputation	Reputed to be dysfunctional	Reputed to be limited in functionality	Reputed to be functional	Reputed to be talented and contributing
Collegiality	Maintains or tolerates contentious atmosphere as shown by inappropriate alliances, generational conflicts, and litigation; climate feels threatening	Maintains overall functional climate but one that is challenged when conflicts develop; climate feels fragile	Promotes professional climate that models tolerance of and respect for diverse viewpoints; climate feels comfortable	Exploits conflicts as potential change agents; department faculty demonstrate mutual respect for students and colleagues regardless of seniority; climate feels stimulating
Respect for Individual and Cultural Differences	Demonstrates intolerance for diversity	Demonstrates limited tolerance but neglects the value of cultural diversity as shown by homogeneity or lack of sensitivity to individual differences	Demonstrates tolerance of diversity but may not systematically promote a climate in which this value is prominent	Purposefully builds across difference to promote a culturally and philosophically diverse faculty; department is "purposefully heterogeneous"

Equitable Problem Solving	Shows substantial bias in resolving problems	Shows some degree of bias in resolving problems	Solves problems in a way that minimizes bias	Develops systems to ensure that decisions are equitable
Program Leadership	Experiences leadership that does not promote departmental progress	Limits leadership functions to single individual routinely enacting decisions without faculty support	Shares leadership across members to accomplish diverse objectives; plans by consensus whenever possible	Shares leadership and actively pursues leadership planning to provide for future development of department
Relationship with University Community	Maintains isolation from the university community	Projects minimal interest due to sporadic involvement in and contribution to the university	Contributes to university service that is tailored to departmental strengths	Shoulders significant responsibility at university level, including leadership role in advancing the university and its mission
Program Involvement in Local Community	Does not connect to the local community	Invests minimally in community activities, driven by personal interests of motivated faculty leaders	Pursues active connections collectively with extra-university community (for example, advisory board, community volunteering) that blend departmental interests with community contribution	Achieves noteworthy departmental involvement in local, regional, or national service

Programs in the middle (developing programs) are spotty in their care of the workspace. Individual faculty members may show some initiative toward their own work areas but perceive the care for the larger environment as solely the province of the janitorial staff. In such programs, pressure points build. For example, faculty will be interrupted in their own work to answer inquiries about directions when the program fails to give forethought to adequate signage. Outdated materials remain hanging and may be frequently commented on by department members (''Someone should really take down that poster—it's five years old!'') but no one attempts to remedy the problem. The denizens of the environment assume such work is ''someone else's responsibility.''

Finally, undeveloped programs simply don't feel like programs. Instead, the work environment features disconnected work spaces that may seem like a string of islands. Social exchanges—whether between faculty and faculty, faculty and students, or students with one another—are perfunctory at best. No one lingers after class, and little or no thought has been given to the importance of common space for impromptu or planned gatherings. Is it any wonder that students are unlikely to ''hang'' in such programs when there are other more inviting workspaces to be had elsewhere?

CAMPUS REPUTATION

People talk. And campuses have lots of people. Whether programs like it or not, the talk generated on campus often reflects prevailing perceptions about program quality. Sometimes campus chatter is an accurate reflection of how the program actually functions. However, adverse campus chatter may not be objective. For example, it may be to the advantage of an individual from a department currently competing for resources with the target department to conduct a smear campaign in case those negative perceptions could swing a decision (say, about office space, faculty lines, equipment) away from the competition. This reality reinforces why it is so important to have systematic, objective data to support claims of quality.

Let's start this time with undeveloped programs. Common criticisms of these are often pegged to the personality characteristics of the most visible, and most unpleasant, department members. Curmudgeons, elitists, slackers, and phantoms tend to top the list of departments that get slammed by their campus colleagues who may not be able to distinguish the negative individual profiles from the activity of the program as a whole. Members of undeveloped programs often spend a disproportional amount of time criticizing other programs rather than doing the harder work of careful self-reflection and continuous improvement. Alternatively, they may engage in baseless boasts and puffery, laying claim to professional expertise and reputation long since moribund, if not altogether departed.

Developing programs do not tend to inspire spontaneous campus-wide praise. Colleagues on campus may be aware of isolated activities of some members of the department, but the positive sentiment for program "stars" doesn't elevate the overall status of the program. In fact, the dominant tone of campus commentary will be more negative than positive. Colleagues suspect or presume the program's faculty are motivated more by self-interest than by a collective vision.

In contrast, effective programs have good (but not stellar) word of mouth. Students seem satisfied with their progress and the caliber of work rendered by the faculty. As a consequence, campus colleagues overhear mostly positive judgments about the contribution of the department to student life and campus quality and willingly share the gist of what they have heard. Yet campus observers will report that the department lacks a sense of professional cohesion, that it appears to be a collection of individuals doing well at pursuing interests that do not jibe well with one another.

A simple litmus test can gauge distinguished department quality among campus colleagues. External reviewers can ask, "Name the top three programs on campus." Typically, colleagues have decided opinions about the programs that have appropriately garnered the most attention through their good work. They may even grouse a bit about undeserved public relations if their own program doesn't fare as well in the public eye. However, it is telling that colleagues can provide a rationale for what constitutes the top campus performers. Normally, the reasons include robust enrollment trends, prize-winning competitive performances by students, and attention-getting faculty activity in the teaching, research, or service realms.

Another quick way to determine a distinguished department is to find out how many of its members serve on powerful campus committees—whether theirs are appointed or elected positions is beside the point. Such leadership is indicative of an important center of gravity that campus citizens, including administrators, look to as a dependable resource. Effective leadership in campus commitments goes a long way toward securing favorable opinions of colleagues.

COLLEGIALITY

Collegiality (that is, a lack thereof) is often cited as the number one reason for tenure failure (see, for example, Diamond, 2002, 2004; Whicker, Kronenfeld, & Strickland, 1993; see also Chapter Seven). However, the impact of uncollegial behavior extends far beyond the adverse effects on any one faculty member's career. A department beset with collegiality problems is virtually guaranteed to produce a program climate that feels distressed, if not toxic. People in such programs focus more on infighting and political intrigue than they do on advancing the departmental and institutional missions, let alone attending to the educational welfare of undergraduate students.

Collegiality problems in undeveloped programs actually manifest primarily in two separate patterns. The first involves the absence of good relationships among faculty members, rendering the department a unit that must accomplish program business across disconnected people. Although they share a discipline, disconnected individuals experience little motivation to go beyond their own limited sphere of academic focus. The longstanding tradition of hiring academics who represent a specialized subarea may exacerbate this problem. If a program needs a Shakespearean scholar to round out the subdisciplines in the department, its members may be dazzled by the scholar's portfolio and give little heed to any potential signals that the personality won't be a great fit.

Unfortunately, the second pattern found in undeveloped programs is far more taxing. In this situation, collegiality falters as subgroups of faculty forge alliances and begin to fight with each other for decisional power in the department. Factions form and program leadership becomes constantly challenged, with forced choice dilemmas about which faction deserves to win any given challenge. Decisions become negotiated or brokered so that proposals that are in the best interest of the program will often be sacrificed to actions, or inactions, that will maintain peace or satisfy camps and factions. Such contentious circumstances do not tend to bring out the best in faculty nor do they contribute to a climate that will inspire students to want to model their behavior after the faculty.

In the most egregious contentious cases, students may demonstrate worldly insight into just how disordered and dysfunctional the department has become. In such cases, students routinely report why Professor X refuses to speak to Professor Y; naturally, students are acutely aware of even worse patterns of behavior than indifferent silence. Students report subtle coercive tactics that constrain their abilities to consort with "the enemy," namely faculty members who are outside the faction with which the student most strongly identifies. Because this combative atmosphere may be the only one students will experience on the way to completing the degree, they may wrongly assume that all programs have a contentious climate.

Developing departments demonstrate surface cordiality but may not experience the synergy that happens when the right people combine their talents to lift the entire program. The departmental mission is not seen as the driving force. Rather, faculty are preoccupied with their own interests while (metaphorically speaking) watching their backs.

In contrast, effective programs experience more lift than drag. Despite individual differences, faculty in effective programs seem to be able to look beyond their colleagues' shortcomings to foster a reliably pleasant and reasonably supportive work environment. They may not completely agree on priorities, but they can work reasonably effectively together.

On the other hand, distinguished programs thrive from the differences that people bring to the table. The faculty conscientiously orchestrate how the various operational obligations can be completed to allow individual members to contribute from their strengths and preferences. When an obligation doesn't naturally align with any specific member's interests, they share the burden. Distinguished programs also tend to be sturdy in the face of conflict. Their members expect to have differences of opinion but have demonstrated through past vigorous discussion that resolving the conflict by careful analysis of all positions can lead to improved solutions. Everyone says his or her piece, and a decision is rendered. Such departments rarely have to vote, as they converge on the most satisfying decisions through consensus. As a consequence, when conflict occurs, it doesn't tend to produce enduring disruptive effects. Instead, group members experience a strong commitment to the solution and an even stronger commitment to the group following the decision.

Respect for Individual and Cultural Differences

Individual and cultural diversity have become important points of emphasis in higher education based on the activities of the last two decades (Ancis, Sedlacek, & Mohr, 2000; Gurung & Prieto, 2009; Moos, 2002). The movement toward purposeful heterogeneity within programs is a complex challenge. For example, traditional departments have been staffed with individuals who were available at the time their jobs emerged. In many cases, this reality means that traditionally trained white males founded the vast majority of academic departments. As more opportunities have opened for underrepresented groups, it has been jarring to traditional practice that may have inadvertently reinforced old ways of thinking.

Distinguished programs have embraced the conversation about the value of being purposefully heterogeneous in the makeup of the department. These programs work to ensure that individuals with widely differing backgrounds and interests will strengthen the vigor of the department. From this standpoint, new perspectives introduced by faculty with such divergent backgrounds can be seen as invigorating. Distinguished programs welcome the challenge and benefit from the clear message to students that diversity enriches. In addition, distinguished programs formally review whether their diversity practices send the right message and make corrections if they conclude that there is more to do.

At the other extreme, undeveloped programs see little relevance in striving for heterogeneity. Faculty members may even denigrate campus efforts to improve cultural diversity, calling them a threat to academic freedom or a distraction from the more important business of passing on the discipline's time-honored traditions and perspectives. In such cases, the program is unlikely to attract new kinds of faculty talent into the program. Students from underrepresented groups complain that the program feels homogeneous and unwelcoming. Regardless of race or class background, all students can legitimately ask why such programs seem removed from the twenty-first century. As a consequence, they remain far removed from the rich collegial practices of the ''Learning University'' (cf. Bain, 2004, p. 175) in which faculty embrace the opportunity to learn from others, including their students.

Programs in the middle—those that are developing or effective—can be characterized as trying to solve the diversity question through patchwork efforts. Faculty may respond to institutional mandates about enriching the characteristics of candidates in the job pool but not show much in the way of dedication toward recruiting diverse perspectives because of the advantages this activity could produce for the sake of the discipline as well as the potential students from underrepresented groups. Although diverse faculty candidates may be interviewed, developing and effective programs often are not focused on successfully recruiting such candidates to be the position finalist. The usual explanation is the lack of a good fit within the department or program—which, under the right circumstances, is not necessarily a bad criterion. Here, however, the goal of changing the program fit is often forgotten.

At the same time, colleagues in developing and effective programs may worry that even if a diverse candidate is hired successfully, he or she may not elect to stay at the institution very long (we might label this the ''projected fit'' problem). Ironically, this conclusion is often reached by pointing to the fact that few, if any, departments have a diverse faculty complement. In other words, diverse candidates will not find a ready-made diverse community;

thus they will choose not to stay, and the cycle is presumed to continue. The obvious problems here include the fact that candidates deserve the right to decide for themselves (once they are hired and work for a period of time) whether they will stay, as well as the fact that buying into the projected fit problem only maintains the status quo of de facto homogeneity.

Equitable Problem Solving

Adverse program climates may not inspire confidence that individuals can get a fair hearing in conflicts. It doesn't matter whether the conflict exists between faculty members, or between a faculty member and a student, or between a faculty member and a chair. If a program gets a deserved reputation for playing favorites, perceptions of the climate will deteriorate.

An undeveloped program is characterized by problem solving in which privilege prevails in the resolution of conflict. Ironically, the problem solvers may be unaware that they are being influenced by the dictates of privilege. For example, senior faculty members may expect their seniority alone to be the decisive factor when conflicts erupt between seasoned and relatively inexperienced faculty. Privilege may be accorded those who

- Have greater access to high-level decision makers
- Have more experience in the setting
- Display a bigger emotional claim (such as number of majors versus nonmajors)
- Talk more loudly or express their ideas more swiftly
- Chronically threaten formal complaint procedures if they can't get their way

By relying on an often unspoken claim to privilege to solve a problem, the undeveloped program may short-circuit more effective discussion. For example, one of us once reviewed a program where the curriculum was thirty years behind the times. Every time junior colleagues attempted to bring the curriculum in line with current disciplinary standards, the senior colleagues would allow the discussion to occur but then hijack the vote at the last minute, often claiming that "everyone wants what's best for the students." The reviewer acknowledged that the intentions of all the participants were heartfelt, but informed the senior faculty—kindly, but firmly—that outdated standards, self-interest, and inertia clearly were steering curricular decisions in unhelpful directions. Only then could serious discussion of cooperative change occur.

In contrast, developing programs acknowledge that bias in decision making can produce less-than-effective decisions. However, the faculty may be unwilling to invest the time to produce a more fair-minded solution. Tension and disagreement are inevitable in such circumstances, and discomfort results. Similarly, effective programs seek to minimize the possibility of bias, but may not do so as systematically as they could. When change comes, it is incremental at best. Thus what could be accomplished in an overall curricular change in one or two years is done more slowly—say, over a five- to ten-year horizon. The problem in such cases is that while waiting for an opinion change or for particular colleagues to retire, larger curricular advances may be occurring at the disciplinary level. In such circumstances, an effective program is continually working against itself.

Distinguished programs establish problem-solving protocols that minimize the influence of bias. Some decisions may be referred to committees appointed to ensure objective evaluation of the issue at hand. In addition, decision rubrics in which the faculty determine criteria for the decision in some formal manner may emerge to help explain and defend decisions. Although the decision process may seem more protracted using such strategies, the end result is that fewer claims can be made that individuals took advantage of being an insider to achieve a favorable outcome.

Program Leadership

Professors have long been evaluated as a central fixture in institutional accountability measures (cf. Halonen & Ellenberg, 2006); however, chairs and other high-level administrators often escape the same kind of evaluative scrutiny although their contributions to program climate may be dramatic. Only recently have discussions about the importance of assessing effectiveness in role become part of the scholarly landscape (cf. Wheeler, Seagren, Becker, Kinley, Mlinek, & Robson, 2008).

The avoidance of this accountability practice is understandable. Because every program that operates in a higher educational context has distinctive elements that place unique demands on the chairs and program directors, such differences militate against common yardsticks for measuring quality. Faculty members may be loath to engage in evaluative practices if they perceive that retaliation for bad news could be possible (i.e., "I won't evaluate you too rigorously so that later, when I'm chair, you won't evaluate me rigorously in retribution"). Unspoken complicity leads to evaluative gridlock.

Most administrators receive very little in the way of systematic feedback on their effectiveness in this important role (Seldin & Higgerson, 2002). Indeed, the caliber of the feedback that gets returned to administrators can be fairly random. Students may base their opinions of administrative effectiveness on a one-time encounter when the student might not have been predisposed favorably to any other point of view but her own. For example, a student makes an appointment with a chair, angling to fast-talk the chair into overriding her professor's B+ judgment about her performance in class. The student argues that she missed the cutoff by less than half a point so the point total should be rounded up but her professor refuses to do so. The student wants the "A−" to which she feels entitled and begs the chair to intervene. An effective chair has no business modifying the grading practices of the faculty member in the interest of academic freedom and equitable treatment of all students in the class, but the chair's refusal is likely to leave the student with a long-standing impression that the chair "doesn't listen to students." In reality, the chair has appropriately defended the principle of nondiscriminatory treatment but that adherence will be lost on the irritated student who failed in her quest.

Similar emotion-laden episodes may dramatically shape how the faculty members feel about their chairs. One refusal of a travel request, for example, can loom large in an otherwise collegial and collaborative chair's record, despite whatever solid grounds might exist to justify the refusal. In our experience, many administrators worry about what they see as "ticking time bombs" created by their reasoned and reasonable refusal to take or permit certain courses of action. In fact, some faculty serving in administrative roles have articulated that they will return to the faculty when the scar tissue of unpopular decisions accumulates sufficiently to render them less effective.

In the absence of a systematic review process, chairs are likely to submit a list of accomplishments from their units as evidence of their effectiveness. This practice may do little to shed light on elements of administrative behavior that contributed to the achievement of the positive outcomes. Indeed, departments with strong members can make even weak chairs look good based on the positive press that comes from spectacular individual achievements.

Undeveloped programs are beset with leadership issues that contribute to an adverse program climate. These include the following common patterns:

- No one wants to be chair. Whatever sap gets stuck with a job will endure it until it is time for the new sap to step in. The aforementioned fear of subsequent retribution squelches new initiatives and maintains the status quo.
- Or worse, the program goes into "receivership," headed by an appointee from another department who may have no background and little sympathy with the mission of the unit. The outsider, although often well-intentioned, is apt to go through the motions to maintain the program, but serious changes are often postponed.
- The chair gets appointed by the dean but does not have full support from the faculty, who had given their support to a candidate that the dean didn't like. Such scenarios will produce a festival of passive-aggressive responses in the hopes that the new chair gets fed up and abandons the job.
- Someone wants to be chair too badly. The new appointment wallows in the prestige and power but mishandles the mundane details, driving faculty to distraction. The worst outcome in this case is when the appointee takes privileges for

himself while pushing his real duties onto a secretary or to other colleagues, some of whom are untenured.

In all these cases and many more, the configuration of leadership will not help the department develop positively, and the climate will suffer. Vast quantities of energy will be diverted to playing politics when they could have been wisely invested in program improvement.

Some operational problems may be addressed in developing programs, but on balance the leadership in such programs will remain problematic. A typical characteristic of such programs involves a leader who may operate too independently from her constituents. Communications are apt to be one-sided, informing rather than based on discussion. The motivation driving the independence may be good-hearted; for example, leaders may want to avoid asking faculty members to be involved in mundane and time-wasting decisions. However, to the extent that the leader bears the mantle of responsibility as a solo endeavor, the program faculty may be unlikely to buy into the leader's plan, which will generate substantially more work in the long run. Whispering campaigns in opposition tend to flourish, but substantive work is slow to come.

Effective leaders construct more positive work environments by sharing responsibilities and by trusting that faculty will deliver on their assignments. These leaders may not engage in much environmental scanning to determine the effectiveness of their strategies, but they do understand that more successful programs will involve investing in program operations activity broadly across the faculty.

Distinguished leaders monitor program climate to give them clues about what is and is not working. They actively seek feedback in both formal and informal ways. They involve faculty members in decision processes not just to solve the problem at hand, but also to retrench commitment to the program. In addition, they conscientiously reinforce contributions by faculty, staff, and students that improve climate conditions. They use challenges to the department (such as a severe budget reduction) as opportunities to engage in extraordinary activity that can build a stronger department through proactive strategies (Facione, 2009).

Relationship with University Community

Programs differ in how they conceptualize their relationship with the university community. Some conceptualizations generate positive energy and facilitate the best work of the department. In these situations, departments reflect a great deal of pride in helping the university accomplish its mission. On the other hand, some conceptualizations reinforce negative perceptions and lack of trust in the university that galvanize harsh feelings and guarantee adverse program climates.

Undeveloped programs tend to be both isolationist and solipsistic. The faculty see little value in making a solid connection with their colleagues outside the department, and their dedication to their own perspectives as "right" and "just" may rule out consideration of other factors that appropriately explain campus politics. The faculty may be united around a shared perception of past maltreatment that they think may justify negative feelings toward the rest of the university. For example, the faculty may fixate on the reallocation of a faculty line to another department as "proof" that the institution has no interest in serving their needs, without determining whether the argument for reallocation was sound. Or they may harbor a grudge when an "undeserving" department is moved into new academic space. In the first case, the conclusion may be drawn without regard to the program's obvious declining enrollments that put the vacated line in jeopardy or the fact that the explosive growth of the other department simply made a more compelling case. In the second, the department may sustain a self-glorifying image of its own importance that is not shared by other constituencies on campus, including the administration. As a consequence, program faculty—in a shortsighted, albeit heartfelt, expression of their disappointment—may make a commitment to do the minimal amount of work to keep the program operational and forgo any other opportunities to make broader contributions to the university.

In developing programs, grudging recognition of university service needs will produce some activity on the part of program faculty. However, the motives for service may be shallow, and the activity generated is apt to be *pro forma* at best. Faculty understand that sitting on committees is required to prevail in tenure and promotion decisions, but they may do little to pursue actual achievement related to their assignment beyond filling space. For example, it might not occur to the faculty member to report the activities associated with their role to the department itself; they simply serve the time. When program faculty performance is lackluster or sporadic with university assignments, campus colleagues will generalize about the program itself based on their uninspiring representative.

Faculty from effective programs recognize that university service is more complex and meaningful than merely filling a seat. They seek opportunities to mix with their colleagues in ways that match their particular talents, and they make a point to bring back reports of their activities to the program to strengthen the program's tie to the group involved in the service obligation. To the extent that their contributions to campus obligations are reliable, energetic, and creative the program climate will, by association, generate more favorable impressions.

On the other hand, an effective program can also be perceived in a favorable, if largely disconnected, way. One of us reviewed an otherwise fine program that was completely isolated from campus affairs. Members of other departments complimented the program on a narrow range of student-related activities but, almost to a person, remarked that they had no idea what else was going on there. A few even said they did not personally know any of the colleagues to speak to or even by name (the campus in question, a small liberal arts college, had fewer than 110 full-time faculty members). As such, the reviewer deemed the disconnection to be a serious failing in a department that could have been distinguished with more investment in the local context.

Campus administrators vigorously pursue members of distinguished programs to supply leadership for the various initiatives that transpire on any campus. A positive program climate provides the best substrate for the development of strong leadership skills. Some of the leadership strength of particular faculty members will be credited to program climates that served as a developmental backdrop for their strengths. When programs are in a position to loan leadership to various campus initiatives, the feedback loop to the department about the breadth of activities at any campus will contribute to a more "plugged in" department and a more vibrant program climate.

Program Involvement in Local Community

Isolationist tendencies also complicate service to local communities for those institutions whose mission highly values this activity. Faculty may construe requests to be involved with the community as a distraction from teaching or making progress on the latest scholarly or creative project. As such, undeveloped programs do little to encourage faculty members to get out from behind the podium or away from the research lab. Without a solid rationale to involve faculty in community enterprises, there is little reason to bring students into the mix to benefit from what the community has to offer.

Members of developing programs are more likely to adopt selected community initiatives that are consonant with their own personal interests. These service obligations may or may not have a direct bearing on the faculty member's discipline. If they do not, the academic value of the community service may be much more constrained, although the public relations value of having a faculty member meaningfully engaged is still worthwhile. Any learning opportunities students could have in the community (such as field placement, internships, research opportunities, volunteer sites) simply are not part of the mix.

Effective programs concentrate on promoting involvement in the local community that will have some salutary effects for the home department. For example, faculty can participate as board members of professional groups in the region that have a connection to the discipline. The community performance has positive effects on public relations for the department and the college or university. Ultimately, such service can develop some alliances in the community that can have some far-reaching financial advantages for the department. In addition, applied learning situations abound when faculty and community come together. Students generally find that service learning helps give their academic learning much more purpose.

Beyond the fundamental good represented in any community contribution, a distinguished program involvement in the community represents a public relations bonanza. "Town and gown" relations are noteworthy. The department embraces opportunities for cooperative ventures. For example, an engineering program may mobilize campus resources to host a robotics competition. For a minimal investment, not only does the project plan showcase the resources the campus may have for the education of future students, but the hands-on nature of the event also provides multiple opportunities for contributions. The activity then can generate a list of potential donors to other related endeavors. Media coverage reinforces the significance of the service contribution, and everyone—current and prospective students, faculty and administrators, community leaders and professionals—benefits.

Conclusion

The claim made in the conversation related at the outset of this chapter—that you can determine program quality in fifteen minutes—was admittedly outlandish. However, careful consideration of the indicators that excited or irritated this group of academic program reviewers led to a comprehensive set of rubrics to help programs make progress in their quality. Taking these in combination with the rubrics described in other chapters of the book, programs have some viable tools to strengthen their programs as well as their claims for distinction. We hasten to add that in some ways the climate of a department or program can serve as a bellwether for how colleagues in it will respond to the benchmarking exercise. Put another way, a program's climate will most likely have an impact on the other seven evaluative dimensions. For this reason, we urge readers—faculty, chairs, deans, and provosts—to pay particular attention to a program's climate and to address it constructively.

Guiding Questions

1. As you tour your own common work spaces, what conclusions can you draw about the vibrancy of the program? What would a visitor conclude about the climate in your program?

2. Why should program climate have such a profound impact on the quality of student learning?
3. How would current undergraduate students in your program characterize its climate?
4. How do you believe other programs on campus view your program's climate? Would administrators concur? Why or why not?
5. What dimensions appear to have the most relevance for identifying the strengths and weaknesses of your program climate?
6. What are the top three programs on your campus? If yours is not among them, what do the other programs do to be successful that your department could learn from?
7. What program climate obstacles keep your program from offering a transformative experience for students and a deeply satisfying experience for faculty?

Chapter Three

First Things First: Attending to Assessment Issues, Accountability, and Accreditation

with George B. Ellenberg

Claudia J. Stanny

Eman El-Sheikh

Our parents told us to be wary of conversations about religion and politics, but within the higher education environment, one is often safer discussing those subjects than opening a dialogue about assessment. Although higher education has been grappling with accountability and assessment for decades, few topics produce such strong reactions among faculty and administrators as the need for a formal assessment structure and process. This is not surprising given that program assessment aims to gauge what happens at the very center of the higher education universe. Responses to the term "assessment" range from "It is useless" to "It is transformative" and touch every point in between. Although some institutions have established strong assessment cultures (for example, Alverno College, Indiana University-Purdue University Indianapolis, James Madison University), it is probably more unusual than usual for a program, much less a university, to be able to claim a deeply rooted, healthy assessment culture in which administrators and faculty carefully and regularly collect data as an integral component of a candid, sustained conversation about program quality and program improvement.

In an era of intense, rapid, and profound change within higher education—change that is often driven by outside forces such as public demand for accountability, legislative responses to the public's priorities, and pressure from accrediting bodies—some faculty members have responded enthusiastically to accountability activities and initiatives. They are comfortable and confident that the data will document their efforts to produce positive outcomes. Consequently, they embrace the opportunity to showcase their work. Others naturally respond with skepticism, delaying tactics, indifference, or outright hostility to initiatives that appear questionable to them or that may hold them accountable in new and unknown ways. At best, faculty questions catalyze a useful dialogue about assessment and how it should be tailored to institutional, departmental, and disciplinary needs; at worst, faculty questions can stultify or negate attempts to design and implement a useful assessment paradigm. With any debate or discussion in higher education, the sardonic adage is often tossed out that the struggles are so bitter because the stakes are so small. In the case of assessment, one must hope that the reverse holds true and that the debates will be healthy and collegial because the stakes are so large. At the very least, a better understanding of faculty responses should help identify ways to overcome hurdles in the way of establishing a vibrant assessment culture.

UNDERSTANDING FACULTY RESPONSES TO ASSESSMENT

Imagine you receive a fateful call from an administrator at your institution. After a friendly chat, the administrator inquires whether you might be interested in some special institutional service to help the entire organization make some much-needed progress. Although the title may differ from institution to institution, the administrator asks you to take on the role of the institutional assessment officer. The offer might be made in response to an impending visit by an accrediting team or to a particularly pointed mandate from the state legislature. The offer might come with a promise of release time or tailored travel to help you get up to speed on the national assessment picture. In either case, your academic life is about to be reshaped, sometimes in dramatic ways, as you shepherd the organization to a new way of conducting academic practice.

For many individuals, this invitation can lead to a transformation of the institution and the faculty. However, for some this new mantle of responsibility will thrust the assessment officer into the very center of campus controversy. It is not an assignment to undertake lightly, for many reasons, but especially because the individual is more than likely to encounter resistance in some form. Perhaps the most important aspect of dealing with resistance, whether you are the faculty member called to serve or an administrator attempting to inculcate an assessment culture on campus, is to realize that resistance occurs for a number of reasons. This is a simple point, but reminding oneself of it helps maintain focus on the issues at hand and to stay away from simplistic explanations. The view from the faculty member's perspective and the view from an administrator's perspective can differ substantially, and clear, two-way communication in the assessment arena is vitally important. In short, seeds of resistance can be sown as easily by administrative mishandling of assessment initiatives as by faculty members prematurely declaring assessment to be a counterproductive influence.

Resistance to accountability as a whole, and to assessment specifically, reflects the impact of broader issues influencing colleges and universities, but the historical context is important as well. Our national culture and our nation's very existence are rooted in rebellion against centralized control. In one view, "It might be sufficient simply to invoke the American tradition of limited government as an explanation of the independence of the higher education sector" (Fritschler, Weissburg, & Magness, 2008, p. 42). Stated another way, resistance can result in positive outcomes because it highlights communication or process issues that may need to be addressed to build a foundation for developing a culture of assessment. In addition, one could argue that education on any level, but especially at the college level, is a complex process and that students may be influenced in ways that are not quantifiable (Walvoord, 2004).

Generational differences may play a role in how faculty members respond to change. Some faculty members view the past as a "golden age" when resources were plentiful; students were conscientious, well-prepared and respectful; and faculty were left alone by legislatures, administrators, and the public to fulfill their missions. Whether or not this halcyon era ever truly existed, older faculty members tend to be more resistant to change than their younger colleagues (Clarke, Ellett, Bateman, & Rugutt, 1996). Young faculty members also may be susceptible to acculturation into a resistance mode in their professional lives as they progress from untenured to tenured status. Part of this acculturation may be driven by their lack of authority, especially as untenured faculty, to question the status quo as described and constructed by senior faculty. If a full professor in one's department decrees that assessment is either impossible or a grand waste of time, that pronouncement carries considerable weight.

Another common response to assessment is that it is a passing fad that can be held at arm's length until it disappears. Anyone who has participated in or observed general education reform, revision of tenure and promotion criteria, or other debates on a campus understands how carefully one must proceed in order to gain faculty buy-in. Assessment is no different in this way, although because of its connotations and faculty preconceptions about it, assessment may be a harder sell.

Higher education culture within the larger American context helps explain some of the resistance to assessment, and broad-based analysis can illuminate the environment from which faculty respond to assessment initiatives, but a more focused discussion offers insight into specific barriers that limit the development of a self-sustaining assessment culture. Faculty reactions to assessment are varied and most often spring from honest questions about the definition, place, and implementation of assessment strategies. At heart, most faculty are really students themselves, with a love of learning and a passion for their respective disciplines, so it is instructive to view them in that light for a moment. Developing assessment models for programs requires the application of critical thinking skills. As most of us know from classroom experience, students respond to critical thinking assignments with varying degrees of success, so it makes sense that the same would be true of faculty when they are faced with their own assessment "assignment." Key among the reasons students struggle with the task of learning to think critically is that the "outcomes of reasoned decisions do not match their personal preferences" (Buskist & Irons, 2008, p. 51). In this case, the faculty member as student may not want to scrutinize assumptions about teaching and learning imbibed from a lifetime in classrooms because this could lead to conclusions that his or her own teaching does not measure up to expectations, that change is needed, or that a course does not contribute as well as it should to departmental goals. This unease may or may not have a basis in reality, but in this case resistance is based on the bliss of ignorance.

Not surprisingly, a significant aspect of how faculty members react to assessment is framed by their views regarding academic freedom and their definition of what constitutes classroom privacy. Documents such at the 1940 *Statement of Principles on Academic Freedom and Tenure* (American Association of University Professors, 1990) offer guidance on academic freedom. Academic freedom is one of the most dearly held faculty perquisites, but with it come responsibilities regarding content, grading, departmental needs, and a host of other factors. Assessing students is central to teaching; assessing programs is central to improving student learning. Faculty typically embrace assessment of their own students (however they may define assessment) as a clear-cut duty that they take very seriously, but may see program assessment as something foisted upon departments by "administrators." Clearly, departmental chairs can reinforce or minimize this perception, but it is a powerful factor in any case.

There are broad philosophical reasons for not embracing assessment, but there are more practical faculty concerns, as well. Whether a faculty member is asked to take on assessment at the departmental or higher level, time is a crucial factor. Faculty rightfully see teaching, scholarship, and service as the proper foci of their energy. If assessment is added as yet another demand, faculty may ask with good reason why it is needed, what form it will take, how much time it will take to do, and what benefits will accrue to students, themselves, their department, the college, and the university. Answering these questions satisfactorily is no easy task, but they must be answered clearly and consistently by knowledgeable assessment advocates if change is to take place.

There are many reasons that program assessment does not always find a fertile environment, but with care and nurture, program assessment can be grafted successfully onto the existing university culture. Our purpose in this chapter is to provide a strong rationale, based on both practical and idealistic motives, for why it is time for departments to examine resistance thoughtfully, take steps to overcome it, and step up to the challenge of developing an assessment culture within their areas of responsibility and promote some tools that might facilitate this transition.

Why Foster Strong Assessment and Accountability Practices?

Faculty experience the current initiative to engage in ongoing assessment for continuous improvement of student learning in the context of multiple demands on their time and resources. The contemporary landscape of higher education includes changing criteria related to scholarly publication to earn tenure and promotion; a press for enrollment growth that may entail larger classes, heavier teaching loads, or both; pressures to acquire new skills with technology for online courses or to enrich the face-to-face learning experience; and greater expectations for community engagement and service. Moreover, because these increased expectations occur in the context of strained university budgets, reduced availability of funding for state-supported institutions, and increased competition for limited research funding, a logical and reasonable question is: What benefits can be expected by committing limited resources to assessment? The new assessment officer will need to have rich and ready answers to that question.

Improve the Quality of Teaching and Learning

Assessment focuses attention on the strengths and challenges students experience in the curriculum (Suskie, 2004, 2009; Walvoord, 2004). Departments engaged in consistent and regular assessment of student learning experience improvements in teaching and learning, and they increase their clarity about "how course sequences fit together, vigorous and helpful faculty dialogue on educational purposes, new approaches to teaching, an improved basis for advising students about their academic progress, and the assurance that all students meet certain standards" (Banta, 1997, p. 7).

One of the nine principles of good practice for assessing student learning articulated by the American Association for Higher Education (American Association for Higher Education, 1992) is *Assessment requires attention to outcomes but also and equally to the experiences that lead to those outcomes.* The continued "attention to the *process* of teaching . . . for the purpose of increasing and enhancing student learning is the defining characteristic of successful outcomes assessment" (Banta, 1997, p. 83), which also includes a commitment to identifying and adopting high-quality teaching practices and other departmental operations (for example, advising practices, strategic planning based on evidence).

The current academic environment is evolving rapidly. Adoption of new instructional strategies related to emerging technologies (such as online instruction, wikis, social networking sites, blogs) raises questions about the impact of these changes on student learning. Assessment of student learning can provide valuable evidence to evaluate these strategies and technologies and help faculty make evidence-based decisions rather than rely on anecdote and intuition (Allen, 2004; Maki, 2004; Maki & Maki, 2007; Massy, Graham, & Short, 2007).

Improve Departmental Coherence and Collegiality

The most important stage in an effective assessment process is the establishment of a regular, evidence-driven conversation about the curriculum and instructional practices that is centered on regular discussions of teaching strategies, and student learning, and continuous reflection on the alignment of the curriculum with program-level learning outcomes. Over time, departments that engage in these conversations will evolve an increasingly coherent program curriculum (Francis & Steven,

2003). These departments will be alert to opportunities to modify and improve instructional practices, advising, and cocurricular activities that improve student engagement in the department (Massy et al., 2007).

Changes in content, practice, or technology can render traditional courses in a discipline obsolete or irrelevant and create needs for new courses. If departments evaluate the coherence of the curriculum with contemporary practices in the discipline and engage in regular examination of student learning, they will be alert to the need for revision sooner than departments that engage in sporadic episodes of examination of their curriculum. Moreover, routine assessment practices will provide tangible evidence for these discussions and decisions. Although effective assessment practices will not ensure that all members of the faculty play nicely during curriculum discussions, a department that establishes a tradition in which curriculum decisions are based on assessment evidence creates habits of interaction that are incompatible with self-serving defense of turf (Massy et al., 2007). Because assessment practices have a public component in terms of the documentation of regular discussions about student learning, these activities can contribute to the public persona of a department that embraces excellence in teaching and student learning (Allen, 2004; Maki, 2004; Walvoord, 2004).

Create Scholarship Opportunities

Faculty curiosity about the impact of their teaching methods on student learning can motivate the development of additional domains of scholarship. The growing literature in the Scholarship of Teaching and Learning (SoTL) and the Scholarship of Assessment is fueled by insights gained from problem areas identified in assessment work (Angelo & Cross, 1993; Cross & Steadman, 1996; Massy et al., 2007; Suskie, 2004, 2009; Weimer, 2006). An increasing number of universities now recognize SoTL as a legitimate component of faculty scholarship and include SoTL criteria in faculty reward systems, including the tenure and promotion process (Henderson, 2007; McKinney, 2007; Weimer, 2006).

INCREASE STUDENT ENROLLMENT AND RETENTION

Departments with mature assessment programs that motivate innovations in teaching strategies and keep the curriculum up-to-date are likely to have the energy and faculty engagement that attract and retain students. Rossman and El-Khawas (1987) noted that some institutions report improvements in the quality of characteristics of the applicant pool following adoption of comprehensive assessment programs. Assessment data are an increasingly important component of marketing programs for academic institutions. When prospective students and their parents are researching schools, they are increasingly interested in direct evidence of alumni success by measures such as admission of graduates to professional schools.

Many students enroll in an institution without a clear understanding of their academic options or a clear commitment to completing a major in a particular discipline. Students who matriculate as undeclared majors, as well as those who declare a major but experience a change of heart after a term or two, are attracted to departments with outstanding teaching and a vibrant, engaging curriculum.

COMPETE SUCCESSFULLY FOR RESOURCES

Strategic planning decisions may be predicated on ''program metrics,'' including assessment of student learning, retention, graduation rates, and other significant outcomes. Examination of trend data addresses questions about the department's relative value in meeting strategic priorities of the institution (Massy et al., 2007; Suskie, 2004, 2009), especially when budgetary crises require difficult decisions about which programs will grow and which programs will be deemed relatively ineffective and therefore dispensable. During difficult times, tangible evidence about student learning based on ongoing assessment can be used to make a case about which programs have merit and to identify programs with potential for growth and enhancement. For example, the University of Missouri successfully used assessment evidence to argue for continued funding support of learning communities

(Banta & Lefebvre, 2006). Similarly, the absence of reliable and valid assessment data about the quality of student learning increases the vulnerability of a program that has little more than informal opinions and traditions to speak in its favor.

Assessment evidence can also provide the documentation needed to obtain additional funding from state government (Banta, 1997). Assessment efforts at Ohio University that documented the quality of undergraduate programs resulted in the awarding of additional state grants for program excellence. Administrators can make good use of documentation of student learning when they solicit funds from donors, legislators, future employers of alumni, and similar groups (Suskie, 2004, 2009). Trend data on the outcomes of greatest interest (such as success on national exit exams) can make a persuasive case for those interested in helping the university reach greater levels of achievement and public recognition.

Satisfy External Pressures and Mandates

Ewell (2007, p. 11) argues that accrediting bodies are "the major external driver of assessment for the past decade." Federal requirements for regional accreditation now require direct evidence of student learning and other mission-related institutional goals (Suskie, 2004, 2009). By 1997, all regional accrediting bodies had enacted accreditation standards related to the assessment of student learning, and 75 percent of states had adopted policies mandating assessment of student learning (Banta, 1997). Accreditation of colleges and universities is a rigorous program of oversight that provides comprehensive review and assurance of sound educational institutions. The Council for Higher Education Accreditation (CHEA) provides broad oversight for regional accreditation bodies. Six primary regional organizations (Middle States, New England, North Central, Western, Southern, and Northwestern) working within the CHEA structure grant accreditation to colleges and universities. Accreditation is mandatory for legitimate recognition of an institution of higher learning.

The work of the Spellings Commission on the Future of Higher Education created a sense of urgency and focused greater attention on the need to engage in credible assessment of student learning (Eaton, 2008b; Miller, 2006). Dicroce (2006) stated, "Indeed there is not a college or university in the land that has not at least started to wade around in the muck inherent in the findings and recommendations of the Spellings commission" (p. B7). Thus the current accreditation environment demands that departments and institutions engage in assessment to maintain their competitive position as a high-quality academic program (Banta, Lund, Black, & Oblander, 1996; Suskie, 2004, 2009).

Qualify for Disciplinary Accreditation

It has become standard procedure for discipline-specific accrediting bodies to require systematic assessment of student learning as a standard of accreditation (Suskie, 2004, 2009). CHEA recognizes twenty-eight disciplinary organizations that accredit bachelor's degree programs (these are listed in Appendix D). All of these organizations endorse and require assessment of student learning as a standard of accreditation.

In addition to mandatory accreditation within the disciplines (Dunn et al., 2007), other disciplinary organizations have developed and promoted program reviews for the purpose of achieving program approval or other hallmarks of legitimacy within an institution. Program approval is similar to accreditation in that programs voluntarily undergo a program review. Criteria for approval tend to be aspirational with program approval serving as a designation of quality. In some cases (cf. American Chemical Society Committee on Professional Training, 2008), disciplinary societies provide graduates of approved programs with certificates validating their educational achievements. In both instances, accreditation and approval, an external body provides validation of the quality of a program and leverage for programs that are vying for limited resources. Additionally, the accreditation process and associated certification of graduates has implications for professional licensure and employment opportunities for alumni of these programs.

Produce Momentum Toward Distinction

Programs that aspire to achieve recognition as programs of distinction should adopt best practices in assessment and pay particular attention to the *use* of assessment evidence to inform departmental discussions about the curriculum and motivate the exploration and implementation of curricular innovation (Allen, 2004; Maki, 2004; Walvoord, 2004). CHEA established the CHEA Award for Institutional Progress in Student Learning Outcomes in 2005. CHEA has now recognized twelve institutions for their work in assessment, either institution-wide or within specific departments or programs (Eaton, 2008a). Banta (1997) identifies several institutions, ranging from community colleges through regional comprehensive and research-intensive doctoral universities, that have established reputations for distinction in academic quality subsequent to adopting comprehensive programs for systematic assessment of student learning.

EVOLVING A PROGRAM-BASED ASSESSMENT CULTURE

The task of the new assessment officer is significantly larger than merely getting some acceptable measurements in place to satisfy accountability demands. Devising sound institutional assessment strategies is an intensive developmental and collaborative process. To be successful in this role, the new officer must work philosophically as well as mechanically if the institution is to sustain its early investment efforts. In effect, the assessment officer may become the most visible organizational change agent at the university (cf. Payette & Shaw, 2008). The scope of the charge of the new assessment officer will vary widely, depending on how seriously the institution has been responding to accountability demands.

Once a program embarks on an accountability strategy, those new to the idea may be easily tempted to think that developing the plan and collecting the data allows them to check off this institutional obligation and move to the next chore that will sustain the program. More experienced faculty recognize that assessment initiates a process that, when appropriately nurtured, can produce a culture of evidence that will sustain assessment and improved student learning. They realize that assessment practice is not only the right thing to do but also the most helpful way a program can chart and execute its preferred course. The process of posing questions about ways to improve on quality simply becomes part of the business of delivering high-quality education rather than resting on established reputation or past laurels.

To develop a true "culture of evidence" (Millett, Stickler, Payne, & Dwyer, 2007), more attention should be paid to the qualitative differences that emerge among programs in the evolution of assessment planning. Our approach to differentiating programs in their commitment to effective assessment emerged in a discussion about overall program quality (Dunn, McCarthy, Baker, Halonen, & Hill, 2007; see Chapter 1). Although we originally geared the work toward monitoring quality in psychology programs, the principles involved in assessment practice can be readily generalized to other disciplines. Summarized in Table 3.1, our approach produced a rubric to capture quality differences among programs that have not been engaged in assessment in a meaningful manner, characterized as undeveloped; those that have gotten under way, but not gotten far in the process, identified as developing; those that have made significant strides in the development of assessment culture, described as effective; and those that have achieved truly distinctive accountability performance, characterized as distinguished. The distinguished group stands out when compared to other programs of comparable size and resources.

The rubric captures specific domains of effort that constitute assessment performance, including assessment planning, data gathering, and use of data for program decisions and promotion. The application of the rubric to any program culture can provide an overall evaluation of the sophistication of the program's stance on this critical issue.

UNDEVELOPED ASSESSMENT CULTURES

In an accountability-enhanced climate, few programs can afford to ignore the need to address matters of quality in an active and meaningful way. Undeveloped programs that somehow still manage to be free from assessment obligations have particular characteristics. Faculty in programs that haven't taken on meaningful assessment practices tend to be self-satisfied; they either do not care about a collective effort toward quality or they assume that the quality is present, often buttressed by their own individual

Table 3.1 Assessment

	Undeveloped	*Developing*	*Effective*	*Distinguished*
Assessment Planning	Does not engage in assessment planning; demonstrates no proactive thinking about program effectiveness	Generates minimal assessment plan to satisfy external mandates, with no intention of follow-through	Accommodates external mandates, but focuses on getting legitimate evidence about program quality	Engages proactively about program effectiveness through continuous, vigorous, and consensual assessment planning
Data Gathering	Does not gather minimal effectiveness data	Gathers limited range of data only when externally mandated; relies on sources of data external to the department	Gathers broad range of data on semi-regular basis and analyzes periodically as required	Collects and analyzes range of data continuously to answer program quality questions; multiple methods and sources may include student and alumni input
Program Improvement	Makes changes in program based on faculty perceptions rather than program effectiveness data	Makes changes in program that minimally link directly to program effectiveness data	Improves program based on data analysis of program effectiveness prompted by external mandates	Regularly improves program based on systematic data analysis prompted by faculty-owned assessment process
Program Promotion	Does not use assessment data in public relations, outreach activities, and resource requests	Reacts to program promotion opportunities with haphazard use of assessment data	Incorporates some elements of program effectiveness data in program promotion activities	Integrates assessment practices into program promotion activities to enhance program

beliefs that each program member is doing a splendid job whether or not that is supported by their respective annual evaluation feedback.

Without any semblance of an assessment plan that can draw together disparate individuals in the unit to talk about their collective goals (Walvoord, 2004), it is obvious that no serious efforts will be made toward collection or interpretation of data. As a consequence, decisions in the program often boil down to which strong personality prevails in the inevitable turmoil that takes place in rarely scheduled program meetings. In such environments, the status quo will prevail, which may not optimally serve the students. It is possible that an accountability process would verify that the existing program is optimally designed and executed, but in the absence of supportive evidence, external evaluators will remain unimpressed. In effect, this approach verifies that it is not a good idea to let the cat guard the cream (Huber, 1992).

Is it possible that a program without an official assessment agenda is necessarily doing unacceptable work? Of course not. However, programs that invest substantial energy in avoiding the production of evidence about their quality—whether that request originates with a dean, a state system, or an accrediting agent—end up with nothing beyond testimony to validate their quality. As economic conditions dictate closer scrutiny of program quality, the risk for the undeveloped program is substantial.

DEVELOPING ASSESSMENT CULTURES

Programs typically launch their assessment practices because they are compelled to do so by external mandates. As a consequence, those who make initial efforts in all areas of assessment activity should probably not be expected to do so with wholehearted enthusiasm. Assessment planning will often show economy of effort, as people with limited-to-nonexistent training try to figure out what it means to have meaningful questions about quality. Faculty members worry that asking assessment questions may expose, perhaps fatally, some areas of weakness in their teaching. Finding just the right questions to assist faculty and departments in improving their teaching practices and student learning without making faculty feel threatened by the process is not easy.

Once the assessment questions devised by the faculty lead to a viable plan, those conducting the program may struggle a bit with figuring out how to gather, interpret, and use the data. Because assessment may not have been part of their job description at the point of hire, they naively speculate about who will be doing the data collection and express concern with the obvious solution that this must be a shared program responsibility. Many developing cultures solve this problem by identifying and appointing a resident assessment expert from among their members, hoping that this person's expertise and activity will satisfy whatever external demands come their way. In such situations, the impact of assessment will be enormous on the anointed one, but minuscule on the program members who have escaped the responsibility.

Developing cultures typically engage in an obligatory annual session to look at quality but may face such prospects with negative reactions ranging from mild dread to loathing. In addition, developing cultures do not readily see a strong connection between the data and the public face of the program, which diminishes their enthusiasm for promoting assessment efforts.

A seasoned department reviewer once reported that she had been asked to come to campus as an assessment specialist whose insights would be valued as the department worked its way through the reporting infrastructure that the administration was requiring. Once on site, she was ushered to a room with cabinets that were overflowing with portfolio materials. The host department was proud of all the data they had collected to verify the high-quality work they were doing, but they acted on the faulty conclusion that somehow the department reviewer would wade through the materials and present them with a validation. Somehow the host institution had adopted the same kind of strategy we often see in promotion and tenure materials compilation: more is better. In this case, absent their attempt to close the feedback loop themselves by interpreting their data, the department made only limited progress in establishing a true assessment culture.

Effective Assessment Cultures

At the point where a program embraces assessment as a tool, the coercive elements of the assessment enterprise tend to soften.

The program begins to select assessment questions that target relative weaknesses. The data-gathering and interpretation activities tend to be more equitably distributed among program members. The program dedicates at least one meeting annually to discussing the nature of their assessment findings and to proposing program modifications to improve quality.

The measurement stories that emerge in these reviews provide a natural vehicle to promote the program. Program members share in the achievement of what is working well and can recount their evidence to different constituents. The stories can sometimes be converted into teaching-learning scholarship, which provides some additional incentives for faculty involvement when this endeavor is endorsed by the institution as legitimate scholarship. In addition, the success of their assessment program may qualify them for additional resources. In such programs, the plans should also easily pass muster from regional or professional accrediting agencies, a fact that can be exploited for student recruitment and program promotion.

Participants in effective assessment cultures begin to recognize that their reporting obligations through assessment mandates can do double duty for their own professional enhancement. Professional societies now routinely feature standing-room-only crowds in the conference offerings that they provide to address common assessment needs. Even in situations where only a few colleagues share enthusiasm about the products and process of assessment, those colleagues will benefit by sharing their assessment insights with their colleagues and in the process build their own cases for favorable tenure and promotion review.

DISTINGUISHED ASSESSMENT CULTURES

The distinguished program experiences a shift in the climate around assessment. Such programs tend to take pride in their achievements and pose sound assessment questions, gather evidence, and use the results in a spirit of continuous improvement as a means of drawing deserved attention to their accomplishments. There is less to fear in the assessment results because the findings usually contain good news about how the program is faring. When so much is going well, it facilitates a candid appraisal of relative weaknesses so that these areas can also be improved with a reduced feeling of risk.

Assessment conversations will be more regularly featured in program meetings because they meet an important perceived need. As a consequence, the whole program tends to be aware of and involved in ongoing assessment activities. The program seeks appropriate benchmark information from relevant disciplinary groups or actively benchmarks its work against comparable programs at similar institutions. Assessment is integrated into the operations of the program, rather than experienced as an add-on requirement (Hutchings, 1990). The plan is modified regularly in response to perceived needs in the program rather than driven primarily by external reporting demands.

In a distinguished assessment culture, program leaders exploit the program's good outcomes to lobby for additional resources, whenever possible. Positive assessment data make a great story that can effectively document program quality for educational officials, prospective students, and concerned parents. In such programs, assessment realizes its full potential as a powerful tool for program enhancement. The program representatives recognize the public value of having positive data to share and begin to show fearlessness in carefully examining their programmatic weaknesses.

One initially resistant department made a dramatic conversion that illustrates the power of shared assessment concerns. From the outset, the personnel in the program balked at what appeared to be added work in identifying measures that would help them understand their own success. Settling on a nationally normed discipline test—and against the advice of local assessment experts—the program personnel were amazed to discover that their students performed in the ninetieth percentile of the test. Suddenly the program had a new story to tell. Repeated test administrations in subsequent years reaffirmed the high-quality work the program faculty were contributing. Inspired by the rich success, the program faculty began actively looking for evidence of other exemplary aspects of the curriculum and also began to show less fear about uncovering areas that needed to be refined. As a distinguished assessment culture, the program regularly shifts the focus of the assessment questions they are asking, but they never tire of telling the successful story that resulted from their original assessment data.

A Rubric for Evaluating the Quality of a Program's Assessment Practices

How does the assessment change agent directly facilitate developmental processes that will give departments good stories to tell? Administrators and program evaluators charged with monitoring assessment quality often start with fundamental questions about departmental assessment practices:

- Was the assessment plan developed and used on time?
- Did faculty collect any data?
- Did they use data to make decisions?

This all-or-none approach does not lend itself very effectively to helping programs develop increasing sophistication in their assessment process. We propose a more detailed strategy involving the development and use of criteria that capture how sophisticated the assessment plan has become. Assessment officials should collaborate with departments or programs to determine how effectively they are meeting these criteria and how their assessment plans are evolving. Such a model employs best practices in assessment and recognizes that collaborative efforts are most productive for creating a culture of assessment (Allen, 2004; Walvoord, 2004) and compares favorably to the "Levels of Implementation" approach proposed by Lopez (2000). In that model, Lopez outlined three levels of implementation that can be used to identify the level of sophistication of an institution's assessment planning and practice.

We propose a simpler rubric that identifies criteria of successful assessment strategies and distinguishes basic assessment plans from those that are more ambitious and well developed. The two-level rubric that includes specific criteria at each level is presented in Table 3.2. A plan that meets the first set of criteria would be considered a satisfactory assessment plan but would merit further development if it fails to meet one or more of those criteria. A plan that includes the first set of criteria as well as some

TABLE 3.2 PROGRAM ASSESSMENT RUBRIC TEMPLATE

	Present	*Not Present*	*Comments*
BASIC ASSESSMENT PLAN CRITERIA:			
Links plan to program outcomes			
Clearly describes context or rationale for selection of outcomes to assess			
Deploys at least one direct measure			
Identifies specific courses or points in the curriculum where data are collected			
Reports data collection			
Documents use of data for decision-making/process improvement; articulates the relation between evidence and decisions made			
Discusses plan and results within department			
Summarizes results in departmental annual report			
MATURE ASSESSMENT PLAN CRITERIA:			
Uses multiple measures to assess student learning outcomes			
Develops sustainable plan in terms of available resources			
Monitors success of plan, using suggestions from previous year(s) if appropriate			
Fits plan to department's long-term goals			

STATUS:

__________ Merits further development (plan is missing one or more of the required elements)

__________ Satisfactory (plan includes all of the required elements for a basic assessment plan)

__________ Well-developed (plan includes all of the required elements and at least some characteristics of a more mature assessment plan)

COMMENTS:

characteristics from the second set would be considered a more mature assessment plan.

Rubric Criteria

Basic program assessment criteria include the following:

- *Links plan to program outcomes.* The question to be addressed by the assessment process should be grounded in the program-level outcomes.
- *Clearly describes context or rationale for selection of outcomes to assess.* The rationale for the specific outcomes or questions should be addressed, taking into consideration the department's goals, resources, and curricular needs. Assessment results from previous years, if any, should be used to identify the outcomes that need to be addressed and the specific questions about the program that the assessment process will attempt to answer.
- *Employs at least one direct measure.* At least one measure, such as an embedded course assignment or a student portfolio, should provide direct assessment of how well students are meeting the intended learning outcomes.
- *Identifies specific courses or points in the curriculum where data are collected.* The plan should identify where in the curriculum data will be collected to assess each learning outcome specified.
- *Reports data collection.* The assessment plan should also indicate whether or not the data collection took place as planned or if there were any changes to the data to be collected.
- *Documents use of data for decision-making and/or process improvement. Articulates the relation between evidence and decisions made.* An effective assessment plan reports that data were collected and describes how these data were used for making decisions about the curriculum, program, or assessment process. A clear link should exist between the evidence provided by the assessment data and the decisions made.
- *Discusses plan and results within department.* An assessment plan that represents the collective input of the faculty is more likely to be useful and sustainable. Periodic meetings to get faculty input on the assessment plan and results and keep them

involved in the process can help build group support for a department's assessment initiatives.

- *Summarizes assessment results in departmental annual report.* The results of the data analysis should be documented in the department's annual report. The relationship between the results and the learning outcomes addressed or assessment questions posed should be clearly described.

The mature assessment plan demonstrates greater sophistication in its design, execution, and evolution. The characteristics of a more well-developed assessment plan include:

- *Uses multiple measures to assess student learning outcomes.* More mature plans may have started out by answering a specific assessment question using a single measure in an earlier assessment cycle. The department may have added measures along the way to provide additional insight into their programs and students' learning outcomes. For example, a specific student learning outcome may have been initially assessed using an embedded course assignment, such as a written report, but may be revisited by reviewing data from student questionnaires. The combined results from multiple assessment measures can pave the way for more informed decisions about the program.
- *Develops a sustainable plan in terms of departmental resources.* A critical aspect for the success of an assessment plan is its long-term sustainability. The development and evolution of an assessment plan should take into consideration factors such as departmental resources, faculty load, and program goals (for example strategic plans, discipline-based accreditation needs).
- *Monitors success of plan, using suggestions from previous year(s) if appropriate.* Assessment results and feedback from faculty should be used to make decisions about the program and curriculum and to evaluate and improve the assessment plan and procedures. Such decisions are important in the evolution of a well-developed assessment plan and should be documented in the department's annual report.
- *Fits plan to department's long-term goals.* Assessment planning should take the department's long-term goals into

consideration in determining the specific learning outcomes to address and assessment measures to employ. For example, for a newly developed program, it may be important to assess how well that program meets the department's mission. Departments that offer multiple programs may benefit from the development of an assessment plan that identifies the similarities and differences among the programs.

Rubric Uses

Identifying the characteristics of an effective assessment plan can help departments develop more useful approaches from the outset of their work. Departments should also be encouraged to use the rubric to monitor the execution and evolution of their assessment plan. Such monitoring of assessment processes can help build a culture of evidence, a crucial aspect of high-quality programs (Maki, 2004; Massy et al., 2007).

Administrators or assessment committees can also use the rubric to monitor and review each program's assessment progress. Faculty developers can review completed rubrics to identify concerns and provide support to individual departments as needed to help them achieve their assessment goals. In addition, the information collected from the rubrics can be summarized at the department, college, or institutional level to document how well accreditation requirements or other strategic priorities are being met.

The rubric was tested in a pilot study in which several departments at a regional comprehensive university (University of West Florida) reviewed their assessment processes and completed the rubric accordingly. In one case, the department was in an early stage of assessment planning and was able to use the rubric to identify the essential aspects of assessment that they needed to focus on. For example, although the department had identified the context and specific courses for collecting data, they had not linked the plan to their specific program outcomes nor identified how the data would be used for decision-making and/or process improvement. The rubric helped the department develop a more effective and sustainable assessment plan from the start.

In another case, a department that had an assessment plan in place for several years also completed the rubric. They found that their assessment plan included all of the elements of a basic assessment plan and most of the characteristics of a mature assessment plan. One criterion that was not being addressed was the use of multiple measures to assess learning outcomes. The rubric facilitated discussions about how additional or indirect measures could be used to augment the existing measure. Even for a department with a mature assessment plan, the rubric was useful in confirming the strengths of their plan and recognizing opportunities for monitoring and evolving the plan.

Tools such as the rubric presented here enable programs to engage in collaborative efforts for developing and sustaining effective assessment plans. They can help programs "close the loop" by using the assessment criteria and results to evolve a basic assessment plan into one that is more mature and grounded in best practices. The development, use, and evolution of such tools reinforce the model that assessment is not an end in itself, but a vehicle for conversation about educational improvement (Walvoord, 2004).

CONCLUSION

Assessment and accountability practices in higher education are not new (Diamond, 2008). However, the seriousness with which higher education is responding to accountability feels new. Accrediting agencies generally adopted a phase-in strategy of assessment effort that allowed institutions to become accustomed to the need to verify quality through systematic assessment planning and practice. The initial phase involved insuring that all institutions at least had a viable assessment plan that seemed well tailored to their missions. Subsequent accrediting visits have stressed the gathering and interpreting of data as a hallmark of the importance of accountability activities. As accreditors move into the era of examining how institutions "close the loop" (for example, what changes should be made in the curriculum to enhance the learning experience for the students?), we are likely to see assessment change agents have their greatest impact on fostering deep and rich assessment cultures in their institutions.

GUIDING QUESTIONS

1. What is the nature of any resistance that program members might show toward the development and use of an effective assessment plan?
2. What would be the single most useful rationale that would motivate more effective assessment strategies?
3. What steps could a program take to minimize risks and maximize rewards associated with sophisticated assessment practices?
4. To what extent has your own program embraced assessment practices as standard operating procedures?
5. What is the level of maturity of the current assessment plan and practices?

CHAPTER FOUR

THE NEW ARCHITECTURE OF LEARNING DESIGN

Focusing on Student Learning Outcomes

Designing a college course is similar to the process an architect goes through in conceiving and planning a building. Both course designer and architect start with a blank slate. Guided by the needs and requirements of the "clients," the designer imagines the end point and begins to fill the blank slate with the necessary components that will stimulate the individuals in that space to achieve the ideal. The architect's intentions are captured in a blueprint; the professor's planning will be apparent in the course syllabus. Whether the end product receives scorn or acclaim will depend on the expertise and artistry of the creator as demonstrated by the durability and quality of the end result.

Historically, institutions of learning articulate an undergraduate degree as a collection of courses representing the current state of content within the respective discipline (Brewer et al., 1993; Lattuca & Stark, 2009). Similar to many architects and designers, faculty are fiercely independent and exercise a great deal of autonomy in drawing up the blueprints that they think fairly capture the content of their disciplines. However, the traditional emphasis has been on whether the design is faithful to the content of the discipline; at best, students' skill development has been an implicit, rather than an explicit goal. Sometimes programs retain courses out of a sense of tradition and add new courses based on emerging trends. Campus-specific criteria (such as credit hour limits) may also be influential in shaping an undergraduate program of study.

Critics of higher education have made a persuasive case that this style of conducting the business of academe has not produced satisfying outcomes (Hersh & Merrow, 2005). As a consequence, a new form of course architecture has gotten traction and is transforming the higher education landscape. Largely driven by pressures related to accreditation, most faculty now face explicit institutional requirements to rethink course architecture from the standpoint of the skills that should be explicitly developed in the process of developing a sound curriculum. The adoption of student learning outcomes (SLOs) means that faculty no longer design courses using a blank slate; the institution obligates faculty to identify the skills that a course can contribute to the department and institutional goals (see Fink, 2003; Suskie, 2009).

Academics have long resisted specific measures of student learning that might be perceived to limit the autonomy of faculty (see Chapter Three for a discussion regarding faculty resistance). Student evaluations, despite their many flaws (Buskist, Keeley, & Irons, 2006; Halonen & Ellenberg, 2006; Germaine & Scandura, 2005; McKeachie, 1997), provide faculty with information about students' likes and dislikes. However, student evaluations offer little in the way of measuring teaching efficacy. Student evaluations also may not formally assess whether students have acquired targeted skills.

How can we make the leap that moves faculty from an emphasis on teaching content to an emphasis on responsibility for developing competent students (Barr & Tagg, 1995)? Although accreditation requires discussion of SLOs, faculty are sometimes reticent to redesign courses to produce student competence. Yet if we want our students to remain competitive in the global marketplace, then quantitative, scientific, and technological literacy and communication skills should be explicitly included as programmatic goals, regardless of major. Therefore, articulation of SLOs not only helps faculty to articulate what students will learn, but allows for improvement of curricula that will develop these skills. Hence moving beyond the cultural traditions of defining a degree exclusively as a collection of courses is long overdue (Dunn, McCarthy, Baker,

Halonen, & Hill, 2007; Kuh, Kinzie, Schuh, Whitt, & Associates, 2005; see also Sullivan & Rosin, 2008).

In this chapter we discuss the rationale for assessing SLOs. We offer recommendations for creating outcomes across domains, linking outcomes to courses, infusing the outcomes in syllabi, and connecting authentic assessment of these learning outcomes to what actually occurs in the classroom. Authentic assessments can be used to improve a single course, to examine proficiencies across several courses or a program's entire major, and to help instructors revise and refine their courses (cf. Fink, 2003).

Brief Background on Assessing Student Learning Outcomes

The assessment of SLOs is challenging (Ewell, 2008; Graff & Birkenstein, 2008). The culture of the academy historically presumed that student learning occurred because scholars imparted the most current research in their respective field of study in the classroom. In this context, the evaluation of student learning was exclusively within the purview of individual faculty members, and course grades reflected measurable gains in student knowledge. Educators did not typically conduct independent summative measures of student learning. If students earned passing grades, which led to completion of a degree, then it was safe to assume that the students acquired the necessary discipline-based information and that they could perform tasks commensurate with entry-level professionals in their chosen fields.

However, an approach to student learning that focuses on specific discipline-related skills goes beyond this traditional view. Ewell (2008) endorsed the emphasis on SLOs as a success measure, and the view that higher education must respond to the call for outcomes-based accountability because it is inherently our responsibility to demonstrate that students are learning the necessary skills to survive, thrive, and be productive contributors in an increasingly competitive global economy.

With the increased emphasis on accountability in higher education (see Bogue & Hall, 2003; Burke, 2004; Maki, 2001; 2004; Schneider & Schoenberg, 1998), colleges—and more specifically, departments and programs—must identify the skills that students should master and provide evidence that students can indeed perform these skills upon graduating (Suskie, 2009). Accrediting bodies and disciplinary associations are keenly aware of this shift in higher education and have begun to promulgate learning outcomes for the respective undergraduate majors (such as accounting, chemistry, biology, psychology). The Council for Higher Education Accreditation (CHEA) requires evidence or assurance of learning in the form of outcomes and they require institutions to provide evidence that students can demonstrate specific competencies (CHEA, 2008). For example, institutions in the state of Maryland, in response to the Middle States Commission on Higher Education, participated in a project to develop SLOs as a measure of institutional effectiveness (Maryland Higher Education Commission, 2004).

This growing emphasis on demonstrating proficiencies means that each academic unit should identify competencies; that is, skills that can be demonstrated at the conclusion of the undergraduate experience. However, a mere summative evaluation of SLOs, although important, does not provide a department with clear criteria for advancing students through the developmental acquisition of skills. In other words, a plan for continuous development and improvement of student learning, as linked to outcomes, should be articulated (Kuh, Kinzie, Schuh, & Whitt, 2005). Indeed, one of the benefits of this goal-focused assessment is that it provides faculty members with a vehicle for engaging one another to determine which skills matter most within a given discipline (see Lattuca & Stark, 2009).

In the wake of rapid and dramatic growth in the emphasis on SLOs by accrediting agencies and other stakeholders, it is not surprising that colleges and universities have had varying responses. The purpose of this chapter is to characterize the range of responses to the various dimensions of SLOs in higher education and to provide some direction to help programs enhance their SLO expertise. Consistent with our general model of evaluation, we characterize the range of performance in SLOs as distinguished (truly exemplary); effective (adequate, serviceable); developing (some strengths, with room to improve); and undeveloped (limited or nonexistent attention). The SLO dimensions we examine include writing, speaking, research, collaboration, and information or technological literacy (cf. Lattuca & Stark, 2009).

Why have we identified writing, speaking, collaboration, and technological literacy as essential learning outcomes? These competencies are consistent with the skills identified by the Middle States Commission on Higher Education and more broadly by CHEA. Written and oral communication skills, critical thinking, collaboration, and technological literacy are central skills that serve as the foundation for all undergraduate degrees (see Table 4.1; Dunn et al., 2007). We want graduates to be able to think critically, work collaboratively, use the most current technologies available, and communicate effectively. Although we believe that these skills are essential for any educated person living and working in the twenty-first century, little has been done to articulate clearly how students can demonstrate these proficiencies.

However, before we delve into performance criteria that reflect the caliber of approach to SLOs, we need to ground our discussion in four basic principles about the assessment process.

GENERAL PRINCIPLES RELATED TO STUDENT LEARNING OUTCOMES

PRINCIPLE ONE: STUDENT LEARNING OUTCOMES HAVE MULTIPLE LAYERS

Student learning outcomes will typically be specified at three levels: within the university mission, at the department or program level, and at the course level.

What is the promise made for student competence at graduation? Will students communicate effectively? Act with integrity? Practice environmental conservation? Clarity provided by the university mission statement makes it easier to identify outcomes at other levels. Good practice begins by articulating outcomes that are grounded in the institutional mission (Center for Teaching, Learning, and Assessment, 2005).

At the department or program level, student competencies are summative and should be clearly articulated as a guide for the development of curriculum. For example, many programs embrace effective communication as an essential outcome.

Table 4.1 Student Learning Outcomes Domain

	Undeveloped	*Developing*	*Effective*	*Distinguished*
Writing Skills	Requires no systematic writing projects	Offers writing projects consistent with individual faculty commitment to writing in some courses	Develops writing skills through limited requirements in targeted classes (for example, may include foundation or writing-intensive courses)	Implements systematic developmental plan for required writing (for example, all senior-level courses are writing intensive)
Speaking Skills	Does not provide systematic opportunities for developing oral abilities	Provides haphazard opportunities consistent with individual faculty commitment to develop oral abilities	Implements limited formal or informal opportunities to develop oral abilities	Requires developmental oral performances to facilitate oral skills that may culminate in presentations in professional contexts
Research Skills	Provides no systematic opportunities or support for student scholarship	Offers selected elective opportunities (for example, research team) for motivated students, but minimal mentorship of students	Incorporates variable research experience as part of the curriculum that accommodates student skill and motivation levels	Requires scholarship from all majors as a performance obligation that integrates content and skill

Collaborative Skills	Offers no systematic instruction or opportunity related to collaborative work	Facilitates opportunities but fails to provide instruction or feedback to facilitate collaborative skills	Provides some training in and feedback for improvement in collaborative skills	Embeds multiple required collaborative activities supported by sound preparation and developmental feedback
Information Literacy and Technology Skills	Does not facilitate students' effective use of information literacy and technology	Provides limited exposure to technology, usually in the context of a single course	Requires experience in multiple contexts to develop a minimum set of technology and information literacy skills	Facilitates refined and creative use of technology and information literacy for professional activities through systematic learning opportunities

Generic examples of departmental expectations for student writing proficiencies might include the following:

- Students will produce a well-written comprehensive analysis of one of the key areas of the discipline.
- Students will write an integrated review of the literature for a topic within the discipline.
- Students will deliver a formal presentation on a discipline-specific topic.

These outcomes explicitly state the competencies that students should possess upon graduation.

Specifying department-level learning outcomes is a daunting but doable task (Allen, 2004). Development of department-level SLOs may be derived from campus-specific criteria, from standards provided by learned societies, or from a combination of the two sets of guidelines. Clear summative departmental SLOs serve as a guide for courses in the curriculum as individual faculty determine how the component pieces of the curriculum will contribute to the target abilities. One approach is to examine the degree program as a whole and identify specific courses that can be linked to outcomes (Allen, 2004; Levy, Burton, Mickler, & Vigorito, 1999).

At the course level, SLOs should be more detailed. It is this course-specific articulation of outcomes that can be most challenging for faculty. Yet if the department broadly defines what students should be able to do at the completion of the degree, the blueprint for developing course-specific criteria is already in place. We should be able to trust faculty to select course-specific outcomes from the larger set of department goals and tailor their assessment strategies based on the outcomes selected (see also Lattuca & Stark, 2009).

Principle Two: Assessment Must Be Designed to Promote and Evaluate the Targeted Outcomes

Linking SLOs (that is, writing, speaking, collaborative, research, and information literacy skills) to specific courses is only the first step in creating a comprehensive assessment plan (see Chapter Three). The second step in developing an assessment plan is to formulate specific assessments tied to the courses.

For example, how might a political science department link SLOs to courses? The first step in this process is identifying how department-wide objectives can be achieved within specific courses. Examples of department-wide goals are as follows:

Students will

- Write a comprehensive analysis of a contemporary political event.
- Describe major principles of political science in a capstone paper.
- Deliver a professional level oral presentation detailing the relationship of political science theories related to a contemporary problem.

Using these department-wide learning outcomes, faculty can develop assignments for their courses that will meet these criteria without compromising their autonomy. For example, a faculty member may require all students to demonstrate a comprehensive analysis of a contemporary political event that reflects the distinctive context offered by that faculty member's course. Table 4.2 provides an example of how this might be accomplished in a psychology curriculum.

TABLE 4.2 LINKAGE OF SKILLS TO MAJOR

	Communication	*Collaboration*	*Research and Information Literacy*
Introductory Psychology	Article Review	Small Group Project	Evaluation of Information Sources
Research Tools (such as Statistics)	Research Proposal	Peer Review	Search for Empirically Based Resources
Content Specific (for example, Abnormal Psychology)	Theoretical Paper	Group Presentation	Use of Empirically Based Resources
Capstone Course	Integrated Paper	Peer Review Group	Use of Texts and Peer-Reviewed Articles

Principle Three: Assessment Should Be Developmental and Inclusive

Assessment of developmentally appropriate SLOs should be formative and summative, developmentally sequenced, and assessed throughout the undergraduate major (Ewell, 2008). Because learning is iterative, SLOs should be explicitly stated in developmental terms across courses (see Diamond, 2008). Within courses, faculty may wish to be even more explicit about the specific skills that students are developing throughout the semester, using effective grading as a means to promote learning (Walvoord & Anderson, 2009). Not only does this level of detail contribute to the larger department-wide assessment process, but it also provides students with a blueprint for the semester and encourages them to adopt the discipline-specific discourse about the skill sets being pursued.

Principle Four: Assessment Itself Should Be Assessed

In Chapter Three we provide a comprehensive guide to developing a department assessment plan. Student learning outcomes reside within the larger assessment plan, and steps should be taken to periodically review the outcomes. Advances in the discipline, changes in professional organization guidelines, and local changes may result in a need to update SLOs. Ultimately, both outcomes and a comprehensive plan for assessment should be articulated and regularly reviewed through a departmental self-study as described in Chapter Twelve. We now turn to the process of articulating specific learning outcomes in each of the domains.

Communication Skills

External constituencies expect graduates to possess a common set of general professional skills as well as to master content knowledge specific to the discipline. Skills associated with a traditional liberal arts curriculum include the ability to communicate both orally and in writing. Increasingly, the ability to collaborate with colleagues is becoming an even more important outcome of an undergraduate degree. Graduates must also be able to think critically and be adept at using information effectively.

Although liberal arts institutions have historically valued writing as an essential skill, virtually every institution of higher learning claims that it is addressing writing as an important student learning outcome (Monroe, 2003; van den Berg, Admiraal, & Pilot, 2006). Despite the perceived importance of writing, few programs clearly articulate mechanisms to ensure the competence of student writing (Dunn, 2006). Indeed, although helpful guides to improving classroom writing and critical thinking are available (Bean, 1996), there is frequently no systematic plan to make certain that students engage in formative discipline-specific writing tasks that are developmentally appropriate.

The process of linking developmentally appropriate assignments to specific courses is, by its very nature, a department-wide effort (Dunn, McCarthy, Baker, Halonen, & Hill, 2007; Grasmuck & Hyatt, 2003). For example, a department may require students enrolled in an introductory survey course to produce an article summary as evidence of elementary writing. In an advanced course, students would demonstrate their ability to integrate several sources in a more comprehensive writing assignment as evidence of writing competency. In this example the linkage of assignments to courses is a collaborative effort agreed on by the faculty—the professionals most concerned with advancing student learning.

Halonen, Bosack, Clay, and McCarthy (2003) specify formative, writing-specific SLOs within the discipline of psychology, and these specific learning outcomes can be more broadly applied to the liberal arts. For example, if we consider that at the conclusion of the degree students should be able to gather resources, organize material to persuade a reader, and present information using conventional expression, a department-wide assessment plan may specify how students can demonstrate these competencies (that is, SLOs) at each level of students' academic experiences. Faculty may expect first-year students to paraphrase simplistic information from basic textbook references. At a more sophisticated level, students in their final year of study would be able to use sources selectively and to integrate content from multiple sources. Similarly, students early in their academic career should be able to organize information in an elementary fashion. A more advanced student would demonstrate an ability to persuade the reader through use of engaging language. We would expect a student completing an undergraduate degree to write a coherent argument based on evidence from scholarly works. Programs will want to not only specify the performance criteria by level and domain, but also identify where, in the curriculum, students will demonstrate these proficiencies.

Despite the increased emphasis on assessment, and the pressure to articulate SLOs, departments continue to struggle to find ways of translating SLOs into a tool for distinguishing themselves as outstanding departments. As illustrated in Table 4.1, using our levels of departmental performance (undeveloped, developed, effective, distinguished), departments can identify how broad SLOs—namely written and oral communication skills, critical thinking, collaboration, and information and technological literacy—translate into distinguishing a program. An undeveloped or poorly functioning department will not have a plan for systematically using SLOs across the curriculum. For example, although a department might intrinsically value good writing, there may not be a systematic writing component deliberately built into the curriculum. Similarly, individual faculty may be committed to developing writing proficiencies in their students, but their individual efforts may not provide the necessary scaffolding for developing competent writers as students move through the curriculum. Writing-intensive courses, although valuable, still do not reflect a systematic approach to produce students with the necessary skills. In contrast, faculty in a distinguished program clearly articulate a plan for developing student writing proficiencies as students progress developmentally through a coherent curriculum, as detailed in Table 4.1.

Because writing is a fundamental skill that is essential for all students graduating with a bachelor's degree, we expect that undergraduate programs functioning at a minimal level require at least one writing-intensive course. In contrast, distinguished programs systematically link writing proficiencies (assignments) to courses throughout the curriculum. Programs using this approach are rare. More often, innovative liberal arts schools have implemented sequenced writing-intensive programs (Hillard &

Harris, 2003; Wolfe & Haynes, 2003). Even within the most innovative of programs, Wolfe and Haynes acknowledged the difficulty of assessing writing and presented a model for linking the general education core with the discipline. The critical element of their model is a sequencing of writing experiences; the drawback is the labor-intensive effort devoted to the project. A distinguished program specifies the products that students must produce at each level of the undergraduate experience, thus ensuring that students graduate as competent writers. Explicitly articulating SLOs or the products of courses also serves to guide the department in developing a discipline-specific curriculum that is distinguished.

Much like the SLOs for written communication skills, those for oral communication should be articulated, at increasingly more sophisticated levels, across the curriculum. For example, a short oral presentation in an introductory course might constitute a basic competency in oral communication. As students advance through a program, they might be required to develop a more comprehensive presentation around a specific topic, and a culminating experience may require students to produce a professional talk that integrates content from the discipline. Departments will want to articulate each of these outcomes in a measurable way in that students should be required to demonstrate competencies (Wiggins, 1990).

COLLABORATION

In addition to identifying SLOs for communication skills, students should also engage in collaborative learning opportunities that mirror professional experiences. Springer, Stanne, and Donovan (1999) suggest that collaborative experiences enhance learning and improve sociobehavioral skills (see also Barkley, Cross, & Major, 2004). Although Springer et al. determined that collaborative learning is beneficial for students in science, mathematics, engineering, and technology (STEM) fields, efforts to integrate collaborative learning into the curricula of many fields are fairly recent. Nevertheless, collaboration is an essential skill that students should demonstrate at the completion of a degree, insofar as it is possible. To accomplish this, programs should systematically provide structured collaborative activities (Thompson, Vermette, & Wisniewski, 2004).

A distinguished program not only links skills to courses, but also scaffolds pedagogy so that students develop increasingly sophisticated proficiency in collaborative skills. For example, students in lower-level courses may need to demonstrate an ability to develop a report with only one peer. As students advance, departments may explicitly require students to produce a project with more than one student colleague, perhaps in teams (see Barkley, Cross, & Major, 2004).

Research and Information Literacy

Seymour, Hunter, Laursen, and Deantoni (2004) provide strong support for the linkage between participation in undergraduate research and the development of strong communication skills. Therefore a coordinated effort to offer authentic, engaging undergraduate research experiences can be an important tool in student skill development (Fink, 2003). These experiences might include assisting with a faculty member's scholarship, or working in student teams to produce a scholarly product or collect data that adds to knowledge in the field. Specific activities will vary depending on the discipline, of course. Student learning outcomes for research skills may be tied to courses, or faculty may wish to develop specific, developmentally based research skills that should be integrated across courses. Research experiences might begin with students working closely with a faculty member to work on a project in progress, and SLOs might be linked to discrete responsibilities assigned to the student. Distinguished programs carefully scaffold increasing levels of research proficiencies throughout the curriculum. The ideal culmination of the experience might be a student-directed independent project, an honors thesis, or a similarly engaging research activity.

In addition to basic research competencies, students should become proficient in their ability to discriminate between valid and invalid sources of information; in other words, graduates should possess information literacy. Emerging technology plays a critical role in virtually every discipline (Laird & Kuh, 2005). Students are increasingly faced with an extraordinarily large volume of information, and selecting valid sources of information is increasingly difficult. The Association of College and Research Libraries (ACRL, 2001) offers guidance for establishing SLOs for information literacy across disciplines. For example, students completing a degree should be able to use appropriate search strategies in professional databases. Too often students believe that they can find all necessary information through a simple Google search or by skimming a Wikipedia entry. Students frequently do not distinguish reputable sources from more general commercially based information. They may not recognize the value of peer-reviewed materials and empirically based reference materials. Regardless of the discipline, faculty want students to develop skills that allow them to distinguish scholarly products from those that are not well researched or empirically based. Strong departments will develop SLOs that specify how students will demonstrate competency in search strategies and evaluation of sources. For example, an effective program may specify that students must be able to retrieve information from the professional literature and produce a summary of the information. As indicated in Table 4.1, a distinguished program will articulate learning outcomes that occur at key points across the curriculum.

In addition to traditional information literacy skills, we suggest that programs consider the role of technology in the professional development of students. For students in most fields, some technological proficiency will be an essential skill after graduation, regardless of whether they enter the workforce or go on to advanced study. Departments may wish to specify that students are technologically literate (for example, that they can use word processing software or statistical software) by specifying competencies. Distinguished programs ensure not only that students receive opportunities to develop technological expertise that generalizes beyond the university, but also that programs explicitly identify proficiencies.

DISCIPLINE-SPECIFIC LEARNING OUTCOMES

CHEA, regional accrediting bodies, and state boards of higher learning mandate that programs specify SLOs for general education competencies. General education competencies (that is, communication skills, critical thinking, and literacy) are often more fully developed within the discipline, and reference to these competencies may be articulated, along with content-based competencies in each discipline.

Many professional societies provide guidance for discipline-specific SLOs. For example, the American Psychological Association (APA) offers guidelines for the undergraduate major (APA, 2007) along with specific developmental learning outcomes across the curriculum (APA, 2008). Similarly, the American Chemical Society (ACS Committee on Professional Training, 2008), in its guidelines for program approval, requires programs to specify SLOs specific to chemistry. For those developing programs striving toward systematically articulated competencies for a student majoring in the discipline, competencies can be a useful tool for curriculum development.

Earlier in this chapter we suggested that SLOs should be linked to particular courses. For example, in addition to the general skills already described (that is, communication, problem solving, information literacy), the American Chemical Society (ACS) specifies laboratory safety skills as an essential competency for students graduating with an undergraduate degree in chemistry. Using authentic assessment practices, SLOs can be used to specify skills that students should be acquiring throughout their academic experience. As an example, early in their chemistry training students should be able to correctly complete information for material safety data sheets (MSDSs); upon completion of a degree, students should be proficient in handling laboratory emergencies (ACS Committee on Professional Training, 2008). A hallmark of a strong chemistry program may be that these specific learning outcomes are linked to specific courses across the curriculum and specified in syllabi.

Crafting a Syllabus

Upon identifying where programs address SLOs in the curriculum, the faculty can specify an even finer level of distinctions in desired performance. Individual faculty may want their students to become more proficient in performing a specific skill. When developing syllabi, specific SLOs can be listed as goals for the course (see O'Brien, Millis, & Cohen, 2008). For example, it might be important for students enrolled in a research methods course (such as statistics or experimental methods) to obtain specific competencies. A partial list of SLOs that demonstrate competency may include the following:

- Articulate a sound hypothesis.
- Operationalize variables.
- Explain logic of hypothesis testing.
- Apply appropriate statistical analyses.
- Interpret the results of analyses.
- Describe benefits and limitations of statistical techniques.
- Identify potential confounds in experiments.

These course-specific SLOs are more detailed than the general outcomes for the major. Using these outcomes, we can create a two-dimensional matrix to link the outcomes to assessment measures used in the course. As illustrated in Table 4.3 (an example from psychology), each student learning outcome can be linked to a measure of evaluation (that is, exams, research proposal, lab assignments, and poster presentation). Through this deliberate process of linking outcomes to measures of student performance, individual faculty can examine how goals for the course are systematically evaluated using existing assessment measures.

USING STUDENT LEARNING OUTCOMES

How can a program reasonably expect to use each of the specified dimensions of SLOs across the curriculum? As a first step, departments may wish to envision what students should be able to do when they graduate. In other words, the faculty must identify SLOs for the major. Departments can then link SLOs to each of the broad general education areas listed in Table 4.1 (that is, communication, research, information literacy) and to discipline-specific content.

Once faculty are comfortable that they have identified SLOs for the major, they can begin specifying competencies that students should be attaining throughout the undergraduate experience. These competencies can then be linked to courses, as well as to specific assignments or authentic assessments across courses.

TABLE 4.3 STUDENT LEARNING OUTCOME (SLO) BENCHMARKS

Student Learning Outcome (SLO)	*Exams*	*Paper*	*Lab Reports*	*Poster*
Objective Measures				
Explain the logic of hypothesis testing				
Operationalize independent and dependent variables				
Use statistical programs to perform analyses				
Describe the benefits and limitations of statistical techniques				
Identify potential confounds in experimental studies				
Recognize and apply ethical research practices				
Describe relationships between theories, experimental, and correlational techniques				
Qualitative Measures				
Conduct a literature search				
Consistently use APA style				
Use formal and professional expression				
Develop plausible arguments to support research proposal				
Relate content from several sources				
Develop logical arguments for conclusions				
Demonstrate effective poster presentation skills				
Articulate sound hypotheses				
Select and apply appropriate experimental design and statistical analysis				

Angelo and Cross (1993) suggest that course objectives should be articulated; however, learning outcomes are more specific and more action-oriented, and they guide the undergraduate experience more effectively. Learning outcomes for courses that are articulated in individual syllabi, with explicit linkages back to the program curriculum, not only help the faculty to be clear about the direction of their course, they also help students to articulate the skills that they learn in the course, and help students to see how learning in the course fits in to the program as whole. Articulating SLOs provides faculty and students with a common path and greater specificity about what students should be learning (Angelo & Cross, 1993). Distinguished departments embrace practices that can be used to demonstrate that students are learning. A distinguished department derives learning outcomes from a departmental mission; their outcomes are clearly linked to the curriculum.

STUDENT LEARNING OUTCOMES AS A DEFINING FEATURE OF A DISTINGUISHED PROGRAM

We began this chapter with a metaphor. Although an architect's plans are made up of individual elements, it is the image of the whole that truly characterizes the end product. Much like an architect's plans, degree programs are constructed using courses that will produce a set of learning experiences that will result in a competent graduate. Putting courses together without the benefit of an underlying structure may not result in the well-rounded graduate of our program that we had hoped for. The bedrock of any degree program is the acquisition of writing, speaking, research, collaboration, and information literacy skills. A degree program thus is not just a collection of courses but a set of experiences that allow students to develop skills that will allow them to be competent professionals. Students take courses that are guided by an underlying plan, one aimed at creating meaningful learning experiences (Fink, 2003). The plan, or blueprint, is in the form of student learning outcomes.

SLOs that serve as the blueprint for a degree program can also be a unifying guide for students and faculty. If faculty are clear about what they want students to be able to do at the end of the program, the department can share in a common goal. SLOs can then become the guide for developing a coherent curriculum that will achieve those outcomes. Departments can provide scaffolding to facilitate student success by appropriately sequencing student learning. Through this process, faculty identify the skills that they want students to acquire, how these skills link to the curriculum, and how they can create opportunities for students to learn important skills in each of their courses.

Our architectural metaphor fails in one important respect. Rather than creating an entity that endures over time, good assessment planning generates a "living blueprint." The goals of assessment require a feedback loop that helps a department determine which aspects of the curricular blueprint should be retained and which need to go back to the drafting board. As a consequence, educators experience much greater fluidity in their quest each term to craft the perfect experience for their students.

Realistically, the pressure to assess SLOs has been imposed by accreditation bodies, governing boards, legislators, and the public at large. However, our response to these pressures need not be simply reactive. As department members, we can use this opportunity to reexamine our course offerings, our curricula, and our teaching. A review of our practices, using SLOs as a blueprint, may result in more positive learning experiences while students are in attendance and more competent graduates when they leave our programs.

GUIDING QUESTIONS

1. Are SLOs developmentally articulated for the major?
2. Are SLOs linked to courses?
3. Have the SLOs been discussed and agreed upon by faculty members?
4. Are the products—the authentic assessments—linked to courses in the major?
5. Are SLOs clearly communicated to students and listed on syllabi? Are the learning outcomes linked to existing authentic assessments within courses?

6. Are summative SLOs articulated for the major? How are the summative measures of SLOs used to assess the program?
7. Is there a systematic review of SLOs when curricula are revised?
8. Do faculty attend to SLOs as a means for demonstrating that students are learning necessary skills (that is, communication, critical thinking, collaboration, and information literacy)?

Chapter Five

Evaluating Curricula

The curriculum is the heart of the discipline. Faculty members have the primary responsibility for curriculum by determining the major content, theories, and perspectives of their discipline that will be transmitted to students. In a real sense, a program's curriculum is effectively an academic plan (Lattuca & Stark, 2009). Not only does the curriculum represent the current state of a given field of study, but in many ways, what faculty impart to students as part of the curriculum becomes the discipline of the future. Whether students continue in the discipline or follow another educational or career path, curriculum encounters provide them with a distinctive world view.

When considering the quality of a program's curriculum, several important issues arise. Does the curriculum reflect the current state of the discipline? Do the courses provide disciplinary content in appropriate context (for example, do advanced courses contain appropriately advanced rather than introductory material)? Are coursework and experiences sequenced to move students through the program in a way that addresses their growing intellectual skills? Is the design developmentally appropriate? Is the curriculum structure coherent to both faculty and students; that is, do faculty and students understand, and can they articulate, why the curriculum is designed as it is? Perhaps most important is the issue of faculty input and engagement in the program design. Faculty that care about the discipline and are invested in what they communicate to students will be engaged in ongoing discussions of the curriculum (see, for example, Fink, 2003).

Disinterested faculty almost guarantee that their program's curriculum will be out-of-date or less than optimal in some way.

Consideration of the curriculum overlaps with almost every other factor we cover in this volume. For example, student learning outcomes (see Chapter Four) cannot be formulated in the absence of a clear understanding of the curriculum. Specific aspects of a program's assessment strategy (Chapter Three) will depend on curriculum design factors. The review process for a curriculum (discussed shortly) is also linked to consideration of assessment.

Issues of curriculum, like other program components covered in this book, tie in to resources (Chapter Eight) in important ways. Programs that are overstressed may be unable to offer an optimal variety of courses to address student interests or to move into growing areas of the discipline. In fact, they may not even be able to cover all major areas of the discipline. However, even a strapped program can have a well-structured and sequenced curriculum (albeit usually a minimalist one) and can develop plans for future growth based on disciplinary standards.

On a positive note, we wish to point out that programs and program faculty typically have a great deal of control and input over this key aspect of their program. Although programs typically do not control the level of resources they receive from the institution, they often control most aspects of the curriculum and its structure (see, for example, Lattuca & Stark, 2009). Thus there is much that faculty can do to improve the experiences of their students by being mindful about, and engaged in, this aspect of their program (Diamond, 2008).

Avoiding Common Pitfalls

A useful exercise when considering curriculum design and structure may be to think of a program's curriculum as a house in which the program lives. When the house was first built, it most likely functioned properly for the residents (faculty and students); each faculty member may have had charge of a particular room of the house (that is, a course or curriculum component), and each room had its own specific purpose. The house as a whole provided comfortable shelter and brand-new, up-to-date living quarters. With the passage of time, however, a house will fall into disrepair unless there is regular maintenance. Old appliances break down, and paint fades. As new faculty members join the program, additional rooms are added to the house. These additions may not "flow" well with the other rooms in the house, or new rooms may be out of proportion to the old structure of the house. Some faculty members may move out of their rooms and into others, leaving their old rooms unattended. Other rooms are abandoned when faculty retire. All of this can result in a poorly designed house that no longer functions well for the residents and is confusing to visitors. Using this metaphor, one can consider whether or not the curriculum of a program best resembles a house that was designed for the current residents or is more comparable to a house whose design no longer functions well for the residents or visitors.

One potential problem is something we can refer to as *curriculum stagnation.* This problem is most likely to be an issue in programs where faculty (due to lack of interest, lack of time, or a focus on other pursuits) are disengaged from the process of curriculum review, or when there is no regular process in place for reviewing the curriculum as a whole. In cases of curriculum stagnation, the program structure and offerings may not have changed in many years, and the curriculum may no longer reflect the current state of the discipline. In extreme cases, new and vital areas of the discipline may be unrepresented in the program. The program is living in a house that has not been maintained and renovated to keep up with new developments.

Another issue may be termed *curriculum drift.* This challenge can occur when piecemeal changes are made to the curriculum over time, without systematic consideration of the impact on the curriculum as whole. For example, new courses may be added when faculty with new specialty areas are hired or when faculty teaching interests change. Older courses may no longer be taught, if some faculty give up teaching them and other faculty do not pick them up. New rooms have been added to the house, and old rooms abandoned, without much thought to how this affects the overall design and usefulness of the house. The curriculum has gradually morphed into something that differs from its original design, and this drift affects the experience that students receive. Connections between individual courses or curriculum components may be obscure to students, and they may experience the discipline as a set of unrelated areas of inquiry, without seeing the interchange and influence among them.

Another issue that complicates the delivery of a high-quality curriculum is the proliferation of numerous specialty courses. Each specialty course tends to be designed and taught by an individual faculty member who typically designs the course as an expression of a passion in research rather than a coherent feature of a well-developed curriculum. Although a well-designed curriculum provides students with choices, including courses in new and emerging areas of the discipline, these choices should not come at the expense of a solid foundation and a coherently designed program (see, for example, Dunn et al., 2010). In extreme cases, faculty members spend most of their time teaching such specialty courses or "pet courses," leaving foundational areas of the discipline to graduate students or adjunct faculty, or uncovered, or barely addressed in the curriculum. Administrators sometimes refer to such offerings disdainfully as "boutique" or "salon" courses. In these situations, the program has added on new rooms that have little or no connection to the rest of the house; for example, a room that can be accessed only by going through a closet. Students may graduate having completed numerous courses in fragmented areas, but with little understanding of the core areas of the discipline.

Another important issue is the suitability of the curriculum for the students at the institution. A perfectly designed house that doesn't fit into the neighborhood (that is, it doesn't work for the specific needs and requirements of its residents and visitors) will stick out like a sore thumb and will not be a popular place. Does the curriculum of the program take into account specific needs of the students it serves by offering appropriately targeted experiences (remedial or advanced coursework, honors experiences, internships or field experiences, supplemental instruction)? Does it provide linkages to future likely careers or educational experiences for this student population (see, for example, Sullivan & Rosin, 2008)?

We address these issues further in the framework presented next. In cases where these problems are extensive, it is worth taking a step back to consider the design of the curriculum in a holistic way. If the program faculty were to design the curriculum from the ground up (demolish the house and rebuild), what kind of design would be optimal? Faculty must be willing to consider whether the current structure of their curriculum best accomplishes their goals, in a way that is meaningful for and coherent to students, or whether it is time to call in the bulldozers.

THE BENCHMARKS FRAMEWORK AND CURRICULUM CONSIDERATIONS

In Table 5.1, we apply the benchmarks approach to an evaluation of program curriculum. Many of the criteria that we list here are applicable to all or most liberal arts, humanities, and sciences courses that are often taught at the undergraduate level. However, specialized and applied fields may have special concerns that go beyond those listed here. Table 5.1 (adapted from Dunn et al., 2007) serves as a guide and a beginning, and should be tailored by an informed examination of the current state of the discipline being represented by the program, as well as the specific goals of the program and its student learning outcomes. Programs differ in their goals and values, and while this framework may serve as a useful starting point for many programs, others will want to begin their review process by creating their own framework. We discuss this further later in the chapter. Another important consideration is that the factors listed in Table 5.1 are not mutually exclusive. Clearly, they interact with and influence one another. For example, the variety of available course offerings is related to content coverage.

In addition to keeping an eye on disciplinary standards when examining curriculum, we also recommend that programs consult other recent work in this area, such as the rubrics developed by the Association of American Colleges and Universities VALUE initiative (Valid Assessment of Learning in Undergraduate Education) (Association of American Colleges and Universities, 2009). Resources such as these provide a rich source of material on student learning for any program looking to redesign, retool, or update its curriculum.

Table 5.1 Program Curriculum Benchmarks

	Undeveloped	*Developing*	*Effective*	*Distinguished*
Content and Skills Core	Does not provide students with appropriate base of knowledge and skills in discipline's core content; curriculum may be out of balance	Provides most of core disciplinary content and skills; some key areas unrepresented, others are overrepresented	Provides all of core disciplinary content but some key areas may be underrepresented; emerging areas may not be covered	All major areas of disciplinary content are represented; emerging and current areas of the discipline are well represented; students are required to complete breadth of coursework
Disciplinary Standards or Guidelines	Curriculum unrelated to disciplinary standards; faculty unaware of or indifferent to standards	Curriculum matches some key standards or guidelines	Curriculum matches standards or guidelines for many or most factors	Program meets or exceeds agreed-upon disciplinary standards and guidelines; active involvement in focusing curriculum on standards
Curricular Structure and Sequence	No coherent structure to curriculum	Has minimal structure with some prerequisites and sequencing of courses	Well-structured curriculum with later coursework building logically on prerequisite courses	Curriculum has a coherent sequencing and structure; students and faculty can articulate the reasons behind the structure; prerequisites are logical and reasonable

(*continued*)

Table 5.1 (Continued)

	Undeveloped	*Developing*	*Effective*	*Distinguished*
Flexibility and Course Variety	Rigid structure of curriculum does not readily allow for variety in courses; includes no variety in courses	Minimal flexibility in curriculum structure and design; some course variety, primarily tailored to pet interests of faculty	Structure allows for some flexibility within limits; offers sufficient variety in course electives to enable some students to pursue interests within the field	Structure facilitates experimentation and growth in emerging areas of the discipline without sacrificing the core; well-designed electives, experimental courses, or concentrations enrich the curriculum
Disciplinary Perspectives	Focuses narrowly on a single theoretical approach	Individual courses may represent multiple approaches; no systematic approach to including multiple perspectives	Inclusion of multiple perspectives in courses across the curriculum	Takes systematic approach to including multiple disciplinary perspectives; coursework encourages student engagement in consideration of competing and complementary views of the discipline
Ethics	Curriculum includes no treatment of discipline-specific ethical issues	Ethical issues treated in one or two selected courses	Infuses treatment of ethical issues across multiple courses	Intentionally and systematically pursues ethics-related learning outcomes throughout all levels of the curriculum

Cultural Diversity	No evidence of attention to the impact of cultural diversity	Token examples demonstrate limited impact of cultural diversity	Diversity concerns addressed through and contained in limited formal course offerings	Diversity reflected systematically throughout curriculum, where appropriate
International Perspectives	No inclusion of international perspectives	Some attention paid to international perspectives in individual courses	Broad inclusion of international perspectives across multiple courses and curricular experiences	Systematic inclusion of global perspectives through coursework, research or performance opportunities, and/or study-abroad experiences; curriculum and course objectives include international focus
Technology	Little to no use of technology to teach or engage students; lack of attention to core technologies of the discipline	Some incorporation of technologies by individual faculty members; lack of support for efforts to include technology	Broad use of technology for teaching and student engagement; some gaps in student experiences with important technologies; technology use may not be fully supported or rewarded	Innovative use of technology to teach, engage students, and provide access; well-developed support and reward systems for technology use; students learn appropriate use of discipline- and career-related technologies

(*continued*)

Table 5.1 (Continued)

	Undeveloped	*Developing*	*Effective*	*Distinguished*
Faculty Engagement	No active discussion of curricular issues by faculty; faculty uninterested in curriculum issues	Some individuals or subsets of faculty are engaged in the curriculum	Majority of faculty feel ownership of curriculum	Program faculty have shared vision of curriculum goals; broad-based faculty buy-in; take responsibility for curriculum
Review Process	Curriculum review activities rare or nonexistent	Sporadic, occasional consideration of curriculum, driven by external pressures	Regular, periodic review of curriculum	Ongoing review and discussion of curriculum; improvements guided by assessment data and by new developments in the discipline

Finally, faculty members should consider trying new teaching models that can involve the perspectives of several different fields while also engaging students. Learning communities represent one effective model (see, for example, Gabelnick, MacGregor, Matthews, & Smith, 1990; Hurd, 2004; Laufgraben, Shapiro, & Associates, 2004; Shapiro & Levine, 1999; Smith, 2008; Smith, MacGregor, Matthews, & Gabelnick, 2004). A student learning community is a small group composed of first- or second-year college students who are motivated to explore a common intellectual question or topic. These students often live together in the same housing or dormitory complex and sometimes take several "linked" courses together, one of which introduces and guides subsequent discussion of the community topic (for example, sustainability, art as a form of activism, leadership). The learning community model requires that faculty colleagues collaborate and plan how their courses will connect with one another, but important outcomes include how students learn from one another as they explore the common topic in depth. Learning communities can help to breathe new life into established or evolving curricula (for detailed but practical guidance on creating a learning community, see Shapiro & Levine, 1999).

CONTENT AND SKILLS CORE

Of primary consideration here is the content taught in the program. At a minimum, the program should provide students with an appropriate base of knowledge and skills in the discipline's core content (for a recent example from the discipline of psychology, see Dunn et al., 2010). This goal involves not only offering appropriate courses to cover all key areas of the discipline, but requiring completion of core courses to ensure that all students completing the program have a strong foundation. Part of this approach should include imparting an understanding of how the discipline intersects with other fields of inquiry. For example, the study of psychology overlaps with biology, sociology, and anthropology, among other fields.

Ideally, the curriculum should also reflect emerging areas of the discipline. Although there may not be course offerings in every new specialty area, some treatment of emerging topics and new developments in the field is important in preparing students for the post-baccalaureate world. Core courses might include units on these new areas, or special topics courses—including upper-level seminars—might deal with emerging areas of the discipline. The curriculum needs to be dynamic and to grow as the discipline grows, but not at the expense of coverage of core areas, and not to the extent that the curriculum becomes a set of unrelated specialty courses.

In addition to the core content, the program should also address discipline-specific skills that students should learn. Most disciplines, if not all, involve specific research methods or techniques of practice. This is an obvious point for professional fields, such as nursing or accounting. However, traditional liberal arts disciplines also require the use of specific methods and skills. For example, students in psychology must learn at least the basics of research design and statistical analysis to be able to appreciate and understand the basis of their discipline. Similarly, without grounding in theory and method to form a framework of inquiry, students in economics may simply learn to apply statistical tools mindlessly to monetary data. Thus a curriculum should include training in these basic skills of the discipline that will be expected of students when they enter the work force or continue on to graduate-level education.

Table 5.1 examines this aspect of curriculum using the benchmarks approach. Curricula of programs at the undeveloped level do not include coursework that covers all core areas of the discipline. In some cases these programs simply do not have the faculty resources to be able to cover all the necessary courses. In other cases the curriculum may be unbalanced. For example, several courses may be taught in one area of the discipline, whereas other core areas are not included at all. In the worst-case scenario, a curriculum may consist of a set of unrelated courses in faculty specialty areas (the aforementioned pet or boutique offerings), with numerous core areas of the discipline completely omitted. For whatever reason (such as lack of faculty expertise or interest), these curricula have serious gaps in coverage of the disciplinary core. Developing programs do a better job at covering core areas, but gaps in key areas still exist. Effective programs ensure that all key areas of the disciplinary core are covered;

however, some key areas may be underrepresented, and they may not do a good job at covering emerging areas. These programs may not be in the best position to grow and change as the discipline evolves. In distinguished programs, students are served by a balanced curriculum that requires coursework in all core areas of the discipline. Students not only graduate with a strong foundation in the discipline's key content but also receive exposure to new and emerging areas of their discipline where the intellectual frontiers are expanding.

DISCIPLINARY STANDARDS AND GUIDELINES

The curriculum should be informed by discipline-specific standards and guidelines that may be available from professional organizations. Some disciplines may have these well spelled out, with specific, agreed-upon standards. Some disciplinary organizations, such as the American Chemical Society, provide for formal approval of undergraduate programs (see, for example, American Chemical Society Committee on Professional Training, 2008). Similarly, the Accreditation Board of Engineering and Technology (ABET) and the Association to Advance Collegiate Schools of Business (AACSB) offer curriculum standards that influence program accreditation outcomes. In other cases, professional organizations may provide only guidelines, ranging anywhere along a continuum from specific requirements to more general advice. Examples include the guidelines developed by the American Psychological Association (2007) and the American Historical Association (2007). In still other cases, professional societies have not converged on agreement of what constitutes minimal or optimal curriculum at the undergraduate level; indeed, at least one discipline, philosophy, declines to recommend specific course work at the baccalaureate level. Where standards and guidelines exist, however, the curriculum design should reflect them.

In the case of undeveloped programs, the curriculum does not reflect, or may be inconsistent with, standards or guidelines published by disciplinary organizations. In extreme cases, faculty may be unaware of standards and guidelines, may consider them irrelevant, or may actively oppose acceptance of the professional group's position. Faculty members in developing programs are aware of existing standards, but the curriculum tends to reflect these standards in minimal ways. In effective programs, agreed-upon disciplinary standards guide curriculum design, which reflects most of the key elements of the standards. Distinguished programs feature a curriculum that not only meets standards for the discipline but goes beyond them to achieve true distinction. These programs are innovators when it comes to curriculum, offering programs that set them apart from others. They may boast a national reputation for excellence in educating undergraduates. Faculty members in distinguished programs may be active in contributing to the national discussion about standards in their discipline, helping to set guidelines that shape the future of undergraduate education.

Curricular Structure and Sequence

Coursework should be sequenced in appropriate ways to build student skills; advanced and specialized content should build on a base of student knowledge in the discipline that is gained in earlier coursework (see, for example, Lattuca & Stark, 2009). The purpose of the curriculum's structure should be clear to faculty and students (Fink, 2003; Lattuca & Stark, 2009). Both groups should be able to articulate why courses are sequenced as they are and to identify the goals of different components of the curriculum (such as foundation courses, specialized content courses, applied courses, capstone experiences). In effect, the structure should provide all stakeholders with a roadmap to developing student expertise in the field.

A well-designed curriculum will typically have a hierarchical structure in which intermediate-level courses build on basic skills learned in earlier courses. Advanced courses should hone student skills and knowledge so that they have achieved some mastery of skills by the time they graduate. Specialized content courses may allow students to pursue interests in particular subfields. In many disciplines, a capstone course in which students are required to integrate and apply knowledge and skills learned throughout their program of study may be an appropriate senior-level experience. For programs in some disciplines, a final senior project (for example, honors' thesis; senior research project; senior recital, exhibition, or performance) may be the formal culmination of a student's undergraduate training. Halonen, Bosack, Clay, and McCarthy (2003), for example, present a developmental rubric for scientific inquiry skills for undergraduate psychology. Comparable rubrics can be applied to skill development in other disciplines; for example, AAC&U's VALUE rubrics (see Association of American Colleges and Universities, 2009; see also Stevens & Levi, 2004).

In addition to appropriate sequencing of courses, well-designed curricula have requirements that ensure that students are exposed to the breadth of the discipline. For example, some programs may require students to complete specific combinations of courses that span all the major areas of the discipline. In programs with very limited resources, faculty must exercise greater attention to ensure that appropriate breadth of study can be achieved in those options the program can afford to offer.

In undeveloped programs, there is no coherent structure to the curriculum. Courses typically have no prerequisites, which means instructors cannot assume students sign up for a given class with any relevant academic background. Without prerequisite requirements, course sequencing is meaningless. Related problems emerge when students may take foundational and advanced specialty courses simultaneously. Most problematic of all, students can actively avoid taking certain courses until they are close to completing their major. Within a psychology curriculum, for example, allowing students to postpone completing their research methods and statistics requirements until their senior year virtually guarantees that important material taught in earlier courses was not understood. These "actively avoided" courses may be quantitative in content (such as mathematics, calculus, statistics, research methods) or assigned to faculty whom students deem to be too challenging or dull. By tolerating students' escaping from courses that would contribute to building skills in a sequential fashion, faculty members collude with student avoidance by offering a less than optimal curriculum design. Obviously, in these programs, coursework rarely builds on information and skills from other courses, because there is no guarantee that all students in the class have a foundation in the discipline. There may be no systematic plan for student skill development, because there is no coherent sequencing of courses to ensure that this happens. In addition, students are unlikely to complete coursework that guarantees exposure to the breadth of the discipline. Students may "pick and choose" courses, ending up with little exposure to important areas of the discipline (for example, a major can comprise any nine or ten courses).

Curricula in developing programs have minimal sequencing; for example, an introductory foundations course may serve as the single prerequisite to all other courses. Students may have some distribution requirements to help ensure breadth of exposure. Effective programs feature a well-designed curriculum in which faculty appropriately sequence courses and expose students to the breadth of subareas of the discipline. In distinguished programs, the curriculum has a coherent sequencing and structure that can be easily understood and readily articulated by both faculty and students. Most important, students understand the logic behind prerequisites and distribution requirements, and they understand the goals of the curriculum as a whole. Effective and distinguished programs often include a capstone experience that serves as the culminating integrative experience for students in the program.

FLEXIBILITY AND COURSE VARIETY

We do not mean to suggest that the high-quality curriculum must consist of a rigid set of unvarying courses. Faculty and students are likely to experience a cookie-cutter or "one size fits all" curriculum strategy as stultifying. However, as we noted earlier, an ideal curriculum design includes coverage of all essential areas of the discipline. The curriculum needs to have a coherent structure that builds skills and exposes students to the breadth of the discipline, but it should also be flexible enough to allow for experimentation and growth into emerging areas of the discipline. A flexible curriculum ensures that students master the skills and content of the discipline, but also provides for student choice so that students can focus on areas of the discipline they find most interesting and applicable to their career goals.

Flexibility can be provided in a number of ways. Elective courses may be offered in specialty areas of interest to students and faculty. Students may pursue independent readings, research, or experiential opportunities that allow them to craft a program that matches their interests. Experimental courses can allow faculty and students to explore emerging areas of the discipline. Some programs may design curricula with carefully constructed concentrations that enable students to specialize while still building appropriate skills and providing exposure to the breadth of the discipline. The ideal program will have a balance between structure and flexibility.

Programs that are undeveloped along this dimension have curricula that do not allow for student choice. The program consists of an unvarying set of courses, and all students complete the same set of courses in the same sequence. At the other end of the continuum, we find distinguished programs whose curricula ensure that students meet learning goals, but also provide for flexibility in program design. They typically offer specialized electives, experimental courses, or other experiences to enable students to pursue their own interests within the program structure. Rich and varied experiential opportunities (such as field experiences, independent study or research experiences, internships, honors research) allow students to apply their content knowledge and skills in ways that are tailored to their interests and career plans.

DISCIPLINARY PERSPECTIVES

Scholars approach most contemporary fields of study from a variety of different (sometimes complementary, sometimes competing) theoretical perspectives that inform their teaching and direct their scholarly pursuits. Students need exposure to the broad scope of different theoretical perspectives to gain an accurate and holistic view of the current state of a discipline.

Undeveloped programs present a curriculum that does not reflect the variety of current perspectives in the discipline. All courses are taught from the same theoretical perspective (sometimes a dated one), and the curriculum does not acknowledge the existence of multiple approaches to understanding the content of the field. Controversies, interpretive disputes, different schools of thought—all are ignored. Students thus come away with a limited or even skewed understanding of current viewpoints and approaches of scholars in the field. Developing and effective programs do an increasingly better job at exposing students to the varying points of view in the discipline. Often this exposure happens piecemeal; it is not systematically built into the program.

At the other end of the continuum from undeveloped programs, we find distinguished programs that intentionally design a curriculum to include all major valid theoretical orientations or perspectives. In these programs, the curriculum gives students the full flavor of the complexity of contemporary thinking in the field. Advanced coursework encourages students to explore their own perspectives and approaches to understanding in the field. Students come away with an understanding of the multiple theoretical approaches, intellectual disagreements, and perspectives that engage scholars and practitioners and give the discipline its richness.

ETHICS

Ethical reasoning, along with its relation to the construal of knowledge, values, and responsibility, is an important component in the development of students during their college years (Perry, 1999; see also Braskamp, Trautvetter, & Ward, 2006). Matchett (2008) articulates several good reasons for explicitly treating ethics in the undergraduate curriculum. First, ethical considerations are at the heart of most, if not all, disciplines. Many aspects of their coursework raise ethical questions in the minds of students, even if instructors do not explicitly cover ethical questions in the classroom. Further, failure to incorporate ethical considerations in a systematic and thoughtful manner can result in a variety of unintended consequences. For example, if students' main exposure to ethics is through learning specific codes of conduct, they may come to view ethical behavior as simply obedience to some higher authority or set of rules (such as an Honor Council or professional code of ethics). If faculty treat ethical considerations in a perfunctory manner in classes, students may come to view ethical decision making as a topic somehow set off from more "serious" or important issues of course content.

How can programs incorporate ethics into their curricula? First, many disciplinary societies (for example, the American Psychological Association, American Anthropological Association, American Political Science Association, American Physical Society) have established ethical codes and procedures. Students should, of course, learn the ethical considerations of the field. These often include issues related to how researchers collect and use data; how they treat research participants, clients, or patients; and how they assign credit for work and ideas in the field.

However, beyond simply learning specific codes of conduct, students should gain experiences connecting the ethical concerns of the discipline to everyday ethical decision making. This goal requires a more in-depth consideration of "whys" and the meaning behind specific ethical codes, and exploration of how ethical codes impact decision making in the discipline. Doing so requires faculty members to consider how the goals of liberal education can be wedded to matters of professional education within courses for preparation for life after college (Sullivan & Rosin, 2008). In addition to infusing ethics into coursework, faculty can model ethical behavior for students. When faculty demonstrate adherence to ethical standards and discuss with students how they (faculty) make decisions in the context of their careers, these strategies can produce powerful learning experiences for students.

The ideal curriculum systematically incorporates consideration of the ethics of the discipline throughout the coursework and experiences provided to students, rather than treating ethics as an isolated topic in a single course (for example a methods course or practicum). The AAC&U's VALUE rubric for Ethical Reasoning (Association of American Colleges and Universities, 2009) is a useful framework for incorporating ethics at different points in the curriculum. In addition, Ozar (2001) provides a model of learning outcomes for undergraduate ethics that could be adapted with a discipline-specific focus, and McKeachie (2002) presents ideas for incorporating consideration of values and ethics into the classroom.

Cultural Diversity

One of the most robust higher education phenomena of the late twentieth and early twenty-first century has been the attention to and emphasis on cultural diversity concerns (Moses, 2002). Nearly every discipline has been touched by the omnipresent criticism that the historical neglect of cultural diversity has been harmful to more complete development of the disciplines. Fortunately, recommendations for including matters of diversity within program curricula and across college and university curricula are available (Branche, Mullennix, & Cohn, 2007). Moving toward greater inclusiveness in the disciplines has been recognized as an important goal not just for the integrity of the discipline but also to facilitate greater access to study by those who previously were denied (see, for example, Gurung & Prieto, 2009).

The movement to incorporate diversity as an essential element in curricular design has not been free of controversy (Brown-Glaude, 2009). Traditional disciplinary scholars may reject the relevance of cultural diversity to their endeavors. However, even in bastions of traditionalism, such as the STEM disciplines, boundaries have become more fragile, opening up new possibilities related to gains through the serious incorporation of diversity. For example, Project Kaleidoscope has demonstrated significant enhancement of diversity concerns being taken more seriously within the sciences (see, for example, Nelson, 2007).

Undeveloped programs may have failed to consider how cultural diversity intersects with their own discipline. This position may be espoused as a "legitimate" expression of opposition to diversity matters, or it may result from failure to see any relevance or connection of such material to the discipline. One byproduct of such unfriendliness is the likelihood that students from underrepresented groups may not feel particularly welcome in the discipline, further compounding the neglect of diversity concerns by the discipline.

Developing programs recognize a disciplinary connection to cultural diversity concerns but are likely to dispatch that connection with isolated examples that are not well developed within a curriculum. For example, a contribution made by a member of an underrepresented group may be highlighted in an attempt to represent full participation, but the program fails to look at diversity issues within the discipline systematically or rigorously.

Effective programs acknowledge that cultural diversity does produce a significant influence; however, the curricular solution may be to create a course ''ghetto''—say, one or two stand-alone courses dealing with women's and minority matters—in which those issues get attention. The course or courses do not rise to the level of a required experience, but department members feel good about making the option available and dispatching the obligation for serious consideration.

In contrast, distinguished programs work toward more systematic consideration of diversity issues so that culturally inclusive courses are created and diverse learning environments are promoted in the process (see, for example, Branche, Mullennix, & Cohn, 2007). When done properly and with thoughtful planning, examples of sociocultural diversity abound throughout a curriculum. Serious discussion transpires about how the discipline has fared based on its inclusive practices. Students experience multiple opportunities to explore this issue well beyond completing an isolated diversity requirement. The AAC&U's Intercultural Knowledge and Competence VALUE rubric (Association of American Colleges and Universities, 2009) provides a framework for how students might be expected to demonstrate learning in this domain. Using these or similar outcomes as a beginning may help faculty think about how to incorporate cultural diversity in meaningful ways throughout the curriculum.

INTERNATIONAL PERSPECTIVES

Friedman (2007) argues that globalization has virtually blended geographical distinctions and that in order to survive we must become more adept communicators. For undergraduates, understanding the global implications of what they are learning will be vital as they enter an increasingly internationalized workforce. Internationalizing the undergraduate curriculum, in terms of both the general education core and individual disciplines, is a relatively new and understandably difficulty challenge. These efforts are fairly new, and many programs are only beginning to attend to internationalizing curricula and including global perspectives.

Initiatives for internationalizing the undergraduate curriculum have been undertaken by the American Council on Education (ACE). With support from the Carnegie Corporation of New York, a two-year initiative entitled Where Faculty Live: Internationalizing the Disciplines (Green & Shoenberg, 2006; Olson, Green, & Hill, 2005) engaged scholars from four disciplines (history, political science, psychology, and geography) to consider skills and content for global literacy at the undergraduate level. The leaders from these disciplines were challenged to develop ways to incorporate global perspectives into the undergraduate curriculum. Each of the participating societies (American Historical Association, American Political Science Association, American Psychological Association, Association of American Geographers) developed specific goals and learning outcomes for undergraduate majors in their respective fields (Green & Shoenberg, 2006). These initial efforts might serve as models for other disciplines or programs working to incorporate international perspectives.

Due to the ease and speed of computer-mediated communication and the development of new social networking tools, even underresourced programs can afford to engage students in international experiences. Webcams, online group collaboration tools (such as Google Groups), online virtual worlds, and other Internet-based technologies have greatly expanded the possibilities for students to interact with others around the globe in ways that were not possible just a few decades ago.

Undeveloped programs are seemingly unaware of the global factors affecting their discipline and higher education in general. The curriculum does not incorporate international or global perspectives, other than as isolated topics in individual courses. Developing programs have begun to attend to global intellectual advances that are shaping the discipline. In developing programs, international issues may receive limited coverage; for example, an elective course within the program may have an international focus. Effective programs, using curricular resources such as Green and Shoenberg (2006), consider how international issues are addressed across the curriculum. These programs take a more systematic approach to the treatment of global issues by incorporating international perspectives in courses throughout the curriculum and in other learning opportunities for students.

Distinguished programs include specific goals and objectives for global learning as part of their curriculum design. This may include required coursework or incorporation of international perspectives in multiple courses throughout the curriculum. In addition, distinguished programs go beyond the inclusion of global perspectives in coursework to provide multiple opportunities for students to engage in international learning opportunities. Such opportunities might include offering study abroad courses in the discipline; hosting visiting scholars or lecturers who provide a global perspective; and providing students with opportunities to engage in international research or performance opportunities.

Technology

Technology plays several important roles in the curriculum. First, we can examine the burgeoning use of technology in the delivery of course content. Chickering and Ehrmann (1996) examined how technology can be used as a "lever" in the implementation of the "seven principles for good practice in undergraduate education" first presented by Chickering and Gamson (1987). They discussed ways technology can be used to encourage contact between students and faculty, engage students in active learning, and develop students' collaboration skills. Many technologies are already ubiquitous in the lives of students (such as social networking sites, rapid hand-held communication and information delivery devices), and the list of technologies that can be used both in and out of the classroom is long and growing (see, for example, Bates & Poole, 2003; Dunn, Wilson, Freeman, & Stowell, in press). Blended learning—the marriage of traditional face-to-face teaching with online learning opportunities—is increasingly common on campus (Garrison & Vaughan, 2008). Other possibilities include the use of student response systems ("clickers") in the classroom (see, for example, Bruff, 2009), video and audio podcasts, online discussion forums and collaborative groups (Palloff & Pratt, 2005), web logs (that is, blogs) and wikis (West & West, 2009), virtual world technologies, "ubiquitous computing," online learning communities (Palloff & Pratt, 2007, 2009), and serious games (see Salen, 2008), to name a few. Because technologies change so rapidly and frequently, this list of pedagogical possibilities and relevant activities will expand and change continually, as well (see, for example, Bonk & Zhang, 2008). Laird and Kuh (2005) report a strong positive relationship between the use of technology for instructional purposes and other effective practices, such as those that encourage collaborative learning and student-faculty interaction. Institutions that are student-centered work to engage students through multiple avenues of pedagogy, including technology.

Of course, technologies used for teaching and learning are not different from those used in the workplace for communicating information and collaborating with colleagues. Programs should actively seek ways to take advantage of technology in ways that engage students and enhance learning, and to expose students to technologies they will likely encounter after they leave the university. In many disciplines, training in the use of technology is a vital part of core training in the discipline (for example, accounting, mathematics, computer science, psychology). Students who graduate without experience with the tools and technologies of their discipline, as well as the ability to use them, will be disadvantaged when it comes to finding employment or going on to graduate-level training.

An additional consideration is the dramatic growth of online and distance education (see Allen & Seaman, 2007). Online education provides options for students and reaches out to populations that otherwise may not have access to programs; for example, students with work schedules or family commitments that make face-to-face classes difficult or impossible. Programs need to consider seriously how online and distance education best fits in with their program goals and future plans. Rubrics and guidelines such as those provided by the Quality Matters initiative can help programs design quality online experiences.

Programs that are undeveloped along this dimension incorporate little to no technology in classes. Faculty members do not use technology to engage students or provide learning opportunities. The lack of incorporation of technology may stem from any number of factors. The program or institution may be so poorly resourced that students and faculty do not have access to necessary technology. Faculty may not have the skills to use technology appropriately. If there is no institutional support to help faculty learn the best uses of technology in teaching, faculty may be on their own when it comes to learning about and incorporating new technologies into teaching. Lack of recognition or reward at the program or institutional level can also be a contributing factor. And in some cases, faculty may be resistant or even hostile toward the use of technology as a means of teaching and engaging students. For whatever reason, students do not receive more than basic exposure to technologies that are important for their discipline or the world of work.

In developing programs, a few faculty members incorporate technology into classes, but appropriate use of technology is not a focus of the program. The level of support for these activities is higher than in undeveloped programs, but faculty members are still primarily on their own when it comes to learning the best ways to use technology. Students' learning suffers due to lack of exposure to up-to-date technologies in their discipline.

Effective programs have a more comprehensive approach to the use of technology. Faculty members actively pursue the best ways to use technology to support student learning. Faculty members are aware of currently existing technologies in the discipline and work to include these in courses.

In distinguished programs, faculty members are proactive about seeking out appropriate technologies to engage students and deliver course content to meet learning objectives. The use of technology is supported by forward-thinking technical support at the institution. Technological innovations that improve student learning are encouraged and rewarded at the program and institutional level. Institutional systems work to provide access to technology for both students and faculty. These programs often actively explore ways to reach out to students via online classes or in "blended" or "hybrid" classes that incorporate both face-to-face and online components (Garrison & Vaughan, 2008). Ongoing assessment activities monitor the use of technology and the ways technology use affects student learning.

FACULTY ENGAGEMENT

A vital curriculum needs active engagement on the part of faculty members (see, for example, Diamond, 2008; Fink, 2003; Lattuca & Stark, 2009). For a curriculum to be dynamic and growing, program faculty must feel a sense of ownership of the curriculum. Engaged faculty members are motivated to continually reexamine the curriculum structure along with the results of their efforts on student learning. As a side benefit of faculty involvement, when faculty are actively engaged in considering and discussing curriculum goals among themselves, this may also become part of faculty-student communication, so that students also reap benefits of understanding the big picture of the curriculum design (see Lattuca & Stark, 2009).

Stagnation is a likely outcome in environments where faculty members disengage from consideration of the curriculum. Work on the curriculum may be regarded as a necessary evil and may not be rewarded, or faculty may be simply overwhelmed with an unreasonable workload; in these cases it is not surprising if faculty show little interest in matters related to curriculum design. These qualities are characteristic of programs we would consider to be undeveloped along this dimension. In developing programs, the majority of program faculty leave the task of considering the curriculum to one or two faculty members who happen to take an active interest. Ownership of the curriculum falls to these few faculty members, and the rest simply go along with these few. In effective programs, the majority of the faculty is engaged in consideration of the curriculum. Distinguished programs feature broad faculty buy-in and sense of ownership of the curriculum. The design of the program's curriculum is seen as something that all faculty members have a stake in. Program heads or other administrators view faculty participation in curriculum decisions as an important, even essential component of faculty responsibilities. Engagement in these programs is not merely pro forma; faculty take seriously the important role they play in constructing an optimal experience for students.

Review Process

A system of periodic review of the curriculum is essential to keeping the program current and ensuring that students are well served by their experiences. The success of any periodic review process is clearly related to how invested faculty members are in the success of their program (see earlier discussion). A faculty that feels ownership of the curriculum and is engaged in assessing student learning will take full advantage of opportunities to frequently review the curriculum, and consider how they might improve it. A curricular review may be part of a self-study and subsequent external review, for example (see Chapter Twelve).

At the undeveloped end of the spectrum, periodic review of the curriculum does not occur. It may simply not be part of the planning process of the program. Courses may be added or deleted as new faculty members arrive and others leave or retire. Motivated faculty members may occasionally add new courses. However, all this may happen without systematic consideration of the program structure as a whole. In extreme cases, faculty may even avoid the curriculum review process. Faculty may (in some cases, correctly) view curriculum review as a time-consuming activity that is not rewarded. Any or all of the pitfalls already mentioned (stagnation, drift, overemphasis on salon or pet courses) are typically the result of this lack of a review process.

Developing programs may periodically review the curriculum. However, curriculum review is not something the program does as a matter of course. Review processes are driven by external demands (for example, accreditation review, demands by administrators for accountability or reform, financial challenges faced by an institution), and faculty show little motivation for curriculum review.

Effective programs engage in program review on a regular basis. The review may be stimulated by external demands (such as the regular cycle of institutional program review) or may come about because of events within the program. For example, program faculty may decide to institute a new concentration and may use that event to engage in a holistic review of the program curriculum.

In distinguished programs, curriculum review is an ongoing process. Faculty stay informed about disciplinary standards and guidelines, and they critically examine their curriculum design based on new standards. Faculty members recognize that emerging areas within the discipline may mean that their curriculum needs updating. New understandings of how students learn may also prompt program review. For example, new research indicating that students learn better when material is taught in a particular sequence may mean that the curriculum should be restructured. Further, curriculum changes are informed by assessment data that indicates areas that need improvement. Faculty members in these programs initiate needed curriculum review, without waiting for external mandates. They are driven by the desire to offer students the best learning experience possible.

Tailoring the Framework

In Table 5.1 we present a framework for examining aspects of a program's curriculum. However, we recognize that programs exist within particular institutional cultures, and that individual programs may have specific missions and goals not reflected in this framework. We recommend that programs consider ways to tailor this framework to reflect their own goals and the learning goals they have set for their students. A careful examination of appropriate assessment data can provide information about what students are learning in the current program and where changes need to be made. What specific characteristics of the student population need special consideration when building the curriculum? Does the "house" designed by the program faculty work as well as it can for students? Does the program or institution have a unique mission? Does the faculty plan to develop a specific focus in the program? Faculty can do research, collect assessment data about how well their current program is working, and brainstorm about characteristics of a curriculum for a distinguished program. They can then develop the criteria for the framework. Given the mission of the institution and the learning goals for students in the program, what would a distinguished program look like? An effective one? What would be lacking in a program at the developing or undeveloped end of the continuum? This type of exercise helps faculty members frame their goals in specific and measurable ways that will keep the curriculum lively, engaging for students, and up-to-date.

Guiding Questions

1. Does the curriculum cover all core areas of the discipline? Is it structured such that students are required to gain exposure to all key core areas? Are important aspects of the discipline missing from the curriculum?

2. Does the curriculum match disciplinary standards?
3. Are some aspects of the discipline or some theoretical orientations overemphasized, to the neglect of others?
4. Is there sufficient course variety to allow some tailoring for student interests or career goals? Does the course variety reflect emerging areas of the discipline?
5. How is cultural diversity represented in the curriculum? How can matters of diversity be infused throughout the courses in the program curriculum?
6. When looking at the role of specific courses, what would happen if you removed a given course from the curriculum? Would the curriculum still meet its objectives? What experiences would no longer be available to students?
7. Are coursework and experiences sequenced in ways that develop student skills? Is there a required capstone experience?
8. Can faculty members explain the rationale for the curriculum and its structure? Can students? What about administrators?
9. Are discipline-relevant ethical considerations treated systematically in the curriculum?
10. What role does technology play in the program? Does the program appropriately use available technologies to engage students?
11. To what extent are faculty engaged with, and interested in, issues related to the curriculum? Do the majority of program faculty participate in curriculum discussions?
12. How recently was the curriculum revised? If your program was designing your curriculum "from the ground up," how closely would this structure match the curriculum you would design today?
13. Is there a plan to revisit curriculum issues on a periodic basis?
14. Are curriculum revisions guided by assessment data?

Chapter Six

Student Development: Solving The Great Puzzle

From the moment the incoming first-year students eagerly take their seats in orientation through the moment the graduates collectively move their mortarboard tassels from right to left, the intervening years offer an extraordinary opportunity for personal change. In fact, these years of college experience offer students repeated opportunities to wrestle with the profound question Alice posed in Lewis Carroll's *Alice in Wonderland*: ''But if I'm not the same, the next question is 'Who in the world am I?' Ah, that's the great puzzle!'' A rewarding college experience can go a long way toward solving the great puzzle of personal identity.

Virtually any course of study has the potential to provide answers to the academic aspects of Alice's question. Dedicated to their disciplines, faculty members want students to be changed in positive ways as a result of the experiences faculty provide. Faculty members typically think of themselves as being primarily responsible for the intellectual development of students rather than for their personal growth. Faculty also simultaneously feel responsible for the evolution of the discipline; they want to recruit worthy students into the disciplines they love, to create future generations of scholars who will follow in their footsteps. When students don't elect to follow in the major provided by any given faculty member, most faculty members still at least strive to promote a positive experience in the discipline, which can contribute to student development and to solving the great puzzle.

Through their own serious efforts in college, students will grow in their cognitive abilities and demonstrate mastery in their selected areas of study. However, the prospects for personal transformation as a result of the college experience must take the full range of that experience into account. This scope of impact can be captured more broadly as "student development." The full range of changes that students experience include not just intellectual changes, but emotional, social, and even spiritual changes that regularly transpire both in and beyond the college classroom.

Change agents for personal transformation in student development include a large cast of characters. Facilitated primarily by the faculty, substantial learning and intellectual development takes place within the formal classroom, studio, or lab setting. Faculty also may enrich student development outside the formal classroom through an array of auxiliary activities, such as study group formation, disciplinary club sponsorship, or invited speaker visits. However, changes in student development are not restricted to faculty input. Student affairs representatives, residence assistants, and even office staff can contribute to positive changes in student development. For example, a student distressed from getting the runaround in trying to solve a scheduling problem may be especially moved by a timely and humane intervention by an academic advisor. As a consequence, the student gains a powerful lesson in treating distressed people humanely and may strive to emulate the advisor's style in future encounters. Such broad definitions of shared responsibility for student development encourage collaboration among the various campus stakeholders, leading to engaging and coherent student development experience as well as robust cocurricular programs.

Solid academic programs are typically concerned with providing more than just content knowledge and skills. Such programs embrace the opportunity to promote positive student development, perhaps even transformation, in their programs. They strive to make student development gains a predictable outcome from planned activity and incorporate an array of opportunities to develop the students' knowledge, skills, and character along the way.

Scrutiny of particular areas of effort can reveal how seriously departments take this responsibility. Indicators of commitment can be found in advising, academic support, student engagement strategies, discipline-based extracurricular activities, and student participation in departmental governance. The purpose of this chapter is to explore those domains of activity in depth and to provide some criteria for gauging how effectively departments attend to student development concerns. However, first let's briefly examine the theoretical foundations of student development that contribute to solving the great puzzle.

STUDENT DEVELOPMENT THEORIES

In the early twentieth century, college campuses became a natural setting in which to apply theories from the emerging disciplines of psychology and sociology (Evans et al., 2010). Although the earliest emphasis in student development stressed vocational guidance, the 1937 publication by the American Council of Education (ACE) advocated for focusing on the development of the "whole student" to facilitate better contributions by college graduates to society as a whole. A subsequent ACE statement (1949) reinforced the "whole student" perspective and stressed the importance of recognizing and attending to the needs of diverse kinds of students.

Formal theories regarding student development began to surface in the middle of the twentieth century (Pascarella & Terenzini, 2005). The focus of student development varies from research that is targeted at a specific aspect of the student experience (such as learning style) to researchers who are more comprehensive or ecological in their consideration of multiple variables that make a difference in student experience.

COGNITIVE COMPLEXITY

One of the first formal theories of student development has proved to be one of the most enduring. Interviewing male students at Harvard, Perry (1968/1999) described how students evolve in their cognitive complexity during the college years. He observed students progressing from a simplistic or "dualistic" view of the world (that is, thinking of the world in "black and white" terms) to more complex and contextual deliberations as a function of their liberal arts experience. Inspired by the work of

Piaget, Perry was particularly attentive to the characteristics of the transition points from one stage of cognitive complexity to the next, including the impact of individual differences (Knefelkamp, 1999).

Later cognitive theories expanded upon Perry's observations. Pointing to the limitations of using an all-male population, Belenky, Clinchy, Goldberger, and Tarule (1986) applied Perry's stages to explain cognitive growth in female students. They posited five separate ''ways of knowing'' that women experience, from the position of *silence,* a mindless and voiceless stance, through a position of *constructed knowing,* which recognizes that knowing reflects thoughts, emotions, beliefs, and the characteristics of the learner herself. King and Kitchener (1994) further speculated about other cognitive transformations that were possible beyond the limits of the relativism stage that Perry described.

MORAL DEVELOPMENT

Kohlberg (1969, 1976) developed a stage theory of moral development that has had a big impact on the understanding of student development. He asked male students at Harvard to reason their way through various moral dilemmas and captured the patterns in their rationales. Kohlberg characterized the students' moral decision making as representing three levels of development. At the *preconventional* level, individuals have not fully grasped or adopted societal norms regarding morality. As such, their judgments tend to be focused more on the individual impact of actions than on societal concerns. In *conventional* reasoning, individuals embrace social norms and appear to demonstrate obedience to authority; in effect, this stance protects the status quo. *Postconventional* reasoners transcend social norms and justify their moral decisions based on a richer understanding of complex moral situations and an appreciation for universal and generalizable principles.

Kohlberg's work remains controversial. Gilligan (1982) argued that an obedience-based schema did not adequately account for moral reasoning in women. She counterproposed a ''care based'' scheme to augment Kohlberg's ''justice based'' theory as more appropriate for the patterns she discovered in women students. Similarly, some critics (such as Heubner & Garrod, 1993; Logan, Snarey, & Schrader, 1990) argue that Kohlberg's stage theory may not accurately portray moral reasoning in all cultures. However, Pascarella and Terenzini (2005) concluded that college enhances moral reasoning skills beyond a level that would be expected from maturation alone.

Identity Formation

Perhaps the most influential of the early theories is that of Chickering (1969; Chickering & Reisser, 1993). Chickering conducted comprehensive psychological assessments of students in their sophomore and senior years with the explicit goal of providing guidance to educators to enhance student development. Supporting the "whole student" philosophy, Chickering identified seven vectors along which development occurs among college students: achieving competence, managing emotions, moving through autonomy toward interdependence, developing mature interpersonal relationships, establishing identity, developing purpose, and developing integrity. He argued that student growth is not a linear process and suggested that students may have to recycle through issues as they become more individuated.

Marcia (1966) targeted identity formation processes in young adults that contribute understanding to predictable student dilemmas. Marcia's four-part taxonomy of identity status reflects the certainty, confusion, crisis, and commitment that can be applied to many elements of the undergraduate journey through college. Marcia posited the state of *diffusion* as an orientation in which students show little motivation in resolving identity concerns. They are vulnerable to conforming, in part because they are unable to make an individual commitment. In Marcia's *foreclosure* state, students prematurely commit to a position because they simply rely on authority figures to forge their direction. For example, students may come to college convinced they should pursue a particular major and show no variation from that decision even when their performances suggest their selected majors might not be good matches for their abilities. Students can also demonstrate *moratorium*, in which ambivalence emerges. Original decisions may prove unworkable, and that recognition can fuel a crisis that can often propel a student into the final status: *identity achievement,* the healthiest of the four stages. Individuals who have achieved identity have thoughtfully resolved the identity crisis and are more willing to take risks and examine multiple viewpoints. For example, a student may abandon the cherished family goal of her becoming a physician in favor of a career in botany because she recognizes the botany major as a better fit with her interests and abilities.

Learning Styles

Kolb (1984) developed the concept of experiential learning to emphasize how the quality or efficiency of learning can differ according to individual preferences for modes of learning. He constructed a four-part taxonomy to describe those differences. *Accommodators* are geared toward action and prefer trial-and-error strategies in their problem solving. *Divergers* show special strengths in coming up with imaginative alternatives in their problem-solving attempts. *Convergers* show a preference for working with technical challenges rather than social ones. *Assimilators* are more comfortable with ideas than with people and prefer theoretical modeling and abstract reasoning to other forms of learning.

In practice, faculty and other student developers may demonstrate their own learning styles in their architecture of learning and cocurricular experience. However, awareness that any given group of students will have variable learning preferences encourages the development of an array of learning experiences that appeal to all learning styles rather than rigidly playing out the preferences of the architect.

Personality Variables

An emerging common practice among student developers is the use of personality inventories to capture individual differences. One of the most commonly used approaches involves the Myers-Briggs Type Indicator (MBTI) (Myers & McCaulley, 1985). Based loosely on Jungian theory, the MBTI captures and contrasts student personality styles along the following dimensions: *extroversion* versus *introversion, thinking* versus *feeling, intuiting* versus *sensing,* and *judging* versus *perceiving.* The resulting personality code communicates distinctive ways in which a student might approach an interpersonal or academic challenge. College officials have used the MBTI to identify or rule out career aspirations, to promote personal insight about style differences among peers, and even to select roommates with the best potential for surviving the strain of living together.

The MBTI has demonstrated beneficial effects for the enhancement of leadership skills (Fitzgerald & Kirby, 1997). Many students attest to the usefulness of personality inventory as a means of giving them insight when they encounter others who behave in unpredictable ways. However, the test is not without its critics (see Pittenger, 1993), who express concern about the instrument's reliability and validity. Although MBTI results may be stable in adulthood, the preferences expressed during the college years may be much more transitory. In addition, MBTI preferences may not readily translate to stable skills sets. Some critics conclude that widespread use of the MBTI in college settings may overreach the inventory's original purpose.

Ecological Models

More recent scholarship in areas that enlighten student development has attempted to produce more comprehensive developmental models that have an ecological foundation. Kegan (1994) created a stage theory based on resolving evolutionary challenges that emphasized the skills needed to cope with complex modern life. He noted that troubles develop in college settings when students engage with what he termed "the socialized mind," or "third order consciousness." Although capable of abstract thinking, students may be swayed by feelings and personal biases and may rely too heavily on designated authorities, such as college teachers, for how to think or believe. In contrast, faculty may have reached "the fourth stage of consciousness," which Kegan called "the self-authoring mind." Most academic professionals can self-regulate and demonstrate independence, but they also may inappropriately expect students to navigate their lives with the same conscientiousness, rather than accept their own role in promoting these changes in students.

Baxter Magolda (2001) conducted longitudinal research on how students move from socialized mind status to self-authorship. She concluded that college environments succeed best in helping students make the transition to appropriate self-reliance when the facilitators provide validating feedback to students about their potential, pay attention to the learner's experience when designing the curriculum and supporting learning experiences, and accept that learners will actively construct meaning out of those experiences in college.

Regardless of the specific puzzle pieces, researchers have tried to contribute to optimizing student development, and universities have incorporated research principles in several emerging best practices that have been widely adopted to enrich student experience and facilitate their development. In this next section, we'll explore some contemporary practices that report success in promoting student development.

EMERGING PRACTICES IN STUDENT DEVELOPMENT

In their landmark article on principles for good practice in undergraduate education, Chickering and Gamson (1987) highlighted the important roles of student-faculty interaction and reciprocity and cooperation among students to foster optimal growth. These practices regularly provide opportunities for strong collaborations to develop between academic units and student affairs divisions on campus. Three popular practices include the employment of the National Survey of Student Engagement for assessment purposes, the use of service learning to promote integrated learning in undergraduate curricula, and the establishment of learning communities to break down traditional barriers to learning.

MEASURING STUDENT ENGAGEMENT

Numerous authors (Astin, 1993b, 1996; Hernandez, Hogan, Hathaway, & Lovell, 1999; Martin, 2000; Terenzini, Pascarella, & Blimling, 1996) have discussed the importance of student involvement for success at the undergraduate level. Involvement, which clarifies purpose and develops a sense of competence, includes several aspects of student behavior, such as the amount of time spent in a given behavior, the level of cognitive focus on the activity, and the extent of commitment to the activity (see Foubert & Grainger, 2006). Perry (1981) suggests that these experiences move students beyond mere tautologies and contribute to increased levels of cognitive development. Astin (1996) reports that academic involvement, involvement with faculty, and involvement with student peer groups are the three types of involvement that have the greatest impact on student development.

Perhaps the best-known effort focusing on the evaluation of student involvement is the National Survey of Student Engagement (NSSE). Numerous campuses administer the NSSE to measure multiple aspects of student engagement at the undergraduate level. Based on responses to key survey questions, NSSE developed five "Benchmarks of Effective Educational Practice" (National Survey of Student Engagement, 2009): level of academic challenge, active and collaborative learning, student-faculty interaction, enriching educational experiences, and a supportive campus environment. The benchmarks are based on student experiences both inside and outside the classroom (such as participation in cocurricular activities and working with faculty on committees or student life activities).

As results from the NSSE make clear, campuses foster student involvement and development through many activities. Academic programs cannot, nor should they be expected to, serve all student development needs, as the entire campus community serves this purpose. Academic programs can provide opportunities that have an impact on students' academic and professional growth and will enhance their engagement with the program, the institution, the discipline, and the local community.

Promoting Service Learning

One promising way to broaden students' intellectual horizons beyond the classroom is through community-based cocurricular experiences. For example, Kuh, Kinzie, Schuh, Whitt, and Associates (2005) offer evidence that service learning enriches classroom experiences. The term "service learning" encompasses a variety of activities that begin in the classroom and are then subsequently applied elsewhere, usually in a community setting. Thus service learning is a form of experiential learning that encourages students to understand how sometimes abstract concepts from a discipline can be constructively applied to real-world settings. Academic programs, then, can provide students with practical community-based experiences that facilitate the achievement of specific learning goals.

Service learning scholars claim a variety of favorable student development outcomes related to service learning. Not only can students achieve discipline-specific objectives, but they can also make gains in cognitive complexity, moral reasoning, personal autonomy, tolerance and empathy, and even "sense of place in the U.S. and global economy" (Jacoby & Associates, 1996, p. 87). Engaging students to a higher degree promotes enduring learning (Association of American Colleges and Universities, 2002; Osborn & Karukstis, 2009).

Service learning also promotes civic engagement, so that students are encouraged to give back to the local community where they currently reside as an expression of citizenship (Eyler & Giles, 1999). Faculty who teach service learning courses hope that these initial community service experiences will encourage students to seek opportunities to volunteer and affect the common good in the communities where they will eventually reside (for a broader discussion of service learning, see Kershaw, Lazarus, Minier, & Associates, 2009). The American Association for Higher Education (AAHE) has produced discipline-specific handbooks for service learning in several disciplines, ranging from philosophy (Lisman & Harvey, 2006) and history (Harkavy & Donovan, 2005) to accounting (Rama, 1998) and engineering (Tsang, 2000).

Faculty interested in developing service learning opportunities for students may not need to develop relationships with local communities on their own. Often, student affairs units can provide community-based experiences to enhance student development, and these experiences can be refined to include student learning outcomes that are specific to a major. Student affairs personnel are often well positioned to provide support for service learning assignments, including introductions, coordination of effort, and even transportation support.

Sponsoring Learning Communities

What may be the most valuable academic and student affairs collaborations can be demonstrated in the learning community movement that has emerged on campuses across the nation. This national movement became viable in the mid-1980s and showed significant growth over the following decade (Smith et al., 2004). Although learning communities may take different forms and functions across contexts, the heart of learning community design includes linked or clustered courses, sometimes thematically linked, for targeted groups or "cohorts" of students. Learning communities also promote student involvement not just in their chosen courses of study but also in community service, providing a perfect platform for service learning.

Advocates of learning communities praise not just their proven capacity to recruit and retain students from diverse backgrounds but their capacity to enhance intellectual growth (Shapiro & Levine, 1999). Such ambitious curricular redesigns "create venues for synergistic activity to occur among people and ideas" (Smith et al., 2004, p. 23).

Departments opting to participate in learning community programs provide students with opportunities to learn discipline-specific content both within the classroom and through informal activities. Roles of faculty and advisors tend to be more personal, and students more comfortably turn to their learning community peers to enrich their learning. When students engage with material in a less formal setting, they learn new applications and the experience further emphasizes the relevance of the discipline-specific content.

The advantages of combining student development theory, discipline-specific learning goals, and intensive faculty development is evidenced in the Documenting Effective Educational Practice (DEEP) project (see Kinzie & Kuh, 2004; Kuh, Kinzie, Schuh, & Whitt, 2005), which highlighted learning communities as a particularly effective strategy to engage students and contribute to the development of their identity. A thorough, comprehensive description of successful learning communities can be found in *Creating Learning Communities* (Shapiro & Levine, 1999).

How Departments Contribute Pieces to the Great Puzzle

Undergraduate programs differ in the degree to which they embrace responsibility for developing the whole student. Generally speaking, faculty in undeveloped programs prefer to draw a bright line between academic responsibilities and the activities that they differentiate as the burden of student affairs; anything that is not strictly academic is also strictly excluded from the job description of professor. However, the growing emphasis on recruitment and retention as accountability measures should effectively broaden the scope of the faculty role in helping students figure out who they are.

Faculty in developing programs recognize the importance of ancillary activities to achieving optimal student development, but they respond to the need in a minimal fashion. Some high-quality work may be accomplished in this area, but typically the burden will be borne by one or two department members, much to the relief of other faculty members who are free to pursue their own priorities.

In contrast, effective programs accept their role in student development and participate more directly in facilitating activities that will promote student involvement. Departments distribute responsibilities across the department and offer useful and timely opportunities to assist students in meeting their development goals. Faculty in distinguished programs tend to embrace student development responsibilities and promote multiple strategies that help students fully realize not just their academic goals but also their optimal personal development. Next we consider how this continuum applies to several specific domains of activity in student development. In Table 6.1 (adapted from Dunn et al., 2007), we use the benchmarks approach to examine how departments perform in several domains of student development.

Advising

Program reviewers often experience the area of advising as one in which even distinguished programs may not excel. Students typically view advising as an intensely personal experience. They want

Table 6.1 Student Development Benchmarks

	Undeveloped	*Developing*	*Effective*	*Distinguished*
Advising	Avoids or minimizes advisement activity	Emphasizes "student responsibility" as a substitute for faculty advisement; primary focus is on course sequencing	Requires interaction between students and faculty advisors at critical checkpoints; some mentoring and career guidance	Comprehensive advising system provides continuously available assistance for course planning, effective mentoring, and career guidance
Academic Support and Intervention	Adopts a "sink or swim" attitude toward student success	Makes referrals to campus-based student success intervention in severe cases	Produces access to departmentally housed strategies for academic support	Provides multimodal forms and locations of academic support
Student Engagement Beyond the Classroom	Does not recognize role of program in student development; does not provide opportunities for student engagement beyond the classroom	Provides minimal opportunities for student engagement with limited faculty involvement	Recognizes important role of program activities in student engagement; out-of-class activities encouraged and valued	Takes a multifaceted approach by offering multiple opportunities to enhance student development, tailored to student needs; activities driven by valid assessment data

Student Organizations	Does not sponsor formal student organizations	Sponsors formal organizations; limited faculty involvement or support	Provides active support for formal organizations that enhance disciplinary identity for students	Sponsors vibrant formal organizations that promote student leadership and engagement through planned learning opportunities
Program-Level Activities and Events	Avoids or minimizes student-focused program activities	Sponsors some student-focused activities	Sponsors array of student-focused activities across spectrum of interests and developmental levels	Promotes student engagement through program activities; actively develops programs focused on student needs and interests
Participation in Department Decisions	Does not allow for student input in program decisions	Includes student input and interests in decision and policy making on occasional or sporadic basis	Provides opportunity for student input in narrow range of program activity	Actively pursues student input in program decisions to facilitate effective policy for the department and provide learning opportunities for students

accurate information about course suitability or predictions about the consequences of their choices, and they often want input at the moment the specific advising question occurs to them. On the other hand, advising, although important, is unlikely to be the top priority for all but a few faculty members. Consequently, students often rate faculty advising response as sluggish at best on what, for them, are urgent and personal matters.

In most undeveloped or developing programs, faculty advisors are typically ''on their own'' when it comes to advising; little support and few resources exist for faculty either within or outside the program. This situation may not be uncommon; Habley (2003) reports that fewer than one-third of institutions provide any form of recognition or reward for advising. Further, only 8 percent of institutions consider advising when making tenure and promotion decisions in all departments (Habley, 2003). Such situations encourage faculty members to see advising as someone else's obligation or to happily hand the burden over to the department or program chairperson.

A worst-case scenario in the developing situation occurs when one colleague makes a serious effort to deliver high-quality student advising, only to become the de facto advisor for all students in the department. Word gets out, and students line the hall to get the benefits from the one faculty member who appears to care about students' destinies. Although some high-quality advising may transpire, the faculty member can quickly become overwhelmed by the intensive advising demands on the member's discretionary time.

Effective advising clearly benefits students (see Kramer, 2003; Pascarella & Terenzini, 2005). However, effective advising demands considerable time, effort, and energy on the part of faculty members, who must understand not only their own programs (course sequences and prerequisites) but other university requirements (general studies requirements, graduation requirements) as well. Faculty members should also be well informed about potential career paths for students, requirements for graduate school admission, employment opportunities in the field, and a host of other issues that are important for student success. Habley and Bloom (2007) describe eight separate roles that effective advisors play in the lives of students: Consumer Advocate,

Intervener, Orchestrator, Dissonance Mediator, Dissonance Creator, Boundary Spanner, Bellwether, and Cultural Guide. Obviously, effective programs recognize that advising goes beyond the "checklist approach."

Advising in such programs not only moves students through the program in a timely fashion but also includes academic mentorship and guidance on career goals and planning as a formal faculty expectation. These programs treat academic advising as an important responsibility not only of individual faculty members but of the program as a whole. They emphasize effective advising in part because the institution acknowledges the importance of this contribution. In these programs, good communication from career planning and student development offices at their institution further supports faculty efforts.

Distinguished programs optimize the advising experience by providing multiple avenues through which students receive guidance. Exhibit 6.1 offers a list of potential advising resources and methods. For example, a program may produce well-designed handouts, checklists, and brochures that students can keep and refer to. An informative and continuously updated website that showcases advising information can be an invaluable advising resource.

In addition to individual face-to-face meetings with students, faculty may provide other options for faculty-student communication. Faculty may arrange group meetings for their advisees, enabling students to meet others who share their interests or questions. They may hold "open advising hours" at a campus coffee shop. Electronic communication options are also numerous. Of course, the use of e-mail is almost ubiquitous in faculty-student interaction. Another option to increase community among students and faculty, as well as provide advising, is to form a group on a social networking site (such as Facebook and Ning). Social networking groups have the added advantage of providing a venue not just for student-faculty communication but also for students to engage with each other. Traxler (2007) characterized the use of social networking as "advising without walls" and lauded the capacity of the strategy to engage digital natives on the technological turf they prefer.

In addition to individual faculty advising, distinguished programs focus on maintaining efficient advising systems at the

EXHIBIT 6.1 ADVISING RESOURCES AND METHODS

Student-Faculty Interaction

Individual face-to-face meetings

Group meetings

E-mail

Electronically mediated advising group (such as a social networking site)

Program-Level Activities

Specialized advising for specific career interests

Symposia on advising topics (for example, careers, graduate school)

Periodic e-mails to all students (such as a weekly ''E-mail news'')

Peer advising group

Orientation to the major course or careers course

Resources for Students

Paper handouts (such as checklists for course completion, handouts on specific topics such as honors thesis procedures)

Program bulletin boards

Website

program level. For example, programs may offer targeted advising for specific careers by having faculty members who specialize in working with students with specific career goals. The program may sponsor activities focused on advising (such as a workshop on getting into graduate school or symposia that bring in alumni to talk about career issues), or it may send out a weekly or monthly e-mail newsletter reminding students of important deadlines, upcoming seminar topics, and other events. An ''orientation to the major'' course or a careers course can serve an important advising function by formalizing the delivery of information in a specially designed class (see Loher & Landrum, 2010; Appleby, 2010).

A peer advising program can be a rich source of information that also contributes to efficient advising strategies for students as they move through the program Peer educator programs have been shown to be effective in a variety of settings (for example, see Copenheaver, Duncan, Leslie, & McGehee, 2004; Ender & Newton, 2000; Foubert & Cowell, 2004; Morrison & Talbott, 2005). In academic programs, specially trained advanced students can provide insight and advice for other students who are just beginning in the program. Benefits of such a program can extend not only to those receiving assistance but also to the peer advisors themselves (Badura, Millard, Johnson, Stewart, & Bartolomei, 2003).

Activities of a peer advising program can extend beyond simple one-to-one meetings between students. For example, the peer advising (PA) program in the department of psychology at James Madison University provides information sessions for prospective majors, presents symposia on careers and graduate school application procedures, and keeps up-to-date information on faculty research activities. Supervisors choose juniors and seniors who have shown an interest in developing their leadership and teamwork skills and in assisting with program activities. The PA program at JMU also focuses on service and community outreach, with fundraisers throughout the year. The PA office also assists the department in numerous ways with student outreach. For example, prospective majors often visit the PA office (which is staffed by peer advisors during weekdays) to get "the student's perspective" on the department. PAs often participate in formal recruitment activities, such as annual events at the university that bring in groups of prospective students. Prospective students who have the opportunity to discuss the psychology department with current students and hear about the academic experiences and career plans of current students can quickly become sold on the psychology department.

Disciplinary organizations may not typically provide guidelines or actively promote best practices for advising. However, national organizations such as the National Academic Advising Association (NACADA; www.nacada.ksu.edu) are rich sources for information on effective advising practices. NACADA's statement of Core Values of Academic Advising (NACADA, 2005) provides guidance for faculty advisors. In addition, numerous excellent books (see Gordon, Habley, Grites, & Associates, 2008; Kramer,

2003) provide resources and help for faculty advisors. Programs and institutions can draw on these and other sources for information and inspiration as they seek to enhance advising.

Academic Support and Intervention

Attitudes about providing outside help parallel the variable enthusiasm regarding advising. Undeveloped and developing programs are minimally aware of ways that the campus may already have moved to provide help for students who struggle; worse, department members simply don't care whether or not the students succeed. In contrast, programs that accept and attempt to meet this serious need can demonstrate remarkable creativity in the modes, locations, and timing of the intervention provided. For example, supplemental instruction (SI) programs for high-risk classes (those in which 30 percent or more of students earn a D, F, or W) can also serve an effective student development role. In SI programs, students who have successfully completed the high-risk course serve as SI leaders. These students are trained to work with students currently taking the course, leading regular out-of-class study sessions.

Not only are students taking the class who participate in SI more successful (see Bowles, McCoy, & Bates, 2008; Stone & Jacobs, 2006), but student SI leaders benefit as well. Stout and McDaniel (2006) highlight potential gains for leaders in not just understanding of the course subject matter but also improved communication skills, enhanced self-confidence and self-esteem, and enhanced professional skills such as organizational and planning skills and learning how to plan for unforeseen events. Lockie & Van Lanen (2008) found four "themes" that characterized the experience of SI leaders, including learning about the diversity of student learning styles, enrichment of their own academic experiences, enrichment of personal experiences, and an enhanced relationship with faculty and understanding of faculty roles. The International Center for Supplemental Instruction at the University of Missouri-Kansas City (http://web2.umkc.edu/cad/SI/index.html) provides information about implementing SI programs, and a variety of relevant resources.

Student Engagement Beyond the Classroom

Exemplary programs that focus on student development and have the support of their institutions will develop projects and experiences that match the needs and interests of their students. We previously noted the roles that service learning (see Kershaw, Lazarus, Minier, & Associates, 2009) and learning communities (see Smith et al., 2004) can play along these lines. However, many programs are turning to specific discipline-based faculty-student collaborations to help promote engagement.

Actively involving students in their own learning appears to be a promising venue for student development, as exemplified by the Student Voices group of the Carnegie Association for the Advancement of Teaching and Learning's Institutional Leadership Program (www.wwu.edu/studentvoices/). Faculty in this program focus on including student voices by engaging students in scholarship of teaching and learning (SOTL) projects (see Bueschel, 2008; Werder & Otis, 2009) so they can more fully appreciate the work intensity that has gone into the architecture of their own education. A high-caliber program could emphasize students as collaborators in faculty SOTL projects to help in developing program assessment tools and analyzing assessment data.

In many disciplines, particularly the sciences, involving students in faculty research is an important tool for engaging students outside the formal classroom (see Chapter Four). Not only do these students learn specific discipline-related content and skills, but they also gain in other ways, including learning to work independently, clarification of career goals, and increasing self-confidence (for example, see Hu, Scheuch, Schwartz, Gayles, & Li, 2008; Landrum & Nelsen, 2002; Lopatto, 2007; Seymour, Hunter, Laursen, & Deantoni, 2004). According to students who participate in research, one of the most valuable aspects of the experience is the opportunity to form personal relationships with faculty outside the classroom, as well as with other students (see Seymour et al., 2004; Falconer & Holcomb, 2008). For faculty interested in engaging students in research, the Council on Undergraduate Research (CUR; www.cur.org) promotes research at the undergraduate level and provides support and information for faculty who involve undergraduates in research experiences.

Programs that are undeveloped along this dimension do not consider or initiate discipline-related activities that can enhance student development. As with advising and academic support, faculty in these programs may consider this to be outside of their responsibility, or they may be so weighed down with other responsibilities that they simply do not have time or energy to expend on these pursuits. Further, faculty may not be rewarded or recognized for these "extra" efforts. For example, in many programs, supervision of student research groups is not considered part of the faculty member's regular load and often unfolds as an uncompensated overload.

Developing programs may provide a few special opportunities for students, but such programs may be driven by the interests and energy of one or two faculty members, who are likely to be inundated with student requests. In effective programs, faculty increase efforts on the part of the program to incorporate such activities, as well as recognition that they are an important part of student development. Programs that are distinguished along this dimension take a multipronged approach to providing meaningful out-of-class experiences for students. Such departments purposefully conduct assessment data to differentiate the methods that may have the greatest impact. Further, faculty receive appropriate recognition for their energy and successful efforts in this direction.

Student Organizations

A program can also promote student engagement through sponsorship of student organizations. These organizations can encompass a full range of options including open clubs for all students interested in the discipline, honor societies, peer advising organizations (just described), and special opportunities for groups of students with special interests (such as specific career goals or a focus on one aspect of the discipline). Student organizations can promote community and cohesion among students in the program. They also provide students with opportunities to develop leadership abilities and a sense of professional identity. Involvement in student organizations is associated with many positive outcomes, including educational involvement, career planning, and establishing and clarifying purpose (Astin, 1993b, 1996; Cooper, Healy, & Simpson, 1994; Foubert & Grainger, 2006).

Beyond local student organizations, faculty may also encourage students to join national or regional professional organizations by promoting this as an option for students and even sponsoring their memberships. Many professional organizations have special categories, often with reduced membership dues, for student members. Through joining such organizations, students connect with the wider academic and professional community outside the university. This opportunity can be a powerful experience for students, as they begin to link their own learning and professional growth to the larger context of their discipline.

Programs at the undeveloped end of the continuum for this factor either do not sponsor student organizations or they give them limited or haphazard support. Faculty support for student organizations (such as serving as a faculty advisor for an organization) may not be rewarded or regarded as valuable, so student organizations represent a very low departmental priority.

Developing programs provide sporadic support for student organizations. The activity level of student organizations in such programs may be dependent on the dedication and energy of a single faculty member. More senior faculty tend to regard the student organization advisor role as low status and typically assign it to the most junior of faculty in the department. If that faculty member leaves the institution or grows weary, the student organization tends to wither. In addition, the success of a variably supported student organization becomes more dependent on commitment from strong student leaders. When involved student leaders graduate, the organization may go dormant unless they have given careful thought to leadership succession.

At the effective level, faculty concentrate on at least one support organization for students that can help them meet their engagement and leadership goals. Students clearly recognize these activities as an enhancement of what is available in the classroom. In turn, faculty remember to explain the value of associating with the student organization and to promote student participation in their meetings with students. Faculty find intrinsic value in facilitating student development through auxiliary activities, regardless of the recognition their involvement earns.

Distinguished programs engage in a wide range of activities that promote vital student organizations. These programs may have multiple student organizations to engage students of different interests. For example, the computer science department at the University of West Florida differentiates student interest groups according to two special purposes. "Bits" represents first-year or transfer students who are brand new to the program. "Bytes" encompasses all other students who, among other activities, can serve as mentors to the "Bits" counterparts. Some activities are executed just for newcomers. Otherwise, faculty can combine the groups for shared advising and career development interests.

Faculty support student organizations through their participation and attendance at events, encourage student involvement, and systematically promote opportunities for students to become involved in professional organizations. Administrators perceive these activities as valuable, and they are rewarded accordingly. Programs of this stature often strive to maintain dedicated spaces for organizations to encourage student activities to flourish.

PROGRAM-LEVEL ENHANCEMENTS

As is the case for formal student organizations, planned activities and events also help students develop a sense of professional identity. Annual events—such as student awards celebrations, poster sessions, or student symposia—can become traditions that students and faculty look forward to attending. Advanced students who participate in such program traditions can serve as role models for beginning students. Faculty members serve in important mentoring roles through their attendance and enthusiastic participation in these out-of-class activities.

A wide range of program events can serve to engage students and build community in a program. Some activities require extensive planning and major expenses; others require no planning other than setting a date, time, and place, and spreading the word about the event. Many of these activities require little in the way of faculty time commitment, but can pay off in large ways when it comes to engaging students in the program. Exhibit 6.2 lists a range of program activities that can engage students outside the classroom.

Exhibit 6.2 Activities to Promote Student Involvement in the Program

- Award ceremonies. These events can recognize both student and faculty achievements. Parents and friends of award-winners, as well as administrators, can be invited.
- Graduation celebrations for graduates and their parents.
- Receptions or gatherings for newly declared majors. This type of event can also serve an advising function, especially if faculty attend and are available to answer questions.
- Student research symposia or poster sessions.
- Symposia on topics of interest, given by guest lecturers.
- Special lectures by faculty on their scholarship area.
- Student-faculty athletic events. The program might field a student-faculty intramural team or have a weekly volleyball or softball game or other event.
- Weekly brown-bag lunch with faculty. This can be held in a break room or faculty members can meet students at a dining hall. Faculty can rotate attendance; for example, each faculty member might attend once during the semester.
- Weekly "milk and cookies" or coffee break for faculty and students. This could be held in a faculty lounge or at a coffee shop on campus or in town.
- Informal gatherings at faculty homes. Examples might include a Super Bowl party or Movie Night.
- Program parties. Social gatherings can celebrate program events or holidays (such as an annual Thanksgiving potluck).

Of course, events should be tailored to fit the student and faculty population and the institutional culture. What are the characteristics of the student population? Are there many non-traditional-age students? Older students may face child-care issues that interfere with their ability to participate in out-of-class activities. Is the student population primarily commuter students, or do most live on or near campus? What is the ratio of part-time to full-time students? Commuter students and part-time students may be less likely to attend events in the evenings or on week-ends. A weekly brown-bag lunch with faculty might be more successful for these students than a weekend picnic or an evening event. Providing a variety of activities allows students to select activities based on their level of interest in the program, as well as their availability to participate. One possibility to enhance positive student development is to require students to participate in some program-level activities. For example, students might need to complete a portfolio involving attendance at selected program functions (such as awards programs, symposia, guest lectures). However, in many cases this may not be practical or desirable.

Undeveloped programs typically do not sponsor student-focused events outside of regular class activities. Faculty members may be actively discouraged from developing outside activities if these activities take away from other activities that have higher value. In some cases, faculty may be so overwhelmed with other duties (such as heavy scholarship demands, unrealistic teaching or service loads, other administrative responsibilities) that they feel unable to help plan, promote, or even attend events.

Developing programs sponsor a limited array of activities, but there may be minimal faculty involvement (for example, the faculty organizer may be the only faculty attendee at an event, which sends a signal about its importance in the eyes of other program members). Faculty often feel relieved of the responsibility to attend if they have made an effort to advertise the event in their classes. Merely issuing an encouraging invitation, although laudable, is not as helpful as demonstrating the event's importance by also attending and participating in it.

Effective programs offer a reasonable but limited range of activities that attract students of differing interest levels. They reward and encourage faculty participation in student-related activities, and individual faculty members value these as meaningful learning experiences for students.

Programs that are distinguished along this dimension sponsor a variety of student-focused activities to engage students of different interests and at different points in the program. In addition, they proactively initiate new activities in response to student needs and interests. They discontinue activities that don't seem effective and may make choices about which activities to choose based on solid assessment strategies. These programs monitor student perceptions of the program both formally and informally (for example, as part of their assessment program), and they are aware of what their students should be getting and are getting out of the program.

Participation in Program Decisions and Governance

Students obviously have a limited role to play in program governance. However, there are several ways in which students can participate in program decisions, particularly those that have a direct impact on students. Allowing students' voices to be heard can have many beneficial effects. Students learn that their opinions matter to faculty; they come to see themselves as contributors to the program, rather than passive recipients of it. They are not just passing through the program but helping to shape it for the future. In addition to the benefits for students, faculty members gain an important source of input on the program structure and program activities. Faculty also have a great opportunity to develop student (eventually alumni) loyalty to the program for the future.

There are multiple venues through which students may provide input to the program and assist with program governance and other activities. The faculty may hold open meetings with students to gather student input and to inform students about current issues in the program. Another possibility is to have an elected or volunteer student advisory committee that meets regularly with the program head or other faculty to provide input.

Student representatives may attend department faculty meetings on a regular or occasional basis. For example, the presidents of student organizations might be invited to faculty meetings. These student representatives not only serve as a sounding board for faculty but can also report to other students about happenings in the program. Of course, students would be excused from discussions of personnel matters or other sensitive issues. Specific committees may also include a designated student member. For example, student input can be very important to search committees or committees that examine curriculum revision.

In addition to serving on committees and giving input, students can also provide assistance to the program. Advanced students can serve as mentors, providing important information and advice to beginning students. Their presence and participation in the life of the department serves as a testimony to new students about the energy, quality, and integrity of the program. When a program is doing its job well, current students often serve as its best advertisement. These students can assist in recruitment efforts, for example, by staffing a table at a majors fair on campus, by recruiting at their high schools, or by meeting with prospective students and their parents. Outstanding advanced students can also represent the program to upper administrators and the university community at large. A cadre of successful students who are pleased with the education they are receiving can speak volumes to administrators about the effectiveness of the program.

Programs considered undeveloped along this dimension do not provide opportunities for student input into program decisions. The dearth of opportunities may indicate that the program faculty are out of touch with, or indifferent to, student concerns. Developing programs seek student opinion on a sporadic basis, often to address an acute problem or unexpected opportunity. For example, a student member may occasionally serve on a selected committee. These programs solicit student input on rare occasions, typically for specific and limited purposes.

Effective and distinguished programs make a point of providing opportunities for the student voice to be heard. Effective programs demonstrate conscientiousness about seeking input for major issues but tend to think about student input as an obligation rather than a useful resource. In distinguished programs, systematic efforts are made to involve students, and they actively participate in program decision making in many ways. For example, these programs may have a formal student advisory committee, or students may serve on committees. Faculty view student opinion as a treasured resource.

CONCLUSIONS

Student development is essential to the life of a dynamic, forward-looking department or program. However, as Kuh, Kinzie, Schuh, Whitt, and Associates (2005) concluded, there is "no single blueprint for student success" (p. 20). Departments can use a variety of strategies to foster student competence, personal integrity, interpersonal relationships, and individual sense of purpose through both in-class and out-of-class opportunities. Students who begin as academic consumers evolve into alumni and, in some cases, even colleagues. As educators, we want them to feel a keen loyalty to our academic program as well as to the larger institution. Given the recent trends in higher education, savvy faculty realize that providing a quality undergraduate education is arguably the most important service they can offer. Ultimately, a department's and its members' willingness to embrace that service can influence how powerfully—or painfully—the puzzle pieces of personal identity can come together.

GUIDING QUESTIONS

1. Is advising a valued and rewarded faculty activity? Do faculty members receive adequate support for advising? Are there program-level advising activities in addition to individual faculty efforts?
2. What is the department's stance regarding the support they are willing to provide students who struggle academically?
3. Does the program provide a range of outside-the-classroom activities that enhance student learning and provide opportunities for student development? Are these activities tailored to the specific needs and interests of the student population?
4. Does the program sponsor a range of program-level events to encourage student involvement? Are these events well attended by both faculty and students? Are students involved in planning and hosting the activities?
5. How is student opinion gauged or solicited? Do students have multiple venues for providing input?
6. Are students involved at all levels of department or program affairs? Are alumni as involved as beginning majors and senior students? If not, how can the situation be constructively addressed?
7. How would students describe their experiences in the program? How have they grown? Do students feel changed as a result of their experiences?

Chapter Seven

Constructively Evaluating Faculty Characteristics

The faculty members in a department or program are the linchpins of undergraduate education: they design the curriculum, create courses, and teach students, preparing them for graduation and life thereafter, including the world of work or possibly graduate school. The life of a faculty member is an autonomous one, a fact that attracts many teacher-scholars to the professoriate. With few exceptions or constraints, faculty members can design their own courses to fit their interests, select books or readings in an unfettered manner, and pursue scholarly interests without much oversight or interference. Generally speaking, faculty can come and go to campus at will as long as they meet with their classes and complete their assigned tasks (such as advising, student club or organization supervision, scholarship, and service and obligations in various contexts).

We believe this relative freedom is what allows faculty members to do their best and most creative work with and for undergraduate students. However, with faculty freedom comes faculty responsibility. Accountability, productivity, and quality are hallmarks of contemporary faculty life (Middaugh, 2001). Teacher-scholars are obliged to seek continual improvement of their professional activities in the classroom, in the program, on campus, and beyond; for example, contributing to the discipline and disciplinary organizations. This presumptive freedom holds true in public as well as private institutions.

Demonstrating one's value to a department and larger institution is usually accomplished by undergoing a performance review. Not surprisingly, some faculty members are wary of external assessment of their teaching and professional activities. Yet evaluation is very much a part of academic life (see Glassick, Huber, & Maeroff, 1997). In this chapter, we discuss the rationale for faculty evaluation and reiterate the importance of formative rather than summative assessment in the constructive evaluation of faculty efforts in and outside of the classroom. Using the developmental benchmarks framework, we discuss ways to assess pedagogical practices, self-evaluation as a teacher, new course development, scholarship, resource generation, professional identity, contributions to the local community, availability to students, service on campus, and ethical conduct. We also discuss the importance of having ongoing faculty development opportunities within a program. Guiding questions concerning how to conduct positive and beneficial faculty reviews conclude the chapter.

THE RATIONALE FOR FACULTY EVALUATION

The history of faculty evaluation is part and parcel of the growth of higher education in the United States. Evaluation typically encompasses three broad areas of faculty activity: teaching, research, and service. The late Ernest Boyer (1990) expanded the understanding of the scope of faculty activity by advocating that attention and credibility both be granted to four types of scholarship: discovery, teaching, integration, and the application of knowledge. On many campuses, multiple forms of scholarship are now considered under the heading of faculty evaluation (O'Meara & Rice, 2005).

As is true for virtually all professional roles, the working assumption is that the quality of the work of the faculty in any college or university can benefit from periodic review. Although faculty performance reviews are sometimes summative (tenure and promotion decisions), in ideal cases they are formative—that is, they are constructive, developmental, and designed to improve or enhance colleagues' contributions to a program. Thus periodic faculty evaluation can

- Inform and guide new faculty through performance expectations
- Improve and refine undergraduate teaching
- Ensure that mid-career faculty do not stagnate but feel appropriately challenged
- Redirect flagging faculty energy
- Promote disciplinary and, increasingly, interdisciplinary engagement
- Encourage service to the department and institution
- Help senior faculty renew their efforts or seek new program responsibilities
- Foster commitment to the goals of the department or program
- Create a sense of fairness among faculty ranks within a department
- Engender camaraderie within a program or department
- Engage faculty in peer-to-peer exchange of ideas and teaching philosophies

The Faculty Review Process

The nature of a faculty review will depend on its purpose. For example, annual reviews serve as a basis for tenure, promotion, and merit raises. Perhaps the review is being done every four or six years post-tenure. Or, the review may determine whether a candidate is worthy of promotion from Associate to Full Professor. Particular circumstances are apt to require slightly different procedures. In what follows, we attempt to portray a general review process but recognize that one size cannot fit all nor can we hope to account for the variety of folkways, traditions, and unique rules found at different institutions.

Numerous scholarly works examine the process of faculty evaluation and its perceived benefits as well as shortcomings. Some works primarily aid administrators (see Arreola, 2007; Buller, 2006; Centra, 1993; Seldin, 1984) and review committee members (Diamond, 2002); others target helping faculty members negotiate the shoals of tenure and promotion reviews (see Diamond, 1995; Seldin, 2004; Seldin & Miller, 2009; Whicker, Kronenfeld, & Strickland, 1993). Pre-tenure faculty members tend to be reviewed annually, whereas tenured faculty may be reviewed on another fixed schedule (such as every six years). In general, programs conduct pre-tenure personnel reviews at least until a tenure decision is rendered. Post-tenure review usually involves an elected committee of colleagues outside the department. Still, conventions vary from campus to campus. In smaller departments, the chair usually evaluates the work of a candidate. In larger programs, a committee, possibly a small group of appointed senior colleagues working in concert with the chair, conducts the review. The candidate usually submits a current version of his or her curriculum vitae (CV) and a portfolio of supporting materials.

PRIMARY MATERIALS FOR FACULTY REVIEW

Exhibit 7.1 lists the supporting materials typically found in review portfolios. We have categorized the contents of Exhibit 7.1 under the three typical areas of evaluation—teaching, scholarly and creative works, and service. A quick glance reveals few surprises, as putting together a portfolio is basically a matter of collecting and organizing relevant documents. Quite a few of the items appearing in Exhibit 7.1 will also be listed in a candidate's CV (such as courses taught, teaching awards, publications, presentations, grants).

Please note that a fourth category in Exhibit 7.1 (''Other'') lists evidence of additional activities faculty members sometimes include in their portfolios. Increasingly, for example, institutions require candidates to write a reflective narrative or self-evaluation about the teaching, scholarly work, and service efforts accomplished during their time at the institution (Glassick, Huber, & Maeroff, 1997). Such reflective critiques should also be forward-looking: how does a colleague intend to develop in the future? Local traditions and folkways often play a role in performance evaluations; such unique forms of professional activity would fall in the fourth section.

One important item is absent from Exhibit 7.1 because it is not a readily quantifiable faculty asset: collegiality. In a collegial environment, faculty members believe that they are part of a ''mutually respectful community of scholars who value each faculty member's contributions to the institution and feel concern for their colleagues' well-being'' (Grappa, Austin, & Trice, 2007,

EXHIBIT 7.1 SUPPORTING MATERIALS TYPICALLY FOUND IN PORTFOLIOS USED FOR FACULTY EVALUATION

Teaching

List of courses taught, with dates

Course portfolios (containing syllabi, writing assignments, in-class exercises, sample student papers, quizzes, exams, among other materials)

Summarized student course evaluations (quantitative)

Written course evaluation comments from students (qualitative, representative sampling)

Copies of course syllabi

Innovations in courses (such as new assignments)

Representative copies of course examinations, including final exams

New course development (proposals, syllabi)

Team teaching experiences (proposals, syllabi)

Grade distributions of candidate's courses

Evidence of willingness to teach less desirable courses

Honors and independent study or research with students

Teaching awards

Scholarship and Research

Current curriculum vitae

Copies of publications (journal articles, chapters, books, monographs, book reviews, compositions, creative works)

Copies of unpublished papers or reports

Papers or posters presented at professional conferences

Invited colloquia, papers, addresses, lectures

Performance or reviews of candidate's creative work

Copies of funded and unfunded grant applications

Service as referee or editor of professional journal

Citation record of candidate's publications (that is, whether peers cite candidate's work)

Research or scholarly awards

SoTL (Scholarship of Teaching and Learning)

Service

Student advising (such as quality of advising, number of majors advised, development of advising materials)

Advisor to student organization(s)

List of department administrative duties (such as search committee service)

Campus committee service, including any leadership roles

Letters of support from committee chairpersons about candidate's activities

Student recruiting efforts

Alumni letters of support (spontaneous or solicited)

Other

Candidate's self-evaluation

Activities in professional societies (for example, officer role, committee memberships)

Campus presentations on disciplinary topics for colleagues and students

Consulting beyond campus (such as academe, government, business)

Community service (such as volunteer work, advising of citizen groups)

---

p. 305). Unfortunately, faculty incivility toward other faculty members may be a growing problem in higher education (Twale & De Luca, 2008). Being a good citizen and working well with colleagues in and outside of a department or program is an understandably important consideration for retention, tenure, and promotion. After all, departments and programs are political arenas and, as Diamond (1995) notes, tenure and promotion decisions are part of a political process. Individuals who have poor interpersonal relationships should be advised to work on their skills in this area (see Whicker et al., 1993). Failure to be collegial means that candidates undergo performance evaluations at their own peril.

Being collegial to students is also important, but we add the proviso that faculty members should draw and maintain appropriate professional boundaries between themselves and the students they teach, advise, or even supervise. The best advice is to be friendly with students, but not to befriend them. The inherent power differential existing between faculty and student roles means that the former must exercise care not to exploit or otherwise take advantage of the latter. Naturally, the issue of romantic or even sexual liaisons between faculty and students is a serious concern, so much so that many institutions now have specific policies forbidding such relationships. Certainly, colleagues should be familiar with such policies, but we stand firm with our original suggestions regarding relations with all students: be friendly, not friends.

Supplemental Materials for Faculty Review: Campus Norms and Peer Comments

There are a few supplemental materials that some institutions gather for review committees to consider, most often when making a tenure decision:

- Teaching evaluation norms for department and college
- On-campus peer comments regarding candidate's teaching
- External solicited letters from disciplinary peers regarding candidate's scholarship

The Office of Institutional Research, or a similar entity, presumably records institutional teaching norms (see the first listed item) that should be used appropriately in the review process (that is, committee members should be trained or ''calibrated'' to interpret them properly). For example, a review committee should be reminded that instructors in the natural sciences tend to receive lower student evaluations than those in the humanities or social sciences. More complex still are evaluation issues concerning gender or race (see Bracken et al., 2006; Stanley, 2006; Philipsen, 2008).

Similarly, on-campus comments from peers regarding teaching can be solicited by the dean in discussion with a candidate's program chair or committee (see the second listed item). Such peer review is an integral part of faculty evaluation. On-campus peer review can be formal or informal. Some colleges and universities require routine visits by peers (often but not always drawn from the same department) to observe a colleague's teaching. These peer observers typically attend a few classes, discuss their observations with the colleague, and then submit a written report to the program chair, personnel committee, or dean. On other campuses, informal peer visitation is the norm. Within a department, for example, junior colleagues may routinely invite senior colleagues to attend their classes and later comment on their teaching style (and vice versa). This kind of ongoing formative assessment promotes collegial relations within a program while also encouraging teachers to borrow or adapt ideas and class activities from one another. In the absence of this sort of informal sharing of pedagogies, untenured faculty members should consider the benefits associated with inviting colleagues into their classroom.

What about off-campus peer review? Peer comments on scholarly work can be solicited from faculty members who teach at similar institutions or those understood to serve as a comparison group (see the third listed item). Candidates may be asked to generate a list of potential referees, which will be added to a separate list drawn up by the chairperson or committee. The dean then chooses referees from the larger list, contacts them, and solicits letters regarding a candidate's record, usually with an emphasis on research, scholarly publications, and creative works. This form of peer review provides a sense of how a candidate is perceived beyond the campus (such as his or her standing within a discipline, influence of scholarship on the field).

THE EVALUATION LETTER

Following a review of the CV and portfolio, the reviewer writes an evaluation letter and shares it with the candidate. The contents of the letter examine the colleague's activities subsequent to the last review, highlighting accomplishments as well as those areas identified as in need of attention. Specific concerns should be clearly documented so that the candidate understands the nature of the problem and how it can be addressed in the future. In turn, candidates should use the contents of the evaluation letter to steer their teaching, research, and service activities until the next formal evaluation. Indeed, the chair or department committee will rely on the guidelines put forth in the letter to assess a candidate's progress. Savvy candidates do an ongoing self-evaluation and seek candid counsel from their chairpersons at a halfway point (such as midyear during a first or second year of teaching), and again, perhaps midway through the probationary period before tenure, to verify that anticipated progress (that is, progress outlined in the prior evaluation letter) is being made. Some institutions have instituted a formal midpoint evaluation process to affirm positive performance as well as to encourage other avenues when a mismatch between faculty performance and institutional expectations becomes apparent.

At the juncture of any formal review, many institutions require candidates to sign off on the evaluation letter, indicating that the candidate received, read, and understood the report. In addition, the protocol often gives candidates the opportunity to appeal the letter's contents in writing before it is forwarded to the next administrative level. If an appeal is submitted, candidates are advised to stick very close to the facts when responding to an evaluation. Clear, dispassionate explanation with supporting evidence is most effective in responding to a negative evaluation. Anger, frustration, accusations, or excuses do not serve the candidate well. In fact, seasoned administrators find that the tone of the rebuttal can reveal aspects of the candidate's character that are likely to emerge under stress. Therefore the wiser course involves clarifying confusion and correcting misinformation, rather than railing against injustice or perceived discriminatory treatment.

Committee Review and Decision

Once the letter satisfies the candidate and department, it is then passed on to the dean, who usually shares it with a faculty evaluation committee (typically composed of elected faculty members) for the actual review. This committee is a college- or university-level committee drawn from academic constituencies reflecting the institution's disciplinary composition (typically humanities, the arts, social sciences, and natural sciences). Colleagues from a candidate's department or program who happen to be serving on the committee are normally excused from the review process (if this is not the committee's practice, they should nonetheless recuse themselves from taking part in this final stage of the review). Committee members then review the candidate's evaluation letter, CV, and portfolio during one or more committee meetings in preparation for developing a recommendation. Astute institutions spell out the protocol for any deviations from normal practice.

The committee communicates its recommendation regarding the candidate (that is, continuation or termination of contract, recommendation for or denial of tenure or promotion or both) to the next level of administration, which may be the academic dean or another academic officer or office. In cases of tenure and promotion, this intermediate officer or office will need to communicate with the next administrative level—at a college, that may be the provost or president; at a university, it is most commonly the provost. In other cases, the dean is likely to communicate the committee's response back to the candidate directly, as well as to the department or program chair. Evaluation procedures will vary depending on custom, tradition, and whether the institution is public or private.

The role of the academic dean's input regarding a candidate's evaluation committee varies from campus to campus. At some institutions, for example, the dean is either a voting member of the committee or an ex officio participant. On other campuses, the dean acts as an independent reviewer. Whatever the local norms, a dean (or provost or other academic officer) will have some input in the ultimate recommendation.

Full-time faculty members who are hired on the tenure-track generally have a six-year probationary period in which to demonstrate their teaching skills, scholarly and creative abilities, and service to the program and wider institution. Toward the end of the six years of service as an assistant professor, a faculty member undergoes a detailed evaluation to determine whether he or she will be granted tenure by the institution. When granting tenure, most institutions also decide simultaneously whether a candidate is worthy of promotion to associate professor. Promotion to the rank of full professor may require some specified number of years of service as an associate professor as well as documented progress consistent with a change in rank (for example, meritorious teaching, scholarship, and service). Progressive institutions and their departments concretely spell out specific criteria and provide examples of the type of performance that is expected at each professorial rank. Less-well-developed institutions offer few criteria or examples, making tenure and promotion decisions something of a mystery and very often a stressful experience both for those being evaluated and for evaluators.

Beyond Tenure

Much of the faculty review process is necessarily focused on providing clear criteria for the tenure and review process. However, clear criteria for maintaining faculty vitality beyond the pre-tenure period are equally important. In the following section we consider specific factors that may emerge during the post-tenure period—the most extensive span of an academic career.

Post-Tenure Review

Ongoing evaluation of faculty performance after tenure is a relatively new and by no means universally embraced process. Within those institutions that conduct post-tenure evaluations, faculty often view the exercise as threatening and of limited value (for example, see Licata, 1986; Licata & Morreale, 2006). Surprisingly, there are still some institutions that engage in little or no review of a colleague's teaching, scholarship, or service once the faculty member receives a favorable tenure decision. The working assumption in such cases appears to be that the granting of tenure anticipates an acceptable level of performance for the duration of a colleague's career.

We do not agree with those who claim that post-tenure review is unnecessary. The nature of post-tenure evaluation is fundamentally different from evaluations done prior to or at the time of tenure. Specifically, post-tenure reviews should be truly developmental; that is, aimed at ensuring that colleagues continue to refine their skills as teachers, scholar-researchers, and colleagues. At the same time, the review should not be a simple maintenance check or pro forma evaluation; rather, as a colleague of ours suggested, it should—must—have teeth. Post-tenure review should be an opportunity for the candidate to review his or her progress while simultaneously having a frank and open discussion with the program chairperson or review committee.

Good faculty members grow as they move through the ranks, and many consciously and conscientiously seek new challenges as well as new avenues to demonstrate their expertise. Some may need to rethink (or retool) their research program or how they go about teaching courses. Others need a bit of guidance; once delivered through effective post-tenure review processes, faculty can direct their energies anew toward new course development, a larger role in departmental or institutional affairs, better advising of students or mentoring of junior colleagues and other relevant activities. Post-tenure reviews can be an opportunity for both the colleague and the program to play to the colleague's strengths while frankly identifying areas for attention and perhaps remediation. Further, a colleague should outline and present a plan (preferably in writing) for his or her intended professional activities during the time before the next review cycle. As was suggested for savvy new professors, we hasten to add that a self-initiated, midpoint discussion with the chair or program director regarding one's perceived progress as a tenured colleague is also a good idea.

Shifting Research Interests: Opportunities in SoTL

When faculty members change their research agenda in the course of their careers, such change is best undertaken with thought, planning, and enthusiasm. The appropriate institutional response typically should support and encourage the colleague's venture. Faculty members can become reenergized by a change in direction; this is the principle that undergirds most institutional practices surrounding professional leaves at regular intervals.

One constructive pathway can be the pursuit of new contributions in SoTL, the scholarly study of student learning to advance and improve disciplinary or interdisciplinary teaching in public ways (see Kreber, 2002; McKinney, 2004). Research in SoTL makes use of self-reflection and analysis, focus group work, interviews, questionnaire-based research, experimental and quasi-experimental research (such as comparing different pedagogies in two sections of the same course), observational research, and case studies, among other research methods. In short, SoTL focuses on identifying those practices that promote learning.

Generally, faculty who conduct SoTL-based research do so by following the standards and practices used within their disciplines. SoTL can enable faculty members to conduct serious and meaningful scholarship that informs and improves what they do daily in their classes. Their findings can, in turn, be shared in professional outlets (such as books, journals, conferences) so that colleagues elsewhere can improve their teaching efforts. For many faculty, embracing SoTL may be a way to jump-start a moribund research program or reenvision the next stage of a career.

AVOIDING FACULTY BURNOUT AND DISENGAGEMENT

The dark side of academic life is the experience of burnout or disengagement from one's disciplinary interests. ''Burnout'' is the common term used to describe serious emotional and physical exhaustion associated with work or career pursuits (see Leiter & Maslach, 2000, 2005). The chief problem is that mounting stress leads to disinterest with and disengagement from work and the workplace. The problem for educators, of course, is that feelings of depersonalization and lack of interest in academic work quickly result in limited or inadequate performance in and outside of the classroom.

Thus an adverse outcome results when a promising colleague receives tenure and possibly promotion, but then effectively stops developing new skills or ceases keeping current with new developments in his or her field of study. Faculty may need to recreate themselves across their careers. The pace of such renewal, however, matters a great deal. Working at too fast a pace creates problems. The race for tenure can often be frenetic, so much so that even the most prepared candidate may have little time to reflect on what really matters in teaching, scholarship, and service. Slower workers risk never finishing projects; a new class never fulfills its promise or seems satisfactory to students or the teacher; an article based on a faculty member's dissertation is still ''in process,'' its author deeming it not quite good enough yet; completion of the chapter or book is close, but never quite finished, so that eventually the scholarly trail to the final polished product goes cold. In the case of a once promising writing project, the colleague's enthusiasm for the work fades with the passage of time, and the manuscript ends up filed away and forgotten.

The academy is rife with case studies of faculty members who peaked at tenure and then began a long, slow slog to retirement. Their early promise ended, they often became trapped in the middle rank. Some become withdrawn and exercise the minimum effort necessary to retain their positions. Others become embittered, adopting a negative posture that often gets turned against the institution that somehow failed to help the faculty member achieve full potential. Too many departments have one or more colleagues who fit this profile, ensuring that even reasonably functional programs must contend with malcontents and energy-draining politics. What can be done to promote more effective relationships to enhance the capacity of any program to optimize faculty achievement?

For pre-tenure colleagues:

1. Articulate formal statements of purpose in the areas that will govern your activity. A short teaching philosophy that can be included in all syllabi to help students understand both style and substance can be helpful. A formalized research agenda, shared with a mentor or supervisor, can initiate new opportunities for collaboration or grant capture. Similarly, a formal service plan can highlight the skill sets the new faculty member has to offer and may identify the kinds of opportunities that will be embraced enthusiastically. These formal statements can also establish context for accomplishments to be reviewed in an official evaluation.

2. Adopt a brisk but balanced working pace that will facilitate satisfactory performance in all required areas of effort, including course development and preparation, scholarship and publication, and service to the program and discipline. Moderation with balance accommodates high-quality family or friend time that may provide the sustenance needed for the long haul.

Fortunately, there are many resources that discuss these issues in detail and offer concrete guidance (see Boice, 1996, 2000; see also Dunn & Zaremba, 1997; Lang, 2005; McKeachie & Svinicki, 2005; Zanna, Darley, & Roediger, 2003).

For newly or recently tenured colleagues:

1. Cultivate a wish list. Faculty members should always keep in mind activities and interests they might like to pursue, such as developing new courses, team teaching, reading in new areas, enrolling in workshops, increasing their service to professional organizations, proposing challenging sabbatical projects, administrative forays, new research and related writing projects. With a bit of forethought, such activities can stave off burnout and promote ongoing renewal.

2. Pursue leadership experience. An often implicit expectation regarding faculty quality is the exercise of skilled leadership. Many communities provide leadership training programs that faculty can participate in; these opportunities provide additional advantages of effectively representing the institution in the community. Contemplate how a provost or president could showcase your leadership, and pursue those options with vigor.

For post-tenure colleagues:

1. Volunteer for mentoring opportunities. Being able to share your expertise and hard-won insights may provide a huge contribution to an eager young colleague. By offering to share syllabi, mutually visit classes, and engage in swapping stories about triumphs and challenges, the post-tenure colleague guarantees engagement that wards off concerns about being labeled as "dead wood." However, evaluate whether the dominant tone of assistance is positive and encouraging or overbearing.

2. Share wisdom and expertise judiciously. Some department discussions grind to a halt when the "ancients" insist on describing in painful detail how a practice or policy evolved. Let others talk first. Wise elders listen rather than being the first to speak.

When evaluation is conducted in a formative and constructive manner, feedback can help to reduce the incidence of faculty burnout and disengagement. We turn now to the role that performance benchmarks can play in faculty evaluation. Such evaluation is important because a department's quality can be adversely affected by the activities of its least functional members (see Studer, 2004). When a department tolerates or accepts mediocre performance (or worse) from some of its members, its overall rating of well-being will be lower in spite of the hard work or achievements of other colleagues. Thus, where faculty characteristics are concerned, the actions of individuals affect the perceived quality of the whole. We believe quality benchmarks offer a constructive way for all colleagues in a program to improve and maintain their roles as faculty members.

Evaluating Faculty Contributions Using Quality Benchmarks

Faculty members affect students directly and have a pronounced effect on what and how well students learn (Angelo, 1993). The best teachers effectively communicate expectations to their students and help them to meet those expectations, cultivating solid college-level performance and learning in the process. Table 7.1 (adapted from Dunn et al., 2007) provides the dimensions of evaluation for faculty characteristics.

Teaching Perspective on Pedagogy

Virtually all faculty members want to be known as good teachers. Given the current economic climate, institutions have the opportunity to recruit highly competent and experienced teachers who can be shaped into great and even distinguished teachers. Thus, regardless of discipline, a quality undergraduate program or department should actively work to attract and retain good teachers. Further, such programs should help teachers develop and refine their classroom techniques across their careers. To make teaching a priority, programs should provide ample opportunity

Table 7.1 Faculty Characteristics for Formative Evaluation

	Undeveloped	*Developing*	*Effective*	*Distinguished*
Teaching Perspective: Pedagogy	Teaches disciplinary material with no concern for pedagogy	Occasionally includes a new pedagogy in a course	Engages students by matching selective pedagogies to appropriate courses	Actively employs new and established pedagogies creatively and effectively in all courses
Teaching Perspective: Self-Evaluation	Teaching is a necessary, if sometimes onerous, part of the faculty role	Teaching is an important part of being a faculty member	Teaching is the most important aspect of being a faculty member; attention to other roles is sometimes postponed	Teaching is the defining role for faculty yet it positively affects all other roles
Course Vigor and Currency	New courses are rarely developed and existing courses are rarely revised, updated, or kept current	New courses are sometimes developed; existing courses are revised or updated only sporadically, often in response to pressure	New courses reflect current disciplinary advances; existing courses are revised and updated fairly often	All courses are always being developed and renewed; content reflects disciplinary advances and current pedagogy
New Course Development	Teaches routine complement of courses; refuses to develop new course(s)	Develops a new course following administrative or collegial pressure to do so	Volunteers to develop new course(s) when need arises	Initiates new course development preemptively, in response to department needs and disciplinary advances

Scholarship	Does no research, publishing, presentation, performance, showing of work, or curating	Creates scholarly work sporadically, perhaps in response to administrative pressure	Active producer of scholarly work who uses program support effectively	Pursues a developmentally appropriate program of research
Resource Generation	No time or energy is directed at generating resources for professional or program support	May be aware of where resources can be obtained but exerts no effort to acquire any	Seeks and receives some funds, usually local rather than foundation-based, with varied success	Uses successful strategies to obtain ongoing funding from a variety of resources
Professional Identity	Has almost no professional identity beyond program or institution	Modest connection with discipline; minimal participation in regional or national organizations	Identity is tied to discipline via appropriate and active membership in disciplinary organizations	Actively contributes to the discipline through service and leadership roles in disciplinary organizations
Contributions to Community	No connection to the local community	Responds only occasionally to requests for community support	Community contributions regularly occur but are linked to personal interests	Sincere contributor to community needs, activities, and events that will benefit from professional expertise

(*continued*)

TABLE 7.1 (CONTINUED)

	Undeveloped	*Developing*	*Effective*	*Distinguished*
Availability to Students	Contact with students is limited to the classroom	Limited presence on campus; limited office hours and e-mail correspondence	Accessible to students and maintains appropriate boundaries (''friendly but not friends'')	Accessible to students and maintains appropriate boundaries (''friendly but not friends''); actively serves as a mentor to students and advisees
Service on Campus	Does no service beyond program responsibilities	Participates on assigned committees	Active in assigned committees; seeks election to others; emerging leader	Serves as a campus leader, one whose opinions and expertise are frequently consulted.
Ethical Conduct	Ignores guidelines for acceptable ethical conduct in discipline	Responds to ethical lapses by enforcing prescribed penalties	Adheres to appropriate ethical standards of discipline	Promotes ethical behavior in teaching, scholarship, and service in program, as well as representative of the discipline

for faculty to attend teaching workshops. Ideally, a department will sponsor one or two faculty development opportunities each year, in which, for example, master teachers can share new pedagogies with faculty members. Colleagues should also participate in any institution-wide workshops, particularly those sponsored by the college or university teaching center.

As shown in Table 7.1, the teaching perspective held by faculty colleagues can matter a great deal. Teachers in undeveloped programs pay no attention to advances in pedagogy. Their teaching is likely to be traditional, even stodgy. They tend to rely on the dominant method used in their discipline, thereby perpetuating the ways they were taught. Usually, lecture dominates, which means there is little time for discussion or even more interactive in-class activities (such as small group work). Teachers in undeveloped programs often eschew new pedagogies because they fear they will not "cover" the necessary material; concern about coverage becomes a means for remaining static. Lecture may be supplemented with question and answer sessions or problem reviews, but little other variety is introduced to improve student learning.

In contrast, teachers in developing programs sometimes have a few fans or a small coterie of student followers. These teachers occasionally add a new pedagogical technique to their courses (such as service learning), but they do not necessarily consider whether it is a good fit to a given course, their teaching goals, or how students learn. Instead, they sporadically rely on one or two pedagogical strategies to "break up" the primary teaching mode used in all of their courses.

In contrast, teachers in effective programs often give new pedagogies a test run and incrementally work them into their courses. They typically adopt a variety of approaches to engage students more reliably. Teachers in more distinguished programs constantly try and succeed with new techniques, and they make a concerted effort to consult the teaching literature in their own field as well as other disciplines. These teachers attend, participate in, and present at pedagogy- or discipline-based conferences to share ideas about teaching. Such colleagues consistently bring back and adapt new ideas to enliven their classroom and their teaching.

Self-Evaluation as a Teacher

Faculty members in distinguished programs define themselves as teachers first and foremost, yet they manage to balance this primary interest with other responsibilities, including scholarship and service. Teaching—that is, questioning, seeking and sharing new ideas, offering wise and informed perspectives—imbues all that they do. A good teacher can also be a good scholar and a good administrator; each role can inform and benefit the others.

Teachers in effective programs place teaching at the top of the list of items defining a faculty member. Unlike those in distinguished programs, however, these teachers sometimes overemphasize their teaching—that is, they lose balance—so that other faculty roles receive less attention and care. Although most of their effort goes into teaching, effective teachers struggle with balancing multiple professional responsibilities, which means that their scholarly, administrative, and service roles can receive much less attention.

Within developing and undeveloped programs, teaching is work; sometimes it is a chore that brings limited satisfaction. A teacher in a developing program sees teaching as a duty, but still an important part of his or her role as a faculty member. The developing teacher may deliver a course that appeals to a narrow segment of the class and may not be particularly motivated to engage the other students, who may be castigated as unmotivated and talentless.

Undeveloped program colleagues view teaching as a required activity bringing little pleasure or fulfillment. They may feel overwhelmed by other demands so they put no effort into improving how they teach or approaching their teaching from a fresh perspective. Alternatively, teaching may have been a required means to an end, such as being able to conduct research in a chosen specialty. Once such a faculty member achieves tenure, there may be little reason to strive for improvement in an activity that is perceived to produce so little reward.

Course Currency and Vigor

One obvious way to assess faculty vitality would seem to be the creation of new courses. After all, the development of new courses and accompanying syllabi is a reasonable way to discern teachers' currency in their discipline. However, new course proliferation, while advancing some faculty development, can mask other problems. In particular, if issues of quality are tied specifically to new courses, then there may be little incentive for faculty members to revitalize existing courses. Indeed, some of these older courses may be essential staples within a program's undergraduate curriculum that make a considerable contribution to the students' intellectual development. Undue focus on new course development, particularly when popular topics are involved, can pull faculty talent and expertise away from the core concerns of student learning and the academic program's genuine curricular needs.

To counter the possible overemphasis on new course development, we recommend that programs focus on the level of currency and vigor found in all courses. This broader focus means that new courses sometimes can be considered as indicators of quality but not at the expense associated with failing to update existing courses. We argue that currency and vigor need to be addressed in all courses, and that the development of new courses must be tied to appropriateness and coherence within the current curriculum. Simply put, the content of all courses should demonstrate both academic currency and vigor, including reliance on pedagogical innovations. Similarly, course syllabi should be updated on an ongoing basis to reflect advances in the discipline and changes in the assigned text or other reading materials.

As a quality benchmark for faculty characteristics, course currency and vigor is shown in Table 7.1. Faculty in undeveloped programs rarely, if ever, revise and update existing courses or develop new courses; indeed, they often refuse to do so, claiming that they were hired to teach only certain courses or that the curriculum "requires" that they teach their current roster of courses. They may even claim that time and effort directed toward new course development has an adverse effect on the existing courses they teach. Faculty in developing programs do not like change, but they will usually agree to develop a new course if their chairperson proffers rewards (such as release time, research space, or desirable teaching times) or when pressure from administrators or colleagues compels them to do so. Faculty in undeveloped programs revise existing courses only sporadically, usually in response to external pressures (such as revised textbooks or curriculum review).

Faculty in effective programs look for ways to ensure that their existing courses are current in content and pedagogy. Thus, to contribute to the well-being of a program, they are often likely to volunteer to develop courses when a need arises. They, too, may seek available rewards, but they do so with an eye to improving the program and helping the students. Effective colleagues revise and update existing courses fairly frequently, often in response to planned changes to a program's curriculum.

Colleagues in distinguished departments initiate new courses in a strategic and appropriate manner, building on curricular strengths but not at the expense of existing courses. They do so by keeping apprised of curricular developments at the national level and when they identify important disciplinary advances that should be reflected in the program's curriculum. Their new courses are not proprietary ventures; rather, these faculty are willing to share the fruits of their labor via team teaching or by passing the course to an interested colleague after teaching it a few times. They update existing courses conscientiously and revise as a matter of course. Distinguished colleagues view course changes as a way to keep themselves fresh while exposing students to the latest disciplinary developments.

One important, if general, point needs to be added regarding new course development: It is in the interests of the program, the director or chair, and ultimately the administration to verify that a new course is truly new. That is, a new course proposal, a draft syllabus, assigned readings, and other supporting materials should be carefully reviewed by program or department members or an appropriate oversight committee.

Scholarship

Scholarship (often referred to as "research") is one of the traditional areas of faculty evaluation. Many, if not most, institutions hire faculty members with at least a modest expectation of some scholarly effort. Writing and publishing discipline-based work is the traditional prize, but Boyer's (1997) call for broader definitions of scholarship opened new possibilities for faculty members who want to add to the storehouse of knowledge through ''discovery.'' According to Boyer and now to many institutions that have remodeled evaluation standards based on this broadened approach, other legitimate avenues of contribution include scholarship of application, integration, and teaching and learning (see O'Meara & Rice, 2005).

Similar to a colleague's orientation toward the development of new courses, an absence or paucity of scholarly work is diagnostically rich. Note that when we use the word *scholarship*, we do so assuming that either the relevant discipline has established standards for what constitutes meaningful scholarship or there is a shared understanding among colleagues about what is or is not an acceptable ''scholarly or creative product.'' Ideally, a program will maintain a written and readily available description of what constitutes scholarship; this document should be shared with all potential hires as well as new and junior colleagues.

When we use the word *scholarship*, we do so in a very broad sense. We refer not only to traditional products, such as articles, chapters, monographs, books, book reviews, and other written matter. We are also including performances (for example, theatrical, musical), presentations, compositions, various artistic works, shows of work, and curatorial activities. Complementing and connecting to these forms of scholarly endeavor constitutes scholarship aimed at improving teaching and learning, including developing and testing novel pedagogies. Conceptions of research have broadened considerably in the last two decades, and faculty and administrators would be wise to initiate or revisit discussions on their campuses regarding the full range of forms that scholarship can take (Boyer, 1990; O'Meara & Rice, 2005). At the same time, attention should be given to the standards used to evaluate scholarly efforts and the scholars producing them (for six guiding standards for such evaluation, see Glassick et al., 1997).

Again, in the ideal case, shared understanding of scholarly expectations should be firmly in place prior to any faculty evaluation. Similarly, institutional expectations and program constraints should be used properly to temper both scholarly definitions and the faculty evaluation process. A program with a heavy teaching load and minimal or no facilities or resources cannot expect its faculty to publish regularly, let alone to place their work in the discipline's top, peer-reviewed journals. By the same token, a reasonable teaching load and adequate resources are not sufficient cause for colleagues to avoid developing scholarly, creative, or pedagogical works.

Colleagues in undeveloped circumstances produce no intellectual work beyond their contributions in the classroom. They may be disengaged from scholarship for a variety reasons, but chief among them may be a real or perceived problem in the program. Perhaps there are serious resource constraints, budget cuts, or excessive teaching demands (for example, too many students, too few faculty to cover courses, necessity of teaching overloads). Alternatively, the problem may be attitudinal. For example, the junior faculty do not produce scholarship because the senior faculty don't bother to do so, and a cycle of mediocrity and a tense atmosphere of recrimination results. As a consequence, no clear scholarship agenda is apparent in their collected works.

Scholars in developing programs produce work but do so in a haphazard manner, often in anticipation of tenure and promotion decisions or in response to critical evaluations and administrative pressure. The danger in this case is that scholarship can be perceived as a sometime or even a once-and-done activity, an obligation to be completed but not necessarily repeated. There is no appreciation or understanding of scholarship as informing, developing, even energizing a faculty member and his or her students, as well as contributing to the larger discipline. The motivation of the scholarly agenda appears to be self-serving rather than offering a meaningful contribution.

In contrast to cyclical bursts of scholarly activity, faculty in effective programs produce a steady stream of scholarship from research agendas that are well suited to the context in which the faculty operate. They remain engaged by disciplinary ideas and sincerely want to contribute to the greater discussion that occurs when work is reviewed by peers. Effective program faculty use the available resources to advance their work.

Faculty members of distinguished programs adopt a longer view of scholarship; similar to being a good teacher, being a productive and conscientious scholar is an important part of how they conceive of themselves as members of the academy. They are likely to evolve a distinctive program of research across their careers, so that one project and its products suggest others, just as the best research questions breed additional questions rather than definitive answers. Distinguished program faculty may (but do not necessarily need to) seek grants or other funding to fuel their efforts; however, what matters is that they regularly engage in appropriate scholarly activities commensurate with program resources and expectations.

Resource Generation

The costs associated with running a program in any college or university are extremely high. Education is expensive, and traditional sources for funding are often tapped out. Thus many institutions encourage their faculty to be entrepreneurial; that is, to seek and compete for grants, foundation monies, and donations that will cover a program's costs or expansion. Colleagues' opinions often vary in regard to whether faculty members should be responsible for doing such development work, but the onus in difficult economic times clearly falls on faculty, particularly if their research agendas demand high-cost equipment that cannot be underwritten by the college or university.

Faculty members in undeveloped programs will spend no time or effort in the search for additional resources. They may claim the effort is futile; they may genuinely believe this responsibility is someone else's—say, the development office or the institution's president. Alternatively, members of undeveloped programs may do too much wheel spinning, searching for resources at the cost of not carrying out other important responsibilities (for example, conducting research, publishing, mentoring). When asked why achievement in these other categories is low, they may claim that little can be accomplished in the absence of additional resources.

A colleague in a developing program may be aware of potential sources of funds, such as an alumni contact or a call for proposals, but is unlikely to exert any effort to acquire them. Although their actual record of receiving funds may be mixed, effective program faculty members are vigilant when it comes to locating funding sources. Although they could be successful at landing grants from foundations or governmental agencies, they often pursue funds from local sources in the community.

Faculty members in distinguished programs are adept at writing fundable proposals and submitting them to appropriate funding sources. They do so strategically and with some regularity so that as one source of funds is depleted, another fills the void. They also recognize that not every proposal will be funded and that obtaining funding is an ongoing effort. This realization means that they continue to seek funding sources for their good ideas, rather than trying once and then giving up in disappointment. They schedule appropriate time for necessary campus approvals. These distinguished resource generators also work well with the institution's development office so that the resource seeking effort is collaborative, not adversarial, and that the skills of any on-campus grants person are used.

Professional Identity

The professional identity of every faculty member in a program matters to the extent that these professionals are in touch and engaged with issues at the forefront of the discipline. Being aware of challenges and controversies at the national level ensures that the program can react appropriately and strategically, especially where faculty hiring and curricular matters are concerned. When colleagues are detached or out of touch with the greater discipline, the program's students can suffer because their discipline-based education may be dated.

Faculty in distinguished and effective programs are active in their discipline. The former often serve in leadership roles in disciplinary organizations, and they are likely to be invited to speak at scholarly conferences or society meetings. These invitations reinforce their special status to their campus colleagues and students. Invitations to serve as a distinguished speaker or lecturer can be profiled in campus public relations activities and bring recognition to the campus and the program.

Effective program faculty may not be leaders, but they routinely participate in professional meetings by presenting their work, bringing students, and maintaining an active connection with colleagues from different institutions around the nation. They take advantage of what professional meetings have to offer, but they do not identify with the sponsoring organization sufficiently to get involved at a higher level.

Colleagues in developing circumstances are less connected nationally but may occasionally participate in or at least attend regional gatherings and organizational meetings. However, their professional identity within the wider discipline is tenuous.

Faculty in undeveloped programs do not have a professional identity that extends beyond their home campus. Their insularity does not serve the program or their students well. As time passes, their disconnection from the wider discipline can turn into alienation.

CONTRIBUTIONS TO COMMUNITY

So-called "town and gown" relations have always been important for colleges and universities. Programs and their faculty members can aid the institution by contributing discipline-based expertise toward helping the community or attempting to help solve some of its problems. In reality, the type of institution influences the type and level of a contribution. A large, well-endowed university may be an economic powerhouse on its own; for example, employing many people who live in and around it. As a result, the institutional ethos may be less inclined to honor faculty service to the community. In contrast, a liberal arts college or a regional university in a similar setting might view the service dimension as an opportunity, if not duty, for its faculty. As a result, the importance of community service might well be reflected in the college or university's evaluation and promotion criteria.

Faculty in undeveloped programs neither have nor feel any sense of connection to the community. Their primary connection is elsewhere—whether to the institution, their particular department or program, or, as is often true today, the national organization that represents the discipline (this is sometimes termed a "guild" mentality). They may live in the community, but they don't feel encumbered by any sense of obligation beyond the confines of their narrowly defined job description.

Colleagues in developing departments sense that the local community is worth supporting; thus such faculty members will sometimes respond favorably to direct entreaties from community groups or local government. They are responsive, but reactive. They may attend a few meetings but are unlikely to become too involved on behalf of themselves or their institution.

Colleagues in effective programs become actively involved in community efforts, but they do so in ways that are connected to their own personal interests (for example, an education professor may offer expertise to a local elementary school but only because his youngest child is a student there). Their service interest may wane when the personal need subsides.

Faculty in distinguished programs respond with enthusiasm to community concerns. They feel connected to the community, and they genuinely want to share their skills while also being a representative of their program and institution. They proactively search out community organizations that would benefit from their expertise, and they make commitments that will serve the community for the long haul.

AVAILABILITY TO STUDENTS

Regardless of whether the student is a major advisee or enrolled in a course, faculty in quality programs are regularly available and approachable to students. The cost of higher education has prompted faculty to be available to students as a matter of institutional accountability. In some ways, too, availability is a proxy measure for a faculty member's connection to students and to the larger program. Less accessibility means less connection, and vice versa. Thus availability acts as a barometer for the amount of faculty-student interaction and advising activities occurring within a program (Chickering & Gamson, 1987).

There are few surprises on this evaluative dimension. Faculty in undeveloped programs tend to exclusively limit their contact with students to the classroom. They list few office hours and actually maintain fewer; the office is a way station for the colleague, not a meeting place. A colleague in a developing program has a slightly higher campus profile; however, office hours are still limited and appointments at other times are discouraged. Corresponding with students via e-mail is a preferred mode of contact; however, it too is usually sporadic and sluggish. Effective program faculty members maintain regular office hours and encourage students to stop by when necessary. When students do, these colleagues establish and maintain appropriate social boundaries: they are friendly but not too familiar with students. Colleagues in distinguished programs behave in the same manner as effective faculty; however, they also act as engaged mentors to students and advisees. They genuinely relish their advisory role and enjoy helping students succeed in the undergraduate years. They take pride in the teachable moments outside of the classroom, and they do so with all students—not just the majors.

SERVICE ON CAMPUS

After teaching and scholarship, service to the institution is usually touted as the third main area of faculty evaluation. Generally, service refers to contributions within a department or program (for example, a hiring committee, library resources in other areas of the college or university, and through professional obligations with disciplinary associations). Service beyond the department is usually some form of faculty governance, such as membership on one or more committees. Programs and institutions suffer when faculty are unable or unwilling to contribute in the area of service.

Faculty in undeveloped programs have myopia when it comes to service outside their department or program. They do not see any value in doing any, or they may perform service beyond the department as a means to an end—gaining tenure—after which they can withdraw from such activities. In some cases, these faculty are responding to program priorities; the program itself may not value such service, and may explicitly prioritize activities such as research over institutional service. Developing program faculty who are more responsible generally carry out their duties on the committees, but they are likely to conduct their activities in pro forma ways. For example, it may not occur to such faculty members to report their committee activities to their home departments; this oversight renders their service less valuable.

Faculty members in effective programs are very active in their assigned committees; more important, they seek nomination and election to other committees within the institution. By doing so they are behaving like good campus citizens and representatives of their program. Their enthusiasm for both appointed and elected roles indicates they are among the institution's emerging leaders. Faculty in programs that are distinguished on this dimension are usually already recognized as established faculty leaders. They are frequently appointed or elected to the institution's most important or influential committee posts, as many administrators and fellow faculty members respect their opinions and often seek their counsel.

ETHICAL CONDUCT

When asked, virtually all faculty members will claim to be ethical individuals, and many disciplines offer detailed ethical guidelines for faculty to follow when serving as teachers, researchers, supervisors, or even consultants. Programs and departments usually affirm some explicit set of standards regarding how faculty should behave as colleagues and, more important, in public and private interactions with students. Accountability pressures, as well as institutional concerns about avoiding legal improprieties, often drive a program's focus on ethical conduct.

Unfortunately, faculty colleagues in undeveloped programs routinely ignore proper guidelines for ethical conduct in program- or discipline-related contexts. Why? Faculty in undeveloped programs may simply be unaware that any guiding standards exist, so they operate in a vacuum. On the other hand, some faculty recognize the existence of standards but genuinely believe that such rules apply only to others who cannot self-navigate. Such cavalier disregard of standards can result in protracted conversations with administrators as well as litigation prompted by students who feel exploited by the faculty member's failure to exercise discretion.

A developing program deals with ethical lapses punitively. When the lapses come to light, erring faculty receive prescribed penalties. Effective programs promote adherence to discipline-based ethical standards; the focus is as much on preventing ethical problems as it is in properly dealing with problems that occur.

Faculty in distinguished programs view ethics as an important component in all teaching, scholarship, and service-related activities. Indeed, they see themselves as representatives of the discipline so that their behavior, ethically speaking, should be above reproach. They are typically well versed in campus or professional standards, and their infusion of ethics across the dimensions of their work rarely results in ethical challenges.

This review of quality benchmarks linked to faculty evaluation considered the features of a scholarly life on campus and in the larger academic community. But what about the bridge between work life and family life? We now turn to the emerging matter of program flexibility and work/life balance.

A Brief Note on Program Flexibility and Work/Life Balance

A recent survey of 8,300 graduate students on campuses of the University of California system reveals that life on the academic fast track may be less appealing than family-friendly work environments (Jaschik, 2009; Mason, Goulden, & Frasch, 2009). Future faculty members represented by this sample of men and women believe that fast-paced, high-pressure academic settings will be detrimental to having a fulfilling family life. In fact, 84 percent of the women and 74 percent of the men polled expressed concern about whether their future work settings would have family-friendly policies. Respondents indicated that teaching-oriented institutions were anticipated to have the most family-friendly policies in contrast to those believed to be in place at research intensive universities.

Although the study's data are based on attitudes and impressions rather than yet-to-be-realized experiences, academic departments and programs should anticipate concerns about family-friendly and related quality-of-life issues during the hiring and evaluation process of pre-tenure colleagues. Pre-tenure colleagues should have the opportunity to ask questions regarding career and family policies, just as departments and programs should be able to make expectations for faculty performance explicitly clear. Neither side should be surprised by the perspective of the other, and we again emphasize that where performance expectations are concerned, candor is essential.

Fortunately, there are various steps that department and program administrators can consider that will make their settings more inviting to prospective applicants. According to Jaschik (2009) and Mason et al. (2009), these include the following:

- Allowing colleagues to temporarily shift to part-time status or to elongate their pre-tenure period without career penalties
- Permitting faculty members "time out" from their careers (for example, "stopping the tenure clock") so that they can attend to child or elder care needs
- Promoting the idea that having children at any stage of one's academic career is an acceptable plan, by implementing appropriate support and resources to aid faculty parents
- Combating the stereotype that "academic stars" are the faculty who move most quickly through the ranks, by acknowledging that different performance models can coexist and that faster is not always better

Academic programs will serve themselves and their faculty constituents—current as well as prospective—well if they pay serious and compassionate attention to issues of work/life balance. This set of issues is clearly relevant to constructive discussions of faculty development and evaluation. We encourage readers to discuss these issues in light of their institutions' traditions, folkways, and aspirations for the future.

Promoting a Program's Future: Closing Words on Faculty Development

When done well, faculty evaluation is more than a process dedicated to deciding contract renewal, tenure, promotion, or even pay raises. Although important on a practical and personal level, these career-related factors are secondary to a program's main goal, which should be to provide a quality educational experience for its undergraduate majors. As we argue in this chapter, careful evaluation of faculty performance can strengthen the undergraduate experience. Constructively evaluating faculty members using clear performance benchmarks is linked to the quality of the program. The use of quality benchmarks for faculty evaluation can identify a program's areas of strength as well as those in need of attention. Yet a program's future success is not guaranteed by solid faculty evaluation alone. In fact, faculty evaluation cannot occur in a vacuum; high-quality programs regularly offer opportunities for intellectual enrichment and faculty development. By *faculty development*, we refer to events and activities that help faculty become better teachers by creating new courses and fostering student development; promoting scholarship and research so that colleagues can pursue a productive career; and providing skills training where leadership, time management, and collegiality can grow (see Gillespie, Hilsen, & Wadsworth, 2002; see also Saroyan & Amundsen, 2004). Relevant events may include a series of teaching workshops led by program or campus experts; inviting speakers to present on issues of pedagogy or professional development; informal peer (collegial) review of classroom teaching and syllabi; and the sharing of classroom activities, projects, and exercises. A forward-thinking program will try to provide several informal and perhaps one or two formal faculty development events each semester. Once a tradition is established (such as time, place, refreshments), attendance and participation will blossom.

Not all faculty development opportunities are program-based, nor must they be. If an institution has a teaching and learning center that sponsors readings, discussions, and workshops, then a program should try to send a representative or two to such gatherings to collect materials that can be shared within a program. These activities can be especially helpful to new and junior colleagues, who can benefit by meeting and learning from colleagues outside the program (that is, the importance of helping a "new face" become a "familiar one" on campus should not be underestimated). Inviting junior colleagues to report on the experience in an informal gathering gives them a chance to act as "experts" by sharing what they learned.

As already noted, whenever possible, programs and their chairs should encourage faculty members to attend professional meetings and conferences where colleagues present new pedagogical practices. Faculty who pursue professional development should not only anticipate having their travel and registration expenses covered; they should also receive the clear message that their participation in such venues is valued by the program. Faculty development works best when colleagues' efforts to improve are acknowledged in a sincere, not pro forma manner. As in high-quality faculty evaluation, faculty development efforts allow a program and the larger institution to demonstrate genuine concern for the progress of individual faculty members.

Guiding Questions

1. Do untenured colleagues currently receive clear evaluations on their progress toward tenure? Is the assessment both formative and summative? Do the formative components appropriately prepare faculty for the summative assessment?
2. Are promotion and tenure policies well publicized and followed by departmental reviewers? Do untenured colleagues feel that the expectations are stated clearly? How do senior colleagues feel about requirements for promotion?
3. Do tenured colleagues receive formative peer assessment? If not, can an evaluation program be developed? How is post-tenure review conducted?
4. Which facets of faculty evaluation are already established measures in your department? Which ones need to be addressed constructively?
5. How will your department's climate (see Chapter Two) affect the development of new faculty evaluation efforts?
6. What faculty development opportunities exist in your program and on your campus? Do colleagues take advantage of these opportunities? Why or why not?

Chapter Eight

Back to Basics: Program Resources

Almost every faculty member, program head, and administrator can relate a personal anecdote about the impact of resources on faculty productivity and teaching: the faculty member without a functional research lab, studio, or practice space; the new hire whose office is located on the opposite side of campus from his or her lab; the student or faculty research project that comes to a halt because promised resources do not materialize; the faculty member who, due to staffing shortages, has to ''gear up'' to teach a core class in which he or she has little or no expertise. Of course, circumstances such as these multiply and become more pressing during times of economic challenge for an institution (Facione, 2009). Each of these examples, and a myriad of others like them, clearly costs faculty time and productivity.

As a counterpoint to these experiences, we can look to the benefits to faculty productivity and student opportunities when a program operates in an environment with sufficient or even plentiful resources. For example, a faculty member, formerly without research space, moves into a newly renovated lab; a new faculty colleague with needed expertise joins the department; a program secures a reliable and sustainable source of funds for essential materials. In well-run programs, such resources pay off in terms of increased levels of faculty scholarship and increased learning opportunities for students.

In this chapter, we consider the importance of resources in helping programs pursue their missions and achieve distinction.

Resources include not only physical spaces (such as offices and laboratories) but also equipment, supplies, materials and the necessary personnel (faculty and staff) to carry out the program. Needs in this domain vary widely across disciplines. In some disciplines, high-quality performance is possible without a significant resource investment. Some programs may need little more than adequate office and teaching spaces, standard office equipment and supplies, and sufficient numbers of faculty with the expertise to provide a high-quality curriculum. Highly skilled teachers can fare well with a reasonable office and adequate classrooms. Other disciplines are resource-intensive, requiring specialized facilities, expensive equipment, sufficient numbers of faculty, and staff support personnel with specific expertise and training. Despite the wide variability, no program can function without at least a minimum of resources.

Adequacy of program resources along the continuum used throughout this book ranges from undeveloped to distinguished. Resource issues are intertwined with the other seven program domains (assessment, curriculum, student learning, student development, faculty, program leadership, administrative support) discussed herein. Whether a program is undeveloped, developing, effective, or distinguished in any of these domains is to some extent dependent on available resources. In fact, in some cases, it is simply not possible for a program to perform at a high level without sufficient program resources.

In our discussion of program resources, we also highlight the importance of adequate institutional support. Although there is much that programs can do to seek out resources and to use them wisely, ultimately the provision of minimally adequate resources rests with institutions and administrators. Decisions about resource allocation should be guided by realistic assessments of program needs, and decision makers should consider whether a program can be viable given the level of resource commitment that the institution can provide. For example, new faculty candidates who need substantial start-up investments may find their options for employment limited to institutions that can afford them. In a similar vein, just as not all institutions can afford to compete at the highest levels in intercollegiate athletics, it may be unrealistic for some institutions to attempt to provide a high-quality program in a discipline that requires large and ongoing investments in specialized facilities, technical equipment, and expensive supplies.

The discussion of resource allocation has taken on new importance recently, as many institutions face the prospect of budget cuts that can severely hamper their missions. Lyall and Sell (2006), for example, discuss the effect that shrinking public funding may have on the future missions of public higher education. As we write this volume, educators in the state of California face severe funding cuts as the state struggles to make ends meet (Chea, 2009; Calefati, 2009), and community colleges nationwide are facing surging enrollments during a time of significant budget cuts (Katsinas & Tollefson, 2009). Private institutions are not immune; shrinking endowments can have the same effects as state-induced budget cuts. These constraints will naturally trickle down to the program level. When budgets are cut, programs may face numerous challenges to their abilities to provide the best for students. These forces can include reducing class offerings, eliminating faculty positions, ramping up adjunct professor employment, and cutting programs. Hiring freezes may mean that class sizes increase or classes must be taught by faculty without the necessary expertise. Construction of new facilities or renovations to outdated ones may be put on hold or cancelled. Necessary supplies and equipment may not be available. All of these factors affect student learning and students' opportunities in concrete ways.

Although we share the hope that the current financial climate will eventually improve, the impacts on higher education will linger for some time. Cancelled programs may not be reinstated, and talented faculty may leave to find work elsewhere. Of course, money is not always as tight as it is in these recession years, but times when budgets are tight or shrinking serve to highlight the importance of resources to the delivery of educational programs.

In Table 8.1 (adapted from Dunn et al., 2007), we provide benchmarks for several aspects of the role of program resources in determining quality. We consider program resources, as well as issues related to resource acquisition, use, and planning. Physical facilities, materials, and equipment are the most tangible set of resources. Faculty members and staff are also vital resources to

Table 8.1 Program Resources Domain

	Undeveloped	*Developing*	*Effective*	*Distinguished*
Physical Facilities	Does not have facilities required to meet minimum program needs, or space may be in disrepair or unsafe	Minimal space needs meets, but space may not function for program goals; lack of appropriate space hampers program growth and activities	Appropriate facilities available for most teaching and scholarly activities	Has access to formal and informal spaces for faculty and student needs, including dedicated, well-equipped lab or other specialized spaces, flexible classroom design, student social spaces
Equipment, Supplies, Materials	Does not have access to equipment, supplies, and materials necessary to carry out the program	Most needs minimally met, but some serious deficits exist in availability of materials; support may be unreliable or unpredictable; equipment and materials budget may be inadequate; many needs not met	Up to current standards; students and faculty are able to function well with available materials	Has access to equipment, supplies, and materials that are up-to-the-minute; cutting edge benefits to students and to faculty scholarship

Personnel	Does not have minimum number of faculty and staff needed, or personnel do not have necessary expertise to provide quality program	Has minimum faculty and staff necessary; some gaps in expertise and work overloads may exist	Functions well, with adequate numbers of faculty and staff; personnel have appropriate expertise	Functions at high level, with appropriate numbers of faculty and staff; provides developmental opportunities for faculty and staff
Administrative Support	Provides inadequate resource support to conduct business or reward faculty	Offers limited support to conduct department business and reward faculty; support may be unreliable	Provides adequate resources to conduct department business and reward faculty	Provides generous support to facilitate program excellence
Resource Use	Wastes resources, or does not allocate resources wisely; resource distribution may be inequitable	Uses resources to moderate advantage, although resources may be inequitably distributed	Demonstrates wise use of resources	Exercises creative use of resources to optimize benefits to faculty and students; distributes resources equitably

(*Continued*)

TABLE 8.1 (CONTINUED)

	Undeveloped	*Developing*	*Effective*	*Distinguished*
Resource Planning	Does not plan for resource acquisition	Engages in sporadic planning; little focus on link between resource needs and curriculum or benefits to students	Engages in continuous and coordinated planning for resource needs	Explicitly links planning to curriculum, goals, and mission; looks forward to new developments in discipline; maintains prioritized list for expenditure of funds
External Resource Acquisition	Does not independently pursue resources beyond budget	Engages in sporadic and limited activities related to resource seeking	Actively encourages resource seeking; maintains close connection with relevant university support offices; publicizes successes	Pursues multifaceted approach to resource acquisition, including alumni, donors, and granting agencies; provides concrete support for faculty grant seeking; publicizes successes to potential donors

be used wisely by programs. Except in highly unusual circumstances, institutions do not have the resources to fully fund comprehensive "wish lists" of all programs. Thus programs typically must compete, either explicitly or implicitly, for available institutional resources. There is much that programs can do to position themselves to garner available resources, including external funds.

Physical Facilities

For some disciplines, without well-appointed offices, study spaces, and space for meetings, it may be difficult for faculty and students to function and to provide a quality program. Other disciplines need space and facilities specifically designed for the work of the discipline. These spaces may include laboratories, testing facilities, practice and performance spaces, or other specialized facilities.

The role of physical spaces in creating community and facilitating student learning is an understudied topic (Temple, 2008). However, there is evidence that the design and configuration of space affects the type of student behaviors and learning (see Dittoe, 2002; Jamieson, 2003; Jamieson, Fisher, Gilding, Taylor, & Trevitt, 2000; Strange & Banning, 2001). For example, some designs support group collaboration, whereas other types of spaces are preferred for individual study or research (see Webb, Schaller, & Hunley, 2008). Classroom design can have a direct impact on learning (see Gifford, 2002). In the sciences, facility design can provide opportunities for student research, promote student-faculty interactions, and set the stage for peer learning by providing opportunities for informal interaction (Project Kaleidoscope, 1998). For faculty and staff, well-designed work spaces can contribute to a sense of being a part of the campus community and can influence faculty morale (Biemiller, 2008; Project Kaleidoscope, 1998). Interaction, collaboration, and productivity in workplaces all can be affected by building design (see McCoy, 2002).

Formal disciplinary standards concerning necessary facilities for training and preparation at the undergraduate level typically do not exist. (One exception is the set of guidelines provided by the American Chemical Society; American Chemical Society Committee on Professional Training, 2008.) However, faculty members often are aware of the amount and type of physical space that is typical for a program of their type. For example, a brand-new biology professor is likely to be uncertain about how much latitude she might have to negotiate needed space for research, as the professor's experience will be limited to the environments that she inhabited as an undergraduate and graduate student. Similarly, performing arts faculty may be unaware of the acoustic features that would be optimal to promote high-quality musical performance. In general, programs scramble for whatever space can be brokered on campus, without regard to disciplinary standards.

Consultants from outside the institution, who are familiar with the resource needs of programs, can be helpful in advising programs and institutions about space needs. Decisions about physical facilities—what is adequate, what is necessary—are intricately linked to program context. Curriculum structure, scholarship goals, institutional context, and immediate and long-term plans for the program should all be taken into account when considering how much and what type of space is adequate for the program. Delivering significant program components online will also be a factor in determining space needs. We suggest a focus on the impact of physical facilities on students. Will students experience disadvantages when competing for jobs or graduate school positions if they cannot receive training on up-to-the-minute technology and equipment? Do new methods in the field require new equipment or new types of space?

Programs at the undeveloped level do not have the facilities to meet minimum program needs. In some cases, the amount of space may be inadequate; in others, the available space may be unusable, or the space may actually impede faculty and student activities and make teaching, collaboration, and scholarship difficult. For example, labs or faculty offices may be inaccessible to students or difficult to access. Adequate classroom space may not be available. In extreme cases, facilities may be in disrepair or even unsafe. As buildings age, they become increasingly vulnerable to all manner of physical decline that can have a direct adverse impact not just on the productivity of faculty and students, but on their health and well-being as well. In these programs, students as well as faculty are often keenly aware of the constraints placed on their activities by the lack of space or the inadequate nature of the facility design.

At a minimal level, certain spaces are required for a program to function. These may include faculty offices, offices or work spaces for staff, teaching space, research spaces such as labs (for some disciplines), and space for student interaction. Faculty scholarship typically requires a private office; individual faculty offices are also important for meeting with students. The available space also should be designed and set up in a manner that facilitates faculty and student work. Programs at the developing level may have most of their minimum space needs met, but they still face serious limitations that adversely affect their ability to carry out their mission and provide optimal experiences for students. For example, teaching spaces, laboratories, or other specialized facilities may be widely separated from faculty offices, so faculty and students spend inordinate amounts of time travelling from place to place. Classroom facilities may be inadequate. Offices of program faculty may be in different parts of the campus from one another, making community-building and collaboration difficult. Individual faculty may feel isolated if their labs or offices are long distances from those of the rest of the program faculty. A program may be housed in a space originally designed with a completely different purpose in mind, one that does not function appropriately for them. Dedicated space for students (for example, student lounge, study areas, offices for student organizations) may be nonexistent.

New buildings and recent renovations are not immune to the challenge. Fancy new facilities that have been poorly matched to their user's needs may end up being just as frustrating to work in as a dilapidated building. Unfortunately, faculty have discovered with dismay that in classrooms retrofitted to accommodate "smart" digital support it may be impossible to write on a board that is now covered with a projection screen. Such bad design can force faculty into teaching styles that must be fitted to the space rather than the needs of the students.

Beyond the minimal level, various types of dedicated spaces add significantly to a program's ability to provide a quality experience for students. Such spaces include (depending on the discipline) student-faculty research labs; studio spaces for faculty and students; performance spaces; spaces for students, such as lounges, study areas, or student organization offices; small group meeting spaces for faculty and students; and a faculty lounge or common room. Shared spaces and spaces that facilitate informal communication (for example, centrally located lounges, "main street" corridors) may be especially effective at promoting collaboration and teamwork (see McCoy, 2002). At the effective level, we typically find programs that have more than the minimal space necessary to carry out their goals. Further, the space is well designed and can be used as intended. Often, spaces serve multiple functions and can be reconfigured in creative ways as needs change. For these programs, space works to promote collaboration and community across faculty and students in the program. Space is designed so that communication occurs naturally. Offices, labs or other specialized areas, and teaching spaces are typically located near one another, and the program has a sense of ownership of the space; it may feel like "home" to them. These programs also typically provide space for student activities.

For programs at the distinguished level, space is well functioning and inviting for both faculty and students. Well-designed offices, student work spaces, and labs, studios, or other specialized facilities are in close proximity, facilitating the development of a sense of community. Dedicated student space (for example, lounges, student work spaces, office space for student organizations) builds community and a sense of belonging among students. Classroom design facilitates high-quality teaching. Distinguished programs use space in creative ways that promote collaboration. In addition, the physical space reflects design with growth in mind. These programs have room to expand for the future and facilities that can adapt as the discipline changes. Distinguished programs often have access to specialized facilities that set them apart from typical programs. These might include specialized lab or field research facilities or uniquely designed performance spaces. Faculty in distinguished programs tend to show greater entrepreneurial spirit in collaborating with community partners to identify and use local resources for mutual advantage. For example, service learning partnerships in hospitals can help satisfy the need to train health sciences students on state-of-the-art equipment. The program benefits by providing student experience in an authentic work environment. The hospital benefits by fostering positive experiences among students who may eventually become hospital employees.

EQUIPMENT, SUPPLIES, MATERIALS

As is the case for physical space, the need for equipment, supplies, and materials also varies tremendously across programs. In some disciplines, teaching and scholarship rely on up-to-date, costly, and specialized equipment, along with a range of materials and supplies. For other disciplines, little is needed in the way of equipment and materials other than working computers and standard office supplies. Minimum resource needs for a particular program must be evaluated in the context of typical standards for the discipline.

How important is it that students receive experience and training using the most up-to-the-minute equipment? In some cases, students may be at a severe disadvantage without such experiences. In other cases, although such training may be desirable, the program may be able to function at a high level, providing students with exemplary learning experiences, even without the most recent cutting-edge equipment and materials.

Programs at the undeveloped level do not have access to the minimal level of materials needed to adequately carry out the program. Both students and faculty suffer from the lack of opportunity to gain experience and pursue scholarship in the discipline. At the developing level, programs have the minimum necessary resources, but the program may be deficient in some important areas of the discipline due to lack of equipment or materials. Typically, the support available does not provide for growth or expansion. In addition, periodic shortages may hamper student and faculty work, and funding for materials, supplies, and equipment may be haphazard. The program may have to resort to frequent requests for additional support for ongoing projects due to lack of reliable funding. Effective programs have reliable access to the resources they need to provide a quality program that matches their mission. Students and faculty benefit through the opportunity to pursue scholarship and gain experience using up-to-date equipment and technology.

In contrast, distinguished programs operate in an environment in which teaching, scholarship, and creative endeavors are enriched through access to appropriate equipment and materials. Student and faculty activities are not limited by a lack of materials and equipment. These programs have reliable sources of funding for their work. They may have access to specialized equipment or materials that set them apart from other programs in their discipline and provide faculty and students with unique opportunities. In addition, faculty in distinguished programs tend to accept responsibility for enhancing whatever materials the university provides by supplementing their resources with funding garnered through successful grant pursuits, or by seeking opportunities to collaborate with other institutions or to partner with community organizations or local businesses. For example, local furniture vendors may be willing to donate furniture items that have been slow to sell, providing badly needed upgrading in exchange for a tax write-off and some public recognition.

Personnel

Faculty and staff may be a program's most important resource. Two factors seem especially salient. First, programs must have sufficient numbers of faculty and the requisite level of staff support to carry out the program. There is typically an ideal relationship between number of faculty members in a program and faculty workload. If the number of faculty is not adequate to teach courses, supervise students, and mentor student researchers, then faculty labor under untenable workloads. Faculty may teach a large number of different courses each term, advise and mentor an overwhelming number of students, and serve on numerous committees. This type of overload can have a negative impact on program quality. Even dedicated and hardworking faculty members cannot compensate for the shortfall. The same holds true for staff. Insufficiently staffed programs have difficulty functioning, and often faculty must spend time performing duties that might be more efficiently and effectively carried out by staff. In addition, staff shortages can contribute to ongoing conflict as staff scramble to avoid blame for the array of tasks that cannot be accomplished. Second, faculty and staff must have the expertise necessary to provide a high-quality program. If a program lacks faculty who are qualified to teach in a foundation area of the discipline, such that important core content areas are not covered in the curriculum, this shortcoming will obviously be detrimental to program quality. It is especially problematic when faculty must teach outside their area of expertise due to lack of appropriately trained personnel. This problem is exacerbated when faculty members cannot "retool" to get up to speed in an unfamiliar area. Likewise, staff should be provided with the necessary expertise and training to provide support. In most cases, secretarial support is the major type of staff support needed, but in some disciplines, individuals with specialized skills and training are necessary for the program to function. For example, laboratory-based disciplines very often rely on in-house technicians to maintain existing equipment, to build or repair apparatus, and to install new technologies. A program in theater may require a full-time technical staff to maintain lighting, stage set construction, and other needs related to rehearsal and performance.

Undeveloped programs do not have the minimum number of faculty and staff needed to provide a quality program. In such programs there may be serious work overloads, such that scholarly productivity, teaching, or both suffer. Programs that are undeveloped may have serious gaps in the faculty expertise because of the lack of faculty members in specific areas of the discipline; key courses cannot be taught, or classes may be taught by faculty who do not have adequate expertise to provide a quality course. So, too, faculty members do not have time for professional development or to update their skills. Burnout, with its attendant negative consequences (see Maslach, Schaufeli, & Leiter, 2001), is a common characteristic of faculty and staff in such settings.

Programs at the developing level have adequate faculty and staff to meet minimum needs. However, there may be some gaps in staffing of certain areas of expertise, and some workload issues. Curriculum development in these programs is hampered due to lack of the faculty and staff needed for expansion.

Effective programs have the numbers of faculty and staff necessary to carry out a high-quality program. Faculty members have the expertise necessary to teach in their assigned areas, and staff members have the training and experience they need to perform their jobs. Faculty members in these programs do not behave as if they are burdened by their workload. They are able to effectively teach, engage in scholarship or creative activities, mentor and advise students, and participate in service activities without experiencing burnout. And such faculty would be poised to take advantage of additional resources that would clearly provide a stimulus to help the program move into more distinguished territory.

In distinguished programs, faculty and staff have workloads that enable active scholarship, effective teaching and mentoring of students, and professional development. Faculty members have the training and expertise to teach their assigned courses, and faculty are supported by active development programs that enable them to keep their skills and knowledge up to date. Staff members also receive support to update their skills regularly. Distinguished programs typically have a proactive plan for growth into emerging areas of the discipline. Considerations of personnel needs are tied to discussions of curriculum growth and expansion, with an eye to providing students with the highest quality experiences. Roles played by faculty and staff in distinguished programs appear to be more refined and interesting. For example, a high-profile department may be host to faculty who capture national awards for quality teaching, advising, research or service. Similarly, staff members may be charged with managing some aspect of community relations or event coordination in addition to the more traditional responsibilities to which staff are assigned.

Administrative Support

The role of administrative support will be discussed more fully in Chapter Nine. However, because consideration of available program resources can hardly take place without taking into account the institutional context and the level of support provided for the program by the institution, in this chapter we address these issues as they relate to resources. When resource needs are ignored or go unmet for an extended period of time, even high-quality programs suffer. Reasons for lack of administrative support may include a lack of clear channels of communication between the program and the administration, negligence by administrators, or even, in some cases, punitive or discriminatory behavior. In some cases, financial considerations can limit support for a program; institutions simply do not have unlimited funding at their disposal. Whatever the reason, lack of support directly affects the program's ability to carry out its mission.

On the other hand, when administrators have a clear understanding of the resource needs of a program and commit to helping the program acquire at least minimum resources, this assistance can free up program faculty to concentrate on the tasks of teaching, mentoring students, engaging in scholarship and creative activities, and building a top-notch program. Concrete material support from the administration also sends a message to faculty that their efforts are valuable, affirming that the institution considers the program worthy of support and investment.

Although administrative support may most often take the form of material support (for example, in the form of space allocation; budgets for equipment, supplies, and professional travel; or new faculty and staff positions), other types of institutional support also can be meaningful and helpful. For example, administrators may enable effective collaborations among programs that maximize access to existing resources (such as space sharing and joint faculty appointments). They can be active in both friend-raising and fundraising. They may promote program activities, either across the institution or in the community. They can ensure that the efforts and accomplishments of program faculty receive recognition and rewards.

Programs at the undeveloped level along this dimension do not receive adequate support to conduct program business. Lack of support may take the form of benign neglect of the program by administrators who may be unaware of or uninterested in the program's needs. In some cases, administrators may not share the disciplinary background and therefore struggle with understanding why particular resources are central to the delivery of the program. In more extreme cases, there may be active denial of needed resources. In addition, accomplishments of program faculty go unnoticed or unrewarded.

Programs at the developing level receive limited support to conduct their business. Resource needs may be addressed at the minimum level to continue the program's functioning, but support may be doled out in a haphazard way such that the program cannot rely on adequate support from year to year. Faculty and student work is hampered; projects may be stopped in midstream because support ceases abruptly or promised resources do not materialize.

At the effective level, programs receive appropriate levels of administrative support. They can rely on adequate support to carry out their mission. Administrators recognize and reward faculty and program achievements. These programs, although receiving adequate levels of support, still may not receive sufficient support to develop further or to expand their program into new areas of the discipline; as such, their frustration mounts. With more systematic, predictable support, greatness could be in their grasp.

Administrators who support distinguished programs are aware of program goals and the resources needed to accomplish them. They regularly recognize and reward faculty achievement in both formal and informal settings. The administration actively seeks ways to promote the program. For example, a chair might highlight faculty accomplishments in a regularly disseminated newsletter to current students and alumni. A dean can acknowledge quality work in formal gatherings or offer congratulations informally for an accomplishment at a coffee break. Administrators encourage program personnel to seek out new opportunities to expand and to pursue their mission in creative ways. Such encouragement from the administration is matched by concrete support. Faculty members in these situations feel supported and empowered to think creatively about the program and its future.

Resource Use

Regardless of whether a program is rich or poor, resources should be used wisely. For example, programs that receive ample support from their institutions may squander their resources. Space may not be allocated for best use, or resources may be wasted or not used for their intended purpose. Even programs that are poorly resourced can use what they have in creative and collaborative ways that enable them to make the most of their limited resources. For example, the lack of on-campus exhibit spaces for museum studies students led to the development of James

Madison University's online virtual museum, where students can design their own exhibits in virtual space (Stevens, Kruck, Hawkins, & Baker, in press). The museum is part of JMU's online campus in the virtual world of Second Life, and receives visitors from both the campus community and the larger virtual world. A program's use of space not only reflects smart management and cooperation among faculty, but it can also be an indicator of the underlying sense of community—or lack of it—in the program (see Chapter Two).

The distribution of resources across program faculty or program functions is also an important consideration. Resources—including space, equipment, and supplies—should be distributed where they are necessary and provide maximum benefits. Even within a program, there may be some research or specialty areas that simply require more resources to function, even at a minimum level. For example, within psychology programs, faculty who specialize in cognitive psychology or social psychology may need little more than up-to-date computers and software to conduct their research, while faculty in other subdisciplines, such as neuroscience or child development, may need specially designed labs and expensive equipment. Therefore, although resource distribution may not always be quantitatively *equal* in terms of square footage allocated or dollar amounts for materials, it should be *equitable* in terms of enabling all faculty members to achieve at comparable levels.

Programs should also actively demonstrate how they use resources in ways that enable the program to enhance student learning, provide scholarship opportunities or creative and performance opportunities for faculty, benefit the community, or any combination of these results. Demonstrating wise use of resources is one tool that programs can use to argue convincingly for additional resources.

Programs identified as undeveloped do not appropriately use the resources they have. Space may be assigned to individual faculty on the basis of criteria other than best use (for example, seniority), or faculty may be put in the untenable situation of having to compete with program colleagues for space. In some cases, faculty may refuse to share "their" spaces, even if it is underused, or when sharing would clearly benefit student learning.

Equipment and supplies budgets may be haphazardly allocated, sometimes even at the whim of a program head. For example, expensive equipment, which may have been the source of a vigorous campaign at some point, may be rarely used or may be used in such a way that it does not have a significant impact on student learning or faculty scholarship. Some program functions may have too much in the way of resources allocated to them, whereas others may go begging. Faculty expertise may not be used advantageously; faculty may teach in areas outside their expertise, leaving essential courses to be taught by those with less experience or knowledge.

Developing programs also typically do not use faculty and staff resources optimally. They do a better job of using resources, yet some resources are wasted or not allocated for best use. Faculty may not be teaching in their area of expertise, or staff talents may be not be deployed to best advantage. Like undeveloped programs, these programs may be negligent about keeping track of how resources are used; thus they cannot demonstrate how their resources benefit student learning or support faculty professional activities.

Effective programs use resources to good advantage. Space and materials are allocated according to need and program function, rather than irrelevant factors (such as the preference of the program head). Faculty share resources when appropriate and collaborate; for example, faculty working on similar projects may share space or equipment. Resources not used as intended are repurposed, so that waste is minimized. Effective programs use resources wisely, but they often do not take the initiative in demonstrating how resources benefit the program.

Distinguished programs, regardless of the level of resources available, use their resources wisely, equitably, and sensitively. Faculty members in these programs are often adept at creative resource use; for example, they find ways to save on some expenses so that other, higher priority items can be funded. They share, collaborate, conserve, and reuse resources whenever possible. A faculty member who can find a good deal on a used piece of equipment that is sufficient for their needs may be able to free up funds for another use. In addition, distinguished programs recognize the value of collaborating across disciplinary boundaries to create more broad-based campaigns when special consideration is needed. A pricey spectrophotometer requested by one department is unlikely to be funded, but when several programs align to make the request and document how the shared equipment could be used across programs, funding is more likely. Faculty members in these programs are especially adept at demonstrating to administrators and other external constituents how they put resources to good use to benefit students, faculty members, or the university community.

Resource Planning

Wise programs think proactively about their future needs. Requests for resources need to come from clearly articulated plans for the future of the program. These plans should be linked to new developments in the discipline, to plans for curriculum expansion, and to scholarship goals of faculty and students. For example, what is missing from the program, in terms of coursework or research opportunities? What is needed to improve the quality of the program and to provide students and faculty with increased opportunities or specialized training or experiences? How is the discipline expanding and growing, and what background will students need as they seek jobs or graduate training? What resources are necessary to provide these experiences for students?

For sciences or other resource-intensive disciplines, advance planning is essential. Faculty members in science, technology, and health science fields know that major resource funding is an ongoing concern, due to the rapid advance of technology. Ongoing resource expenditures are important in other areas as well, such as visual and performing arts. In some disciplines, major expenditures for resources or space may not be necessary. Still, all programs should have a clear plan that articulates their resource needs and links them to their growth and development.

Undeveloped programs have no articulated plan for future resource needs or how resources will be acquired. They may passively wait for resources to be allocated to them, or they may repeatedly ask the administration for additional resources, without having well-developed ideas for how the resources will be put to best use. Even worse, undeveloped programs may respond negatively to administrators' requests for resource planning, refusing to cooperate or plan in an appropriate fashion until resources appear. Sometimes "diva moments" by frustrated faculty in institutional planning sessions can lead to a reordering of priorities that will ensure continued disappointment and frustration for the faculty. A cycle of disregard can develop, impeding faculty-administration relations and program success.

Developing programs engage in some planning for resource acquisition. Planning in these programs typically is sporadic, rather than a continuous and ongoing process. Developing programs are not in the habit of focusing on the link between the curriculum and resource needs. As a result, they may frequently find themselves in the situation of lacking necessary resources. Or, when funds become available unexpectedly, the program may miss out because they do not have an updated plan in place for their use. One related phenomenon in this arena is the failure to synchronize strategic planning and budgeting processes. Both activities are essential, but without an obvious connection between the two, both processes are doomed to be ineffective. In effective programs, planning for resource acquisition is a continuous and ongoing process. Faculty members in these programs engage in conversations about what they will need to pursue their missions, and they develop a plan for acquiring it. If funding becomes available, they are in a position to use it wisely.

Distinguished programs have well-articulated plans for resource acquisition that are explicitly linked to the mission, goals, and curriculum. Faculty are mindful of how new resources will benefit students. Program faculty members are forward-looking; they are aware of new developments and growth areas in the discipline, and they keep this in mind when planning resource acquisition. For example, will advances in the discipline require future resources? Distinguished programs typically maintain a prioritized list of needed resources, so that, if funding becomes available, they are able to demonstrate a need and a plan for using any additional funding. A final indicator of programs functioning at the distinguished level involves the regular consideration of the larger contextual issues that face administrators charged with such important decisions. Typically, representatives from these programs understand that their program will not be the only worthy cause under consideration and work effectively to take their competition and other constraints into account as they develop the most persuasive argument possible. If their resource needs cannot be met, distinguished programs show grace in disappointment, recognizing that an optimistic response can generate goodwill that can help in future campaigns.

External Resource Acquisition

A final consideration for resource acquisition involves seeking funds from sources external to the institution. Rarely is an institution capable of funding every item on a program's wish list. Wise programs recognize this fact of life and proactively seek external funding. Faculty or programs may apply for grants from funding agencies (for example, governmental agencies, foundations). In addition, programs may work in close coordination with their institution's development office to seek private donors and alumni contributions toward needed resources. A program can assist in these efforts by maintaining active relationships with alumni and by using their website and other materials to publicize and promote the successes of students and faculty.

In undeveloped programs, there is no consideration of seeking external funds for resource needs. Faculty members feel no encouragement or support in seeking grants for resources. In some cases, faculty may regard such activities as "not my job" or may be actively discouraged from seeking grant support by their colleagues or program head. These programs typically have no connection with their institution's development office or with grant support offices on their campus. In fairness, many senior faculty may have been hired during an era when external resource generation was simply not part of the higher education landscape, so they may be particularly resistant to redefining the scope of activities that constitutes the role of the professor. Similarly, pre-tenure faculty are not in the best position to focus their scholarship activities on highly competitive funding sources.

In developing programs, individual faculty may occasionally seek grants, but these may be isolated efforts that are not consistently supported or encouraged. When unsuccessful in grant pursuits, the faculty may abandon the attempt rather than persevere to refine the proposal to achieve success. Efforts appear to be token rather than serious attempts at external resource generation. The program may maintain minimal contact with the relevant institution offices and may make some efforts to maintain alumni connections or seek donors, but these efforts are not systematic or sustained.

Effective programs have a system that encourages appropriate grant-seeking activities, and typically several faculty actively pursue funding to support student activities or their own scholarship. These programs have connections with their institution's development office and offices that support faculty in seeking external funding. They publicize their successes and make active efforts to maintain contact with alumni.

Distinguished programs seek external funding with gusto, using multiple venues and approaches. They have a strong connection with their alumni and make targeted funding requests from appropriate individual donors. When unsuccessful in their grant quests, they redouble their efforts by examining factors that would make their proposals more competitive; they recognize that persistent efforts will produce the greatest likelihood of achieving their desired goals. They maintain a website that touts the program and the successes of students and faculty. Potential donors receive information about program needs as well as how donations will benefit students, faculty, and the institutional community. Their cultivation of potential donors is coordinated with the institution's development office. Faculty receive systematic information about grant opportunities that may have unique appeal to their research interests. Faculty are encouraged to pursue grant funding and are actively supported in these efforts. Such support may take the form of reassigned time to pursue funding. In sum, a distinguished program demonstrates a range of highly successful external funding.

Conclusions

A program cannot perform a high-quality job of fulfilling its mission without some resource investment in the way of adequate space, faculty and staff with appropriate expertise, and funds to cover essential supplies and equipment. In rare circumstances, a program with only minimal resources may be able to perform at a distinguished level through creative sharing of resources and conservation measures ("getting by with less"). However, better-resourced programs are simply in a better position to provide optimal experiences for students and to foster faculty productivity.

In closing, we wish to reemphasize the important and often direct connection between resources and student learning opportunities. Well-resourced programs feature classrooms that are designed to enable teaching and learning and work spaces that provide for collaboration and community building and enhance peer-to-peer and student-faculty interaction. These programs include external funds that allow the program to demonstrate success in achieving the mission and goals.

What strategies can programs adopt if they have insufficient resources but still wish to strive for the most optimal program possible?

- Monitor whether space or materials are being put to good use and consider reallocating resources in an equitable fashion to benefit the maximum number of students and faculty.
- Brainstorm about how space, equipment, and supplies might be shared or "stretched" to cover as many needs as possible.
- Seek out possibilities for sharing research space across departments or institutions.
- Employ every possible strategy to use resources wisely and to seek out new resources.
- Consider ways that community resources can be used to provide opportunities for students and faculty.
- Seek resources simultaneously from multiple sources—granting agencies, alumni, foundations, donors.
- Demonstrate to external constituents the role of resources in providing the best-quality experiences for students.
- Communicate in a clear and systematic fashion with administrators regarding their resource needs and the benefits that will flow from additional resources.

We recommend that programs review their resource allocation and projected needs on an annual basis as a proactive rather than a reactive exercise (that is, simply filling out an annual report with a cut-and-paste from the previous year's effort). We realize that departments and programs are apt to respond to such an exercise with skepticism unless there is a good-faith effort on the part of the administration to review requests with an eye to actual and eventual funding. By performing an annual request exercise with integrity, an academic program can demonstrate to faculty members, students, and administrators that they have a sincere commitment to being good stewards where resources are concerned.

GUIDING QUESTIONS

1. Has the program made a realistic assessment of their needs in the following areas: physical facilities; equipment, supplies, and materials; and personnel? Can they articulate their needs by relating them to their curriculum structure, scholarship goals, the institutional context, and their immediate and long-term plans?
2. Does the program have adequate and well-functioning physical facilities, including teaching space? If a program uses specialized facilities (for example, labs, practice spaces, performance spaces, testing facilities, off-campus research facilities), are they available, safe, well-designed, and up-to-date?
3. Does the program have sufficient equipment, materials, and supplies to provide a quality experience for students? Is necessary equipment functional and current?
4. Does the program have sufficient numbers of faculty and staff to fulfill its mission? Do faculty and staff have appropriate expertise to perform their jobs (teaching in assigned areas, providing technical support)?
5. Does the program use resources wisely? Are resources distributed equitably, in ways that enable all faculty to do their jobs?
6. Does the institution provide a realistic level of support for the program resource needs? Is there clear and direct communication between the program and administrators about resource needs?
7. Does the program have a plan for how future resources will be directed? Has this plan been effectively communicated to administrators and program faculty?

8. Does the program seek external funding, where appropriate, to augment resources? Is there a culture of being proactive about resource seeking?
9. Does the program actively publicize its work and accomplishments in ways that demonstrate the effective use of resources?

Chapter Nine

The Art, Science, and Craft of Administrative Support

Higher education administration is a mysterious enterprise. Every academic unit lays claim to a particular niche in an organizational hierarchy or superstructure of the college or university. In addition, every unit has an infrastructure, consisting of relationships, practices and policies, funding mechanisms, and other "structures" to help the business of the unit unfold. However, a well-functioning program uses an almost imperceptible administrative structure to advance the goals of the department. In fact, the operations and influence of departmental administrative practices may not be obvious until something goes wrong.

To achieve the important goal of educating undergraduates, a well-functioning administrative support structure is essential. Although faculty function autonomously, they must also learn to work effectively and efficiently within the administrative systems that support their academic pursuits. In this chapter we examine dimensions of administrative practice that contribute to a well-functioning department and productive faculty. We use the term *administrative support* to refer to issues related to program administration and function; these include mission, bylaws and procedures, faculty performance evaluation, teaching assignments, scholarship support, and recognition practices. For each dimension we describe the range of possibilities for administrative practice, from those academic units that experience exemplary practices (that is, the distinguished) through those that are insufficient (that is, the undeveloped). We detail the criteria that constitute a strong administrative foundation in Table 9.1 (adapted from Dunn et al., 2007), and we conclude with a set of recommendations to optimize administrative practices.

The Role of the Mission

An administrative colleague of ours likes to use a nautical metaphor in describing the importance of a shared mission: "Get them into the boat, get them to focus on the same point on the horizon, and then get them rowing in the same direction." Academic programs must have a clear direction to function optimally (Morrill, 2007). Although a shared sense of mission can develop over time, without formal consideration or intentional development of a mission statement, the act of airing shared expectations to identify commonalities and gaps is the preparatory step for developing and using a mission statement. A mission statement should include a vision—an aspirational statement that provides direction for the department. The mission statement sets context for future direction and can help guide departments toward a common goal (Tierney, 2002). Although the mission statement is of paramount importance for guiding the department, the mission statement is only the first step in developing a broader strategic plan (see Rowley, 2001).

Undeveloped programs may plod along, delivering an inherited curriculum; their understanding of their mission may be implicit, unspoken, and unchallenged. Although an undeveloped program may deliver some high-quality educational experiences for their students, the faculty project an image of disjointedness in which individual missions trump collective interests. Faculty not only actively avoid discussions about a shared vision, but they also are likely to be cynical about external initiatives related to mission clarification. In such cases, the mission may simply devolve into getting students across the finish line.

In developing programs, faculty surrender to external pressures to engage in visioning exercises. They develop a mission statement but still distance themselves from the process. Whatever concept paper gets officially developed also tends to end up

Table 9.1 Administrative Support Domain

	Undeveloped	*Developing*	*Effective*	*Distinguished*
Mission	Shows no interest or investment in developing a mission statement	Creates a mission to respond to external demands but shows little reference to the mission	Develops publicly stated mission statement through faculty consensus and shows some linkage between activities and the mission	Tailors mission to the goals of the university and actively uses and evaluates the mission to improve the major
Bylaws and Procedures	Does not adhere to institutional policies, bylaws, or systematic procedures	Creates bylaws or systematic procedures but may inconsistently adhere to them; bylaws may not be appropriate or functional	Consistently applies functional policies and bylaws	Adheres to up-to-date bylaws and regularly reviews bylaws to ensure best practice
Evaluation	Operates in the absence of criteria for personnel decisions, resulting in unpredictable outcomes	Maintains guidelines for personnel decisions but may not abide by them	Maintains viable and appropriate criteria to guide personnel decisions with minor problems in adherence	Regularly reviews content and process of guidelines for personnel decisions to ensure clarity, fairness

(*continued*)

Teaching Assignments	Assigns inappropriate faculty responsibilities (such as chronic overloads, inequitable assignments)	Assigns large teaching loads with reasonable distribution of assignments	Assigns equitable and reasonable responsibilities	Actively attends to quality-of-life issues through flexible teaching assignments, service, research, and other collaborative efforts
Scholarship Support	Discourages scholarly activity through insufficient support	Expects scholarly activity but may not provide appropriate support	Provides adequate support for scholarly activity	Promotes and enables vital engagement, with an array of scholarship and opportunities
Recognition of Achievements	Ignores achievements of faculty and students	Inconsistently recognizes faculty and student achievements	Recognizes faculty and student achievements but praise may be perfunctory	Actively pursues recognition opportunities to honor student and faculty accomplishments

on the bookshelf, never to be looked at again until the next external mandate arrives.

Effective programs take the issue of developing a shared mission seriously. They invest time and effort in the process, and recognize that their discussions strengthen relationships across the department. Faculty also work to develop a mission statement that fairly and equitably captures the spirit of those discussions, which is no small achievement, given the complexity of the task.

Kuh, Kinzie, Schuh, and Whitt (2005) suggest that vibrant universities are guided by a shared sense of purpose among all constituents. To be effective, a department's mission statement must be guided by the broader missions articulated by the college or university in which the unit resides. We can compare the comprehensive visioning process as analogous to a Russian nesting doll. Providing the outer shell, the university describes its values and intentions. University missions typically include a general statement about the importance of student learning, high-quality research, and community service, but they can often be rather vague (Morrill, 2007). Underneath this structure, the college uses the university statement as a guide for its own mission statement, tailoring its specific content to fit well with university objectives. Finally, as the most interior structure, the unit or department then devises a mission statement that fits comfortably within the missions of the college and university. Exhibit 9.1 provides examples of how a unit can produce coherence in mission statements.

Mission statements can vary in length from a pithy sentence to protracted text, but the most effective mission statements are focused, memorable, and meaningful. Not only must departments take into consideration the broader university context, but they must consider the characteristics of their students, the nature of their respective disciplines, and realistic budgetary limitations. The focus should be on advancing those activities that are central to their respective disciplines. Although a program chair may provide leadership to develop the mission statement, the effective chair does so with the collective input from faculty. Faculty buy-in enhances the likelihood that the mission statement will have traction.

Distinguished programs elevate the importance of mission-related practices to keep the faculty in the boat, focused, and

EXHIBIT 9.1 EXEMPLARS OF MISSION STATEMENTS

University of West Florida Mission

As the only university in Northwest Florida, the University of West Florida combines the advantages of a collegiate culture with the capacity for high quality scholarship and graduate programs. Dedicated to helping students realize their full potential, we favor small classes with fully qualified professors who deliver personalized, caring and innovative education at both undergraduate and graduate levels. Although UWF officially maintains the status of a moderate-sized, regional comprehensive university, many UWF programs and faculty members have achieved national prominence. UWF's research enterprise emphasizes applied research, simultaneously creating opportunities for student engagement and growth. By pursuing and nurturing mutually beneficial community partnerships, UWF enhances the educational, cultural and economic development of the region and beyond.

College of Arts and Sciences Mission

The College of Arts and Sciences challenges students to meet high standards of academic excellence, develop their creativity, and increase their civic engagement as they acquire a broad knowledge base. Faculty actively involve students with discipline-specific concepts, theories, frameworks, and methods as they engage in a full range of scholarly activities and professional service. From a curriculum that emphasizes values and ethics, students develop assessable skills in critical thinking, communication, and project management that provide essential tools for dealing effectively with life in a world of accelerating change and growing diversity.

Department of Music Mission

The Department of Music offers a personalized education at the baccalaureate level to equip students to perform at professional levels and to think critically as musicians and educators. This personalized education is augmented by numerous performances and ensemble opportunities. The department sponsors musical performance both alone and in conjunction with the Theater and Art Departments to reach out to both the university and the community.

---

rowing toward the same horizon. The mission is not static and should be revised as a program's situational context evolves. External pressures will likely shape priorities at the university level, and these changes will necessarily be reflected at the department level (McGuinness, 1996). Given the nature of change, a distinguished program actively revisits the mission and uses the mission statement, through consensus, to move the department forward in creating a vibrant and positive culture.

Before we leave this section, we should address one growing problem: when resources are strained, university administrators frequently ask both chairs and faculty members to "do more with less." As the minutiae of "doing more" multiply, routine tasks and activities from the academic year sometimes make it harder for departments to engage in long-range planning. Increasing demands on faculty time make it even more difficult to maintain perspective and move collectively toward a shared vision of educational excellence. However, distinguished programs make the investment in clarifying their mission, because this strategic collaboration can help them identify activities that enhance their impact as well as those that do not fit with their mission. The mission statement can become a weapon for guarding against taking on assignments that dilute the program's primary focus.

Encoding Expectations in Bylaws and Procedures

Bylaws, policies, and procedures—whether governed by the university, college, or unit—offer important guidance for all members of the university community. For example, university procedures for tenure and promotion, along with appropriate appeals procedures, provide an overarching structure that facilitates the tenure process across units. Instructions for assembling tenure and promotion materials, processes for submitting materials, and university deadlines appropriately guide the process (see Chapter Seven). Similarly, university policies may stipulate how courses will be maintained if a faculty member becomes ill or is engaged in professional development opportunities such as a stint in administration or a term as president of a professional organization. These policies may also offer guidance for responding during emergencies. Some institutions will be rich with written guidelines, whereas others may muddle along by implicit understanding. Usually environments that offer explicit structures are easier to navigate. Greater legal protection is conferred by administrative practices that provide clear and explicit direction for the multitude of decisions faculty and administrators will face. However, regulations that produce inflexible policies are fraught with potentially cumbersome results. All members of the university community, but particularly junior faculty, need to be fully informed about current administrative practices as well as changes that might affect their ability to work within the system. Therefore, in addition to university guidelines, programs should create and regularly revise bylaws and procedures that facilitate optimal functioning at all levels.

Bylaws provide broad structure for department operations. Items typically addressed in bylaws include voting procedures, committee composition, parliamentary authority, and the rights and obligations of the chair. In contrast, department policies and procedures are more detailed and include criteria for faculty evaluation, rules governing summer school teaching, and policies related to pedagogy, among other areas.

Bylaws, policies, and procedures are only useful to the degree to which department members accept and observe these established protocols. Crafting useful bylaws, policies, and procedures can be a difficult process. Although faculty do not typically express interest in developing administrative procedures, their interests should be at the heart of the shared governance process. Clear guidance for development of these documents should be forthcoming from the office of the dean or other administrators. Exhibit 9.2 contains suggestions for items that should be included in bylaws or procedures. Bylaws, policies, and procedures should be sufficiently broad but include only those elements that are useful for conducting department business. If the department guidelines are too specific, they may impede department progress by limiting faculty autonomy, flexibility, and creativity.

Faculty in undeveloped programs may be oblivious to the existence of relevant regulations or policies that might influence their behavior. Alternatively, undeveloped programs may simply not have gotten around to putting their practices into words, thus leaving open opportunities for simple misunderstandings or serious turmoil. Not only do ill-defined policies and procedures allow for a negative climate, but a lack of clearly articulated procedures can result in a grievance or litigation.

Exhibit 9.2 Components of Effective Bylaws, Policies, and Procedures

Bylaws

Structure of the department

Membership (such as professors, lecturers, adjuncts)

Chair responsibilities including procedures for election and removal

Voting procedures

Committee assignments

Department-specific tenure and promotion criteria

Department organization (sub-areas of a department)

Policies and Procedures

Summer school teaching policy

Curricular policies

Grievance procedures

Conflict resolution practices

Faculty meetings

Emergency class coverage

Developing programs may have initiated a partial set of bylaws, policies, and procedures but tend not to use them effectively. As such, each new problem that arises may prompt a sense of crisis. New regulations pop up in response to each problem. Consequently, the new rules may not be very well developed due to the program's focus on solving the crisis rather than developing a comprehensive strategy that will prevent future problems. Similarly, rules created by a developing program fail to consider long-range planning. In general, developing programs are reactive rather than proactive in establishing their governance procedures.

Effective programs establish a fairly comprehensive set of regulations to address those aspects of the department business that must be systematically administered. When the policies are well developed and the department is functioning effectively, faculty typically abide by the regulations they have created. They recognize that bylaws may need revision as the department evolves, yet they do not tend to make those modifications on a systematic basis. In well-functioning units, faculty consider the documents a useful reference manual rather than a rigid structure that imposes an oppressive climate (see Chapter Two). If a department applies a rigid structure, then clearly the program is underdeveloped rather than effective.

A current and comprehensive set of department bylaws and operating procedures that not only addresses old problems but anticipates and averts future difficulties is the hallmark of a distinguished program. Operating procedures derived through consensus can keep a program functioning and moving forward, even in times of leadership change or other transitions. The irony is that faculty thriving in distinguished programs rarely have to refer to the manual to function smoothly. The regulations have been so well crafted that appropriate behavior grows naturally out of the interaction of its members. Perhaps part of that liberation from the manual comes from the solid investment in crafting regulations that effectively capture great administrative practice in the first place.

PROVIDING EQUITABLE EVALUATION SYSTEMS

Conclusions derived during annual evaluation, tenure, and promotion processes represent high-stakes moments in the professional lives of faculty. Although nearly all academic programs evaluate faculty progress in the three pillars of performance—teaching, scholarship, and service—programs vary dramatically in the degree of direction they provide to faculty. Clear evaluation criteria are the cornerstone of an equitable system (Altman, 2000; Theall, 2002).

Undeveloped programs may have no explicit performance standards or the standards may be ambiguous, and this lack of clarity contributes to a negative climate (Leaming, 1998; Tucker, 1993). Favoritism may substitute for objective evaluations when programs fail to clearly articulate criteria for promotion, tenure, and merit. In such circumstances, faculty are at the mercy of the objectivity of the current chair. If the program is administratively unstable, a faculty member may experience evaluations by multiple chairs who may not draw the same conclusions about the quality of faculty performance from similar levels of achievement over time. This problem underscores some advice a colleague of ours provided to pre-tenured faculty: "Chairs may come and go, but a publication is your friend for life.'' In the absence of crisp guidelines, faculty must be high achieving in as many endeavors as possible to reduce their risk of a negative outcome due to supervisory instability.

Faculty in developing programs recognize the importance of providing performance guidelines that reduce ambiguity. For example, limited criteria may be available for the tenure and promotion process but not for the annual evaluation process. Unfortunately, the criteria may be insufficiently developed to help with critical decisions, or the administrators implementing the system may ignore the university, college, and department regulations. These programs may experience a great deal of lost time in conflict resolution and grievances as a consequence of decisions that do not have well-established guidelines.

In contrast, effective programs create viable performance standards that reduce ambiguity about what the program expects of an individual faculty member. Each faculty member has an understanding of the relative importance of teaching, scholarship, and service. In addition, administrators in effective programs clarify where and when evaluations take place and describe opportunities for redress if conflict emerges. However, the quality and clarity of the standards themselves may not encourage faculty to achieve their full potential.

A distinguished program crafts standards that not only fit with the department and university missions but also serve to inspire faculty and promote collegiality (Diamond, 2000). The criteria demonstrate enough flexibility to recognize faculty contributions in a variety of teaching, scholarship, and service activities that serve the mission. Such criteria provide clear guidance about how faculty members can optimize successful outcomes. For example, although a publication in a top-tier journal will necessarily be weighted more heavily than a presentation at a local conference, it might also be possible to obtain a comparable rating by publishing several articles in less prestigious outlets. Following is one approach to clarifying expectations related to teaching performance evaluations. Regardless of how a program operationalizes its criteria, the distinguished program encourages a diversity of contributions that strengthen the collective efforts of a department, and the department performance standards reflect the relative merits of those contributions. Distinguished programs recognize that a perfect evaluation system will remain elusive, but they strive to make the system as perfect as possible, taking steps to provide clear criteria that accurately reflect the expected scope and quality of contributions. They also systematically revisit and revise those criteria to ensure their currency.

Example of Evaluation Criteria: Performance Indicators for Teaching

Because high-quality teaching is critical to the university's *regional comprehensive* mission and vision, excellent performance is required for all tenure and promotion decisions. Teaching includes all teaching and learning activities in and out of the classroom that result in relevant, appropriate course outcomes, including the following:

- Face-to-face classroom teaching at main or branch campuses
- Online teaching
- Teaching in distance learning circumstances
- Research group supervision and mentoring
- Continuing education assignments
- Advising

Departments must use scaled performance indicators that clearly delineate the differences between the performance levels of *distinguished, excellent, good, fair,* and *poor.* Departments must not merely list the performance indicators without providing guidance about the relative importance of the indicators that are required for each performance level. Moreover, those indicator measures must both cohere with university criteria described in this document and fairly capture unique characteristics of their disciplinary and departmental cultures.

The following sections provide guidelines for departments in how to make appropriate judgments for tenure and promotion recommendations on quality of performance (i.e., poor, fair, good, excellent, and distinguished).

Teaching Performance Indicators

Distinguished Performance

Distinguished performance demonstrates that the weight of evidence supports an unusually high degree of quality in teaching as shown by the following indicators that build upon performance indicators for excellence.

Performance indicators that may be used to support distinguished ratings:

a. Numerical student evaluation data document clear statistical exceptionality
b. Narrative statements emphasize powerful impact on learner or transformative learning experiences
c. Teaching awards honor high caliber of performance
d. Leadership evident in the promotion of high quality teaching and curriculum development in the department

Excellent Performance

Excellent performance represents *consistent high quality* teaching with positive outcomes for students as reflected by the performance indicators below.

Performance indicators that may be used to support excellent ratings:

a. Student evaluations document consistently positive impact on learning
b. Teaching philosophy provides foundation for coherent course planning and activities
c. Syllabi outlines comprehensive, clear, and appropriate performance expectations
d. Assessment practices enhance student learning and contribute to department needs
e. Goals and course content routinely provide evidence of successful continuous improvement effort
f. Pedagogical practices facilitate optimal learning conditions
g. Student support practices facilitate optimal student development
h. Advising, mentoring, and student supervision practices receive consistent favorable review
i. Special teaching assignments (e.g., honors, capstone, General Studies) executed with expert skill
j. Appropriate standards of academic integrity promoted, including respect for students and their rights
k. Participates voluntarily in professional development activities to improve teaching quality and flexibility

Good Performance

Good performance demonstrates overall teaching effectiveness but some *minor* areas for concern. In general, the weight of evidence suggests that teaching performance is below what is required for tenure and promotion decisions.

Performance indicators that may be used to support good ratings:

a. Student evaluations data document adequate impact on learning
b. Teaching philosophy expressed in course planning and activities
c. Syllabi provide reasonably clear and appropriate expectations
d. Assessment practices support student learning and contribute to department needs
e. Goals and course content give evidence of continuous improvement effort
f. Majority of pedagogical practices are appropriate and effective
g. Majority of student support practices are appropriate and effective
h. Advising, mentoring, and student supervision practices are appropriate and effective
i. Special teaching assignments (e.g., honors, capstone, general education) executed with reasonable skill
j. Maintains appropriate standards of academic integrity, including respect for students and their rights
k. Participates in teaching development activities when directed to do so

Fair Performance

Fair performance demonstrates some positive teaching outcomes but produces *major* areas for concern for the department. The weight of evidence suggests that teaching performance in this performance category is below what is required for tenure and promotion decisions.

Performance indicators that may be used to support fair ratings:

a. Student evaluations data document areas of moderate concern (ratings below the department average)
b. Teaching philosophy may not be clearly expressed in course planning and activities
c. Syllabi need to provide clearer and more appropriate expectations
d. Assessment practices show some difficulty in supporting student learning and meeting department needs

e. Goals and course content reflect limited continuous improvement effort
f. Some pedagogical practices need attention
g. Some student support practices need improvement
h. Advising, mentoring, and student supervision practices need improvement
i. Special teaching assignments (e.g., honors, capstone, general education) could be executed with greater competence
j. Occasional challenges related to academic integrity
k. Some indications of disrespect for students and their rights
l. Does not typically participate in teaching development activity

Poor Performance

Poor performance demonstrates *serious* problems in attaining success in teaching role as reflected by either (1) a combination of *many* negative indications, or (2) fewer but more *extreme* behaviors that produce substantial negative outcomes on students and their learning. In general, the weight of evidence suggests teaching performance is *well below* the department norms. Because of the high priority placed on teaching, this level of performance requires major remedial work.

Performance indicators that may be used to support poor ratings:

a. Student evaluations data document consistent and substantive problems (ratings well below the department average)
b. Teaching philosophy missing, poorly articulated, or poorly expressed in course activities and planning
c. Syllabi fail to establish clear and relevant expectations
d. Assessment practices are inadequate to support student learning and department needs (e.g., learning outcomes are inadequate, inappropriate, or missing; testing strategies are not effective or fair)
e. Goals and course content reflect no continuous improvement efforts
f. No assistance rendered for department assessment plan
g. Pedagogical practices are unsound (e.g., disorganization; late, missing, unhelpful feedback; standards too lax or too challenging; routinely poor preparation; disengaging, chaotic, or hostile classroom environment)
h. Student support practices are unsound (e.g., late or absent for class, not responding to e-mail, not keeping office hours, showing favoritism)

i. Consistent and very negative ratings in advising, mentoring, and supervision of student's scholarly or creative activities
j. Special teaching assignments (e.g., honors, capstone, General Studies) avoided or poorly executed
k. Chronic academic integrity concerns identified including evidence of disrespect for students and their rights

Source: Principles adopted at University of West Florida, 2008.

DETERMINING EQUITABLE TEACHING ASSIGNMENTS

Although faculty lives consist of teaching, scholarship, and service, only teaching translates into heated discussions about "workload." Institutions vary in their expectations about what constitutes a fair teaching load. In research-intensive contexts, teaching workload will be minimal, perhaps one or two courses per term, so that faculty can devote more time to research, performance, or creative efforts. In contexts where teaching has greater priority, the teaching workload will be more extensive. For example, it is not uncommon for community colleges to assign five courses per semester; however, in these contexts, scholarship demands may be minimal or nonexistent.

Good teaching requires time to identify appropriate student learning outcomes, prepare content, design effective activities, and provide students with feedback. When teaching is coupled with the competing demands of scholarship and service, stress can result from having too little time to do all things well. Therefore the balance of activities and extent of teaching load must be taken into consideration when making teaching assignments. Teaching load encompasses not only the number of credit hours but also the number of students, number of different courses taught by a faculty member, specific demands of the course (for example, significant grading responsibilities), and venue for delivery of the course (for example, online, hybrid, or traditional).

Balancing the needs of the department with the obligations of faculty is a difficult process. Undeveloped programs fail to provide reasonable or equitable assignments. For example, chairs may give privilege to senior faculty members who routinely get to choose preferred courses and teach at preferred times. If their teaching assignments reflect boutique courses in esoteric interest areas, the course may produce low enrollments. Put another way, undeveloped programs do not effectively use their faculty resources (see Chapter Eight). This practice can result in a double paradox: the most expensive faculty members employed by the institution produce the least; at the same time, the faculty who contribute the most effort in generating student credit hours receive poorer treatment.

A related problem for undeveloped programs is abuse of overload assignments. At some institutions, and especially during times of severe financial challenges, faculty may be required to take on additional teaching responsibilities. Chronic teaching overloads and the accompanying burnout (see Maslach, Schaufeli, & Leiter, 2001) negatively affect faculty morale through diminished quality of life as well as potentially threaten successful tenure and promotion decisions due to failure to complete research or creative projects.

Developing programs pay greater attention to matters of fairness in making assignments but do not fully succeed. In developing programs the chair may attempt to balance teaching assignments for some faculty, but assignment of courses is not systematic and transparent. Due to limited resources, faculty may be required to teach numbers of students that strain the capacity to teach in an effective and pedagogically sound fashion.

In effective programs, administrators attend to the variety of aspects that the teaching load comprises and work to assign an equitable distribution of responsibilities. Key to this process is attention to flexible and creative teaching assignments. For example, effective programs may create systems that provide credit for specified numbers of thesis supervision or directed studies. Technically, load takes into account all of the diverse activities faculty members must accomplish to deliver a strong program.

A distinguished program manages to strike a balance between autonomy for individual faculty and a common goal of serving students. Administrators demonstrate genuine concern for the quality of life of individual faculty members. For example, they take into account extraordinary challenges in the personal lives of faculty (for example, protracted family health problems) and work creatively, through workload assignments, to help valuable faculty weather the storm. They may also call appropriate time-outs in the tenure clock if conditions warrant this kind of largesse without creating other inequities.

SCHOLARSHIP SUPPORT

An institution's orientation toward and support for scholarship are two crucial issues that affect the quality of scholarship that faculty produce. The orientation toward scholarship is present in two forms—explicit written guidelines and implicit cultural expectations for what constitutes evidence of scholarship. Support for scholarship includes providing faculty members with time, proper facilities, and appropriate financial support to accomplish their research agendas (see Chapter Eight for further discussion of resource issues). Bland, Weber-Main, Lund, and Finstad (2005) provide a thorough examination of best practices for promoting and supporting faculty research.

Undeveloped programs fail in both arenas. Institutional expectations about scholarship fail to set the bar; consequently, faculty may not develop skills to produce high-quality scholarship, and there is no predictable negative consequence for failure to engage in scholarship. If no additional supports or even encouragements are forthcoming, it is easy to see why faculty would become discouraged and focus their efforts on activities that are more highly rewarded (for example, service, teaching, external obligations).

In contrast, developing programs provide some limited guidance for clarifying productivity targets. However, they fail to deliver support in the way of time, funding, or equipment to accomplish the task. In such situations, scholarship patterns are likely to emerge in fits and starts rather than as sustained and successful research agendas. Situations in which faculty scholarship is expected, but not supported, can especially undermine faculty success, morale, and confidence.

Effective programs succeed in providing the guidance that gives faculty members a sense of purpose about their scholarship. Clear criteria reduce the stress associated with tenure, promotion, and determination of merit. Whenever possible, more subtle, implicit expectations should become articulated in a manner that facilitates sound decisions about which scholarly products will be more satisfying and profitable to pursue. Effective programs develop specific strategies to enhance time management. For example, scheduling teaching assignments to free up larger blocks of time may enable faculty members to pursue creative activities more efficiently. Similarly, if there is an expectation that scholarship will be focused (for example, empirically based, service learning focused), then the appropriate infrastructure will be in place to support these focused activities.

Administrators in distinguished programs recognize and support the full scope of faculty scholarly activities. For example, they understand that individual faculty may have different goals for their scholarship at different stages of their career. In a well-functioning and supportive environment, distinguished programs welcome the diversity of scholarly activities (see Halpern et al., 1998; Myers & Waller, 1999; O'Meara, 2005). Faculty feel inspired to set high goals, and they experience sustained appreciation for their accomplishments.

RECOGNITION OF ACHIEVEMENTS

Academic life is rife with intrinsic rewards: the light in the students' eyes caused by a sudden insight, the intellectual fun of designing a new course or creating a new composition, the joy of welcoming a new colleague into the program, and the renewal of energy associated with getting a "do over" with every new term. However, the academy is also an intensely competitive environment in which individual accomplishments can and should be celebrated for multiple good effects. Not only does a high-achieving faculty member get appropriate attention and reward, but the program itself can grow in stature from well-designed recognition practices.

Faculty in undeveloped programs regularly experience administrative neglect in relation to their personal and professional successes. No matter what the accomplishment, faculty achievements may be ignored or minimized. In especially unstable programs, individual accomplishments may even be belittled, as interpersonal jealousies may come into play and result in active attempts to sabotage a colleague's success.

The approach to recognition for accomplishment in developing programs is scattershot. Intermittent recognition of accomplishments may create the perception of inequity. For example, a particularly visible community service activity may be rewarded in a public forum. However, an equally important activity (for example, innovative teaching) may not rise to a level of visibility that allows for adequate recognition. Minor accomplishments may cause an avalanche of public attention, whereas major achievements may engender a collective yawn. In such programs, standards of excellence have probably not been well articulated. Alternatively, individual faculty may be extremely productive in ways that may or may not be consistent with the departmental mission. Although there may be some attempts to recognize faculty achievement, the events may be poorly organized and do little to reinforce praiseworthy behavior.

Effective programs do a better job of identifying laudatory ideals and also of following through with deserved recognition. A well-functioning department allows for flexibility in terms of recognizing individual accomplishments. For example, a program may have an exemplary researcher located across the hall from a professor who is widely known for the extra hours devoted to effective student advising. Effective programs find ways to honor both types of contributions. A well-functioning department not only acknowledges important service contributions but also provides tangible support for these activities. Recognition systems should be more than perfunctory and should consistently foster positive, mission-consistent contributions.

Distinguished programs unambiguously identify the types of activities, scholarship, and service that warrant recognition. Not only do such programs actively create and participate in campus-based recognition systems, but they also maximize their opportunities to recognize faculty contributions within the department. Additionally, these programs participate in national recognitions. Many disciplinary associations provide opportunities for recognition of teaching, scholarship, and service. The most effective administrators seek out opportunities to nominate faculty for local, regional, and national awards. In distinguished programs, evidence of distinction mounts, especially when external awards and recognition validate the quality of the program, faculty, and students.

FORGING DISTINGUISHED ADMINISTRATIVE PRACTICES

Several strategies can assist programs in the quest for distinguished practice. In closing this chapter, we recommend the following actions:

1. *Mission:* Embrace strategic planning. Throw out the old mission statement and start anew. Think about where you want the department to be five years from now and organize intervening steps accordingly. Programs often benefit from a formal retreat to accomplish this goal on such a large scale. An outside facilitator can sometimes be useful to ensure that all voices are heard and considered.
2. *Bylaws:* Transparency is essential for thriving programs. In the spirit of shared governance, faculty should feel comfortable identifying problem areas and proposing changes. Discussion of needed changes should be public rather than behind closed doors. Regular meetings facilitate the exchange of information, the capacity to act nimbly in response to emerging institutional demands, and the opportunity to evolve policies that serve all program members.
3. *Evaluation:* The fastest way to achieve program distinction is by making shrewd hires. It is important for departments to recruit and retain faculty who are culturally diverse and who bring a diversity of perspectives and experience (Bland, Weber-Main, Lund, & Finstad, 2005). When programs have given performance expectations careful scrutiny and come to consensus about what constitutes superb performance, this will influence how subsequent position advertisements are developed. By hiring strong talent that is well suited to the mission and retaining those individuals through sound administrative support, the program can make substantial progress on a distinguished reputation in a short time frame.
4. *Workload:* Workload assignment should be a public process. When the rules and regulations about how course scheduling takes place are equitable and reasonable, a public discussion can foster mutual understanding and a sense of camaraderie about the shared activity ahead. Administrators can avoid

being trapped in inappropriate allegiances to the members of the program.

5. *Scholarship:* Distinguished programs have a knack for helping their members contribute from their individual strengths. For some faculty, their scholarly and creative activities will be of paramount importance. Other faculty may disengage from the scholarly enterprise in pursuit of other activities that express the program's mission. Administrators should help such individuals find meaningful ways to make significant contributions, but they may also need to neutralize any resentment of the additional support and resources that may be required for the research-oriented faculty to thrive.
6. *Recognition:* Administrators should ensure that multiple opportunities are available for recognition of accomplishments in all three areas of faculty responsibilities—teaching, scholarship, and service. Whenever possible, recognition and awards programs should also be tailored to acknowledge contributions at various levels of career development (that is, early career faculty, senior, or distinguished contributions). It is particularly important to recognize contributions of faculty in areas that are mission central but potentially undervalued by the university community.

CONCLUSIONS

In this chapter we highlighted the importance of the underlying infrastructure that serves to support all aspects of faculty performance—research, teaching, and service. A clear mission and a well-developed strategic plan are essential for guiding a vibrant program toward continued excellence. So too is a clear set of bylaws to guide equitable practices. The climate of a department is directly related to the strength of planning, bylaws, and equitable treatment of faculty and ultimately the overall functioning of the department. In fact, equity is at the heart of fostering the development of a distinguished program. We believe that providing appropriate support for scholarship, equitable assignment of faculty load, fair evaluation practices, and acknowledgment of outstanding contributions for all areas of faculty responsibility will result in a truly distinguished undergraduate program.

GUIDING QUESTIONS

1. Is the departmental mission current and actively used to guide departmental decisions?
2. Are department bylaws present, current, and distinct from procedures? Do department bylaws and procedures facilitate the activities of the department?
3. Are criteria for faculty evaluation clearly articulated and transparent in their application?
4. How are teaching assignments determined? Are courses assigned in a flexible, efficient, and public manner?
5. How is scholarship interpreted and supported? What kind of scholarship works best in the context?
6. Do faculty feel sufficiently recognized for the scope and quality of their work?

Part Two

Benchmarking in Practice

Chapter Ten

Benchmarking Quality in Challenging Contexts

The Arts, Humanities, and Interdisciplinary Programs

Jane S. Halonen

with Gregory W. Lanier

Assessment in the arts and other areas of the academy is assuredly not easy, and mandates for developing cultures of evidence to address quality in higher education remain highly controversial (Miller, 2006). Faculty, in their responsiveness to assessment mandates, can be categorized roughly as follows: those who are receptive to assessment, those who are less than thrilled with assessment and all that it entails, and those who are neutral. Assessment-receptive faculty members accept, and some even embrace, accountability practices, because measuring impact sets direction and gives meaning to the work. At the minimum, assessment-resistant faculty feel annoyed by accountability requirements and may have legitimate concerns about the value of the process, given the sometimes inordinate amount of time and energy invested in assessment practices. At the extreme end of negative response, some assessment-resistant faculty may actively avoid participating in assessment activities in the hopes that higher education somehow will come to its senses and resume the practice of trusting faculty to manage their own classrooms without unwelcomed intrusion. Assessment-neutral faculty don't have feelings one way or the other about assessment. Full disclosure: to date, we have never met anyone who belongs in this neutral category. Like sex, religion, and politics, assessment and accountability provoke robust reactions.

In this chapter, we deal with the arts and humanities—areas that are, for good reasons, populated with faculty who may need to be persuaded about the need for and utility of assessment in their disciplines. In contrast, many academic disciplines have a head start in their receptivity to accountability practices, because identifying targets, actively monitoring progress toward the targets, and even comparing performance to relevant benchmarks would all seem to be natural outgrowths of the commitment to delivering high-quality education. For example, measurement is a fundamental principle in science and social science; therefore, arguments against the production of measurable evidence to support claims of quality not only run counter to the accepted disciplinary culture but seem a little foolish. As a consequence, the natural and social sciences appear more ideally suited to the expectations for managing accountability.

Similarly, the business and education disciplines, as well as other disciplines that must adhere to specific accreditation standards, are often better prepared to address accountability expectations. Business programs have extensive practice in managing by objectives and adhering to requirements of the Association to Advance Collegiate Schools of Business (AACSB). Education programs must meet standards defined by the National Council for Accreditation of Teacher Education (NCATE) that reinforce the importance of strong accountability practices.

However, our experience as liberal arts administrators has shown us that many disciplines and disciplinary hybrids tend to be resistant to assessment planning and practice. (A psychologist, Jane has served as a chair of two psychology departments and a dean of the behavioral sciences in a women's college; she currently serves as the dean of a college of arts and science at University of West Florida, a regional comprehensive university. A Shakespearean scholar, Greg has not only served as the head of fine and performing arts and chaired the departments of music, theatre, and English, but also currently serves with Jane as an associate dean of the college of arts and sciences, with primary responsibility over the honors and interdisciplinary studies programs.) Faculty and administrators in the arts and humanities often may be less open to accountability practices because the disciplinary cultures in those areas tend to view measurement itself as a reductive, distasteful, and deadening enterprise. Many disciplines in the arts and humanities prize diversity in interpretation and multiplicity in perspective, often insisting that there is no "right" or "discrete" knowledge that can (or should) be shared or replicated even if all of the parameters of the investigation are exactly and precisely replicated. Therefore the need to establish quality through the hard numeric evidence of data for accountability purposes may not be a good philosophical fit with the discipline's core methods and problem-solving strategies. In addition, programs that don't have an obvious departmental home, such as interdisciplinary humanities or social sciences programs, present many similar difficulties for measurement-based accountability practices. In total, these challenges often take a toll on accountability practices and program evaluation efforts.

The purpose of this chapter is to explore typical challenges to benchmarking practices that tend to befuddle the arts, humanities, and interdisciplinary studies. We rely on quality benchmarks systematically to frame our arguments, including examining the following domains: curriculum development, assessment planning and student learning outcomes, program resources and administrative support, faculty characteristics and program climate, and student development. We conclude each section with a set of recommendations that can help propel faculty and their programs in the right direction to become more effective in achieving legitimate cultures of evidence. We genuinely believe that our teacher-scholar-administrator colleagues in the arts, humanities, and interdisciplinary studies will be pleasantly surprised by the utility of the benchmarking exercise for improving their programs and the educational experiences of their students.

Our experience in this endeavor is drawn from direct interaction with a wide range of faculty and programs: the humanities in general, the interdisciplinary humanities and interdisciplinary social sciences programs, and a school of fine and performing arts (comprising the departments of music, art, and theatre). Consequently, the examples we use will be particularly familiar to people in those disciplines. However, we suspect that the principles we identify as relevant across these programs will also apply to other disciplines in which creativity and performance take precedence over other liberal arts modes of learning.

We also acknowledge that the quality of programs across these content areas varies from impeccable quality with prominent national reputation to genuine dysfunction, disinterest, and ongoing struggles. However, our focus addresses what makes the faculty reluctant to engage in assessment. By concentrating on the characteristics of areas in which an assessment and accountability culture is *undeveloped*, we hope to propose some strategies that can encourage a constructive, more receptive stance toward accountability.

Curriculum Development

Achieving convergence on a defensible common ground appears to pose a particular problem across the arts, humanities, and interdisciplinary programs, although the reasons for convergence failures may differ among those areas. The problems entail an absence of historical consensus about the educational goals of the respective disciplinary domain, resource limitations in relation to scope of design, and haphazard design practices.

Absence of Historical Consensus

One common feature across these special programs is that each discipline may struggle to identify a canon of agreement about what is most important to learn in their respective disciplines. Many disciplines reject the notion of a canon as outmoded or unnecessary. There may be some foundational work in a discrete artistic specialty or skill; however, there is little agreement about basic characteristics or curricular experiences that foster a coherent artistic knowledge base or skills set. Similarly, humanities scholars may not recognize where their interests converge because the specific disciplinary interests within the unit may share very little overlap. Traditions in those programs with an undeveloped status may simply encourage faculty independence in curriculum matters rather than foster broad-based consensus.

Curricular decisions that were once sacrosanct in the humanities come into question once the faculty give serious thought to the range of authors and artists, periods and movements, and cultures and ideologies that students should experience. To take just one commonly disputed example: should every English major study the works of Shakespeare? Twenty years ago, that question might have been dismissed as sophomoric, but now many institutions grant degrees in English to students who have never studied the Bard. Similarly, twenty years ago one would have been hard pressed to find any courses in literary theory offered at the undergraduate level on the vast majority of campuses; now, however, literary theory courses appear to be more indispensable than Shakespeare. The upgrading of a program's curriculum at least suggests that the faculty exert energy to keep the curriculum current; however, in *undeveloped* programs the curriculum may be more a manifestation of esoteric faculty interests than legitimate common ground.

Interdisciplinary studies programs in general have also long been criticized for a lack of common foundation, knowledge base, and focus (see Slattery, 2006; Wineberg & Grossman, 2000). Interdisciplinary programs typically draw students with almost no shared background beyond some random overlap of those courses required by the general education curriculum. Once they begin pursuing the interdisciplinary degree, the range of course offerings can be so broad and flexible that no two students have anything like the same educational experience.

Resource Limitations and Scope of Program Design

Given the state of the global economy in the years just before and during this writing, no liberal arts or interdisciplinary program has carte blanche to build programs that can't be justified in relation to student credits hours generated; however, available funding sometimes will force arbitrary choices about what can and should be included in program design. Scholars with narrow or esoteric specialties could be added to any special programs at will if budgets didn't intervene to forestall more grandiose plans. However, resource constraints dictate that all curricula must be delivered within some realistic parameters.

In some instances the unchallenged belief that an expanded range of curricular choices guarantees high quality keeps programs in undeveloped status; in this case, the faculty equate quantity with quality even though a broad range of options is probably not, in itself, an indicator of quality. In each program the range of subject opportunities offered by the discipline must be purposefully determined within the constraint of available resources and with an eye to delivering a high-quality educational experience for the student. Choices and compromises—which invariably amount to cuts in either range of options or depth of focus—must inevitably be made to deliver a quality learning environment.

Given that a university-level program of any kind presumes that there is an intellectual core, an art department cannot function properly without an art historian and art history classes to trace the trends, developments, and breakthroughs within the discipline over time. But beyond that core, choices of direction soon mount; in a time of limited resources, the number of available faculty lines quickly limits those choices. Certainly painting and drawing are fine arts core skills that need staffing, but after the department adopts those "core" activities, which subdiscipline is most essential? Ceramics or printmaking? Weaving or performance art? Digital art or jewelry making? Intaglio or photography? If the reach of the art department becomes too wide in an attempt to serve all comers, then dilution can quickly erode quality and produce students who become dabblers in many crafts, but masters of few or none. An undeveloped program will often vociferously advocate for more lines based on the mistaken belief that broader representation of the field will automatically engender better quality.

Haphazard Program Design

Curricula in special programs have sometimes evolved in contexts in which faculty advocated maximum control over selection by students (Tchudi & Lafer, 1996). These conditions give rise to even greater challenges about establishing the coherence of curriculum. If the student can select even as many as six to eight courses from a single discipline, then the chances are very, very slim that any two students who share what is often called a "major area emphasis" will have taken more than three of the same courses. Nearly all departments in interdisciplinary programs offer far more than the six to eight courses needed for an interdisciplinary degree.

Linda Suskie, executive associate director of the Middle States Commission on Higher Education, concluded that poor curriculum design is a natural outgrowth of the slapdash manner in which the faculty treat interdisciplinary issues. In a personal communication on September 1, 2006, she stated:

> I've seen too many interdisciplinary programs in which the faculty "construct" the program by listing every course at the institution that has anything to do with, say, Asian studies; students choose whatever courses they like from the list (perhaps by choosing one from Column A and two from Column B); and a "major" is born. These kinds of interdisciplinary majors are virtually cost-free to the institution, especially if these students are taking otherwise under-enrolled classes, but don't give students the kind of purposeful education they need today.

As a result of this approach, interdisciplinary programs can become, as a colleague of ours used to sneer, the equivalent of "majoring in sophomore surveys." Convergence on a "core" goes a long way to ensure pedagogic quality and to limit the dilution of learning by tangential exposure to unrelated subject matter.

Recommendations for Curriculum Development

To encourage forward momentum for undeveloped programs, the following suggestions may be helpful in curriculum development:

1. Establish consensus about educational goals, but acknowledge them as mutable and specify when the goals will be revisited in the future. Incorporate systematic plans to revisit the consensus to take full advantage of emerging areas of importance and "sunset" those that are in decline. Adopting the

curriculum plan as a living document can sometimes reduce the intensity of turf wars.

2. Design course curricula to address content requirements that fit reasonably with available resources. Discourage course proliferation, particularly because unrestrained growth cannot be justified when a leaner curriculum will suffice.
3. Establish the right infrastructure, including a selective and limited list of core courses, a sequence of specific methods classes, and a meaningful capstone class.

ASSESSMENT PLANNING AND STUDENT LEARNING OUTCOMES

Developing an assessment plan forces the kind of conversation that faculty should have about establishing and maintaining the integrity of any program (Walvoord, 2004). However, these practices may be especially unpalatable to undeveloped programs. In this section we consider three topics that can help produce positive energy for benchmarking, including transforming traditional practices into assessment, identifying robust student learning outcomes, and promoting professional standards.

TRANSFORMING TRADITIONAL PRACTICE

Objective accountability practices have long been a standard practice in the arts and humanities, but may not have been recognized as legitimate assessment methods. Nearly every theatre, music, or art major has endured at the very least one audition, juried competition, or portfolio analysis. Therefore, the culture of directly assessing student performance is well established in the fine and performing arts; however, faculty may not be well prepared to see these traditions as a manifestation of sound assessment practice. Similarly, as a group, English professors are arguably the best essay graders in the universe, but they generally abhor assessment since they associate the activity with teaching to discrete and specific outcomes. Therefore, assessment practices can be seen as directly opposed to the goals of literary exegesis.

In general, evaluation practices in the arts and humanities are transacted rigorously; faculty members closely read and then score each and every essay; they attend and adjudicate every recital; and they scrutinize and evaluate every project portfolio. Faculty expertise provides individualized feedback on each student's performance roughly in isolation, but during the appraisal the faculty member keeps in mind that a near infinite variety in interpretations, approaches, presentations, and conclusions can (more likely, should) be reflected in each individual paper or performance. On the surface, this opportunity to achieve unique creations seems at odds with accountability systems that reduce achievement to discrete and specific behavioral criteria.

Therefore, we realize that a persistent challenge that besets assessment in the arts and humanities often is countering the misconception that assessment necessitates lock-step learning. The key for the arts and humanities seems to be shifting the perception away from the belief that assessment is about specific things that the students must learn and toward an understanding that assessment more profitably concentrates on the skill sets that characterize the discipline.

Standard evaluation practices in the arts and humanities traditionally involve numerous, highly complex, but nevertheless holistic, judgments about what the student has done or submitted. For example, when reviewing a theatrical audition, the evaluator makes complex judgments about the student's diction, enunciation, voice projection and timbre, posture, quality of movement, eye-contact, characterization, stage presence, among other qualities, all within the span of two one-minute contrasting dialogues. Consequently, the evaluative focus is exclusively on the moment with little room for consideration of the steps and processes by which the student got to that moment. The same conclusions can be drawn about paper and essay evaluation in which the appraisal—the grade—is primarily, if not exclusively, a very complex and holistic judgment about a final product.

To ask that a faculty member shift focus from the student's performance toward his or her own pedagogical practices, as well as the place and purpose of those practices within the design of a larger component (that is, the curriculum as a whole), represents a major paradigm shift away from standard disciplinary evaluation practice. If nothing else, the effort needed to sort through the complexities of making judgments about the quality of a performance or paper and to isolate a single specific component or outcome such as "critical thinking" in the humanities is immense; that can be reason enough for faculty in these areas to resist the assessment movement. Consequently, high quality and successful assessment practices appear in those programs that have made the shift away from "What has the student learned?" to "How is the student learning?"; further, we should acknowledge that such a shift marks a major departure from historical practice in the arts and humanities.

Identifying Robust Student Learning Outcomes

Out of the struggle to craft purposeful and significant student learning outcomes (SLOs) in the arts and humanities, one critical shaping question often emerges: what is essential to the knowledge base of the discipline? Unlike professional programs or others with strict accreditation standards, programs in the arts, humanities, and interdisciplinary studies often do not have easily identified skills or a roster of essential knowledge that facilitates rapid consensus and approval from the faculty. Therefore, when done well and taken seriously, the discussions that must occur to establish essential learning outcomes can be fraught with tension, conflict, and petty rancor—if not downright uncivil turf wars—fueling even greater justification to resist participating in assessment activities.

Assessment-resistant contexts often demonstrate intrinsic preferences toward multiplicity and diverging perspectives, sometimes resulting in SLOs that are so hopelessly broad that they can include anyone, anytime, and anything (such as "Engage in the entire world of discourse and debate from politics to education"). Conversely, SLOs can be so narrowly constricted that they speak to only a subset of a subdiscipline, in which case it takes hundreds of SLOs to cover the territory. Achieving balance is a desirable, but often a very difficult task.

Once faculty can be persuaded to make the fundamental pedagogical shift toward assessment planning in the arts, humanities, and interdisciplinary studies, the respective programs face major challenges. Faculty in these areas do not, as a rule, trend toward number friendliness, so even if a solid assessment approach exists, methods need to be devised so that the dreaded number gathering can be done as quickly and simply as possible. Once the data have been gathered, programs must establish mechanisms for the meaningful analysis of the data and appropriate modification of courses and programs as well.

Quality programs in these areas do yeoman service in adapting assessment methods to existing practice or finding other avenues for "authentic assessment" (see Paris & Ayres, 1994; Wiggins, 1990). For example, faculty (and local professionals, if available) can use simple Likert scales linked to specific performance components at "end of the year" auditions in bachelor of fine arts (BFA) Theatre programs. The data from such activities can quickly reveal strengths and weakness of the curriculum. If the scoring shows that none of the students in a musical theatre BFA program can master a basic jazz dance step, then something is wrong with the amount or focus of the dance training. Item 1 in Appendix C is an example of a rubric used to convert audition performance to data-rich material that departments can use for evaluating program quality.

Similarly, disciplinary style sheets can provide direction to students as well as a rubric for evaluators in assessing student achievement. Item 2 in Appendix C is an example of a holistic rubric that serves double duty in assessing writing performance. Students get concrete feedback about what improvements should be made in their individual work; programs receive feedback about what areas require greater concentration if they strive for improved programmatic quality.

Many, if not most, of the challenges discussed above also influence interdisciplinary programs because so many of those programs have extensive humanities components. The diffuse nature of many interdisciplinary programs can make it impossible to identify what the students are learning at all, much less how they are learning it. Item 3 in Appendix C is an example of an effective assessment plan with student learning outcomes for an interdisciplinary program.

Once the initial set of learning outcomes has been established, faculty quickly discover that the process is iterative; further quality enhancements will begin to ripple out as the faculty revisit, tweak, alter, and again tweak the SLOs toward an even more ideal curriculum practice.

In the arts, the creative and expressive nature of the central activities poses special challenges. Outside the purview of psychology and the neurosciences, emotion is by nature difficult to either codify or quantify, but it is often precisely the emotional aspect of a theatrical show, musical performance, or art exhibition that stands out as a foremost indicator of quality. Outcomes that can capture these characteristics do well to keep excellence at the forefront (an example from art might be: "Convey a complex idea effectively through purely visual means"). Further, the arts pose a special problem in the capturing of data to be used for the assessment of learning outcomes, as so many artistic products are ephemeral. All theatrical performances have very limited runs and are difficult, if not impossible, to archive (even the best video recording will not capture the entire experience of live theatre), so as a capstone project it provides the perfect opportunity to judge the quality of many aspects of a theatre department's instruction and curriculum. But the assessment data must be gathered right then and there, during the performance, or it will be lost forever. Therefore quality assessment plans in the fine and performing arts will include mechanisms to capture and evaluate the performances and shows as they happen (some ways of doing this are American College Theater Festival [ACTF] adjudications in theatre, the scorings of musical competitions, and art show juries). Finally, good assessment practices call for multiple well-trained judgments in scoring situations that include both faculty and professionals (for example, the artistic director of a professional opera). This practice provides multiple perspectives and hence more reliable data.

Professional Standards

Professional performance and behavior standards can also play a significant role in determining program quality; they are a bedrock of disciplines like nursing, engineering, education, and clinical lab science, among others. However, the concept of professional standards may pose a particular threat to arts and humanities faculty.

Arts programs have diverging ideas about the prominence and purpose of professional activities. In some arts programs, the standards of performance and behavior may be explicit, formally taught, and practiced at many steps throughout the curriculum, culminating in refereed or juried exhibitions. If the institution or program has adopted the practice of regular evaluation of the behavior and efforts of the student during recitals, shows, or exhibitions, then it is rather easy to demonstrate quality, especially if the review involves professionals from outside the institution (for example, members of the local symphony orchestra or representatives from the American College Theater Festival [ACTF]).

Conversely, some programs (English, philosophy) will resist standards of professionalization as antithetical to the pursuit of the discipline; some faculty will appeal to the lack of any professional entity that even remotely reflects the program as in the case of interdisciplinary studies. Finally, even when faculty members accept such standards, they may be comfortable with implicit, rather than explicit, standards. Some students will no doubt pick up appropriate comportment by observing and modeling the faculty or more advanced students, but if the standards are not articulated and regularly reinforced, an infraction of professional expectations is increasingly likely. For example, a theatre performance can be blighted by, on the mild end of infraction, late or ill-prepared performers, or more egregiously, inappropriate alcohol use and even fisticuffs backstage. This outcome is especially problematic because lapses or violations of expected ethical behavior may occur in very public contexts that can shape community opinion and consequently adversely affect community opinion and support.

These hindrances can be overcome when the faculty, in concert with the students, pull together to establish standards of conduct. There are many examples of honor codes for student behavior in general across the collegiate and university landscape that might serve as models. For example, a recently adapted honor code for musical performance classes produced the following statement that the choral director read and discussed on the first day of class: "As Argonauts, we act with integrity and professionalism. As musicians, we work in harmony to achieve excellence." The statement amplified the basic honor standards of the university by clearly providing the perspective of the performing arts. In sum, indicators of quality to look for in this area are expressed codes of conduct, handbooks, opportunities for outside professionals to give feedback on student behaviors, and the like.

Recommendations for Assessment Planning

Faculty in undeveloped programs need to be persuaded that benchmarking can offer advantages that will get them moving in an assessment-friendly direction, including the following:

1. Although faculty can sometimes express legitimate confusion about the meaning of SLOs, they rarely have difficulty writing strong letters of reference for deserving students. Scrutinizing a handful of letters to harvest outstanding characteristics for some of the program's best graduates can often provide a starting point for this important conversation.
2. Emphasize what should be already recognized as existing effective practice. Find good rubrics already in play in the program and discuss ways that the practice, if not the rubric itself, might be more broadly applied to produce a helpful database for accountability purposes.
3. Concentrate on no more than a handful of SLOs that would be broadly accepted by the program faculty. Formally select outcomes that allow the program to showcase what the faculty do well. Determine how these outcomes can be embedded in existing curriculum, especially a capstone experience. Reassure hesitant faculty that positive assessment results can build a program's reputation.
4. Identify clear advantages that will result if faculty and students can build professional codes that clarify expectations. Faculty will improve efficiency by reducing the time they spend resolving disappointing student performances. Students end up with fewer surprises when it's time to request letters of recommendation if they clearly know their performance targets and when they achieve them.

PROGRAM RESOURCES AND ADMINISTRATIVE SUPPORT

Undeveloped programs that neglect accountability end up at heightened risk during economically troubled times. In this section, we look at the problems that stem from a lack of impact data when a program tries to secure adequate program resources and maintain administrative support.

THE SAGGING BOTTOM LINE

In general, programs in the arts and humanities seem to be more vulnerable to the resource fluctuations that beset the higher education landscape (a statement that is particularly poignant as these words are being written during the global economic breakdown of 2008–2009). Because nearly all of the programs in this area simply are not players in the ''grants and funding'' game, they are almost exclusively dependent on the funding that flows from the institution in general, with some assistance from endowments (particularly in the area of scholarships, in the case of the fine and performing arts). The arts specifically are resource intensive compared to the rest of the humanities landscape. Most history and philosophy faculty usually can be satisfied with adequate supplies of paper, library access, and a computer; however, the special natures of the fine and performing arts require much higher per-capita levels of funding.

Due to both the disparity in need and a general lack of external funding sources, the financial health of these areas can be additionally threatened by an unsympathetic stance toward the arts and humanities by the upper administration. To take one prime example, at many institutions the practice regarding equipment purchases or upgrades (beyond those that may occur at the moment of program start-up or the advent of a new hire) routinely follows the model that is quite successful in the hard and soft sciences: administrators will front the costs for such purchases in exchange for an agreement that later successful grant proposals funded by outside agencies will generate overhead. This method has little efficacy in a department of English or an interdisciplinary program, as those areas have no exceptional equipment needs. Consequently, the multiyear and multimillion-dollar research grants that provide so much support for hard and soft science activities simply don't exist to the same degree for arts and humanities programs.

On the other hand, the arts in particular enjoy greater access to gift resources because of local arts devotees in the community. However, even when there is considerable financial assistance for the arts, that funding may not flow exactly where and when it is needed. In general, most universities experience strong community interest in establishing scholarships that aid students pursuing the fine and performing arts, yet support for the maintenance of old facilities and the acquisition of updated equipment is harder to obtain unless it can be linked to a drive for flashy new performance spaces.

Questions about appropriate resource distribution for the arts and humanities abound and swiftly escalate during times of economic hardship. When times get tough, administrators under duress may demonstrate the unfortunate tendency to view the arts and humanities as extras or "fluff," which makes them quite vulnerable to budget cutbacks. When the stars align in this unfortunate configuration, arts programs are particularly vulnerable; those holding the purse strings can succumb to the temptation to do it on the cheap.

This regrettable approach has two major impacts on quality in arts programs in particular. First, the decision to withhold necessary equipment replacement or maintenance funding can quickly lead to major safety issues. For example, a chop saw for picture frames will work just fine if the blade guard is damaged or removed, but the danger factor for the student operating the saw increases exponentially. Second, even if programs decide to mount lean productions or projects regularly to contain costs, that decision greatly diminishes the educational preparation for the students. Music students, for example, should have access to professional-level instruments, such as very costly Steinway grand pianos, to develop their talent to a professional level. Similarly, a play may be mounted with contemporary clothing on a minimalist set and still provide good training for the actors on stage, but a constant diet of such unadorned offerings appreciably degrades the training of the technical theatre students who need to tackle the challenge of attempting a Broadway-level extravaganza to develop their talents and skills fully.

THE WOBBLY COMMITMENT

If you are in the theatre department, perhaps the most discouraging words you can hear from the provost are "I don't do plays." Special programs may have a particularly difficult time engaging firm commitments from administrators who don't demonstrate any affinity for those disciplines. An undeveloped program that doesn't generate a good defense through solid accountability data simply has no way to develop traction in the minds of those who will determine the funding and the fate of the program. Demonstrating the necessity of a program by documenting its educational impact is the only way to ensure it gets both the attention and the crucial resources it needs.

RECOMMENDATIONS FOR RESOURCES AND SUPPORT

In the end, durable administrative support and predictable funding are bottom-line indicators of quality for arts and humanities programs. How can undeveloped programs begin to organize their energies to secure more stable working conditions?

1. Program advocates need to make the case for a continuous stream of funding for maintenance and necessary equipment upgrades and replacement, along with reasonable increases in resources that match increases in the student population. Comparisons to comparable programs at peer institutions, especially when the comparison finds the home institution wanting, can sometimes be more persuasive than an undocumented complaint about funding shortages. Charts and graphs may be able to drive home the point more efficiently than long-winded texts.
2. Program advocates should orchestrate at least an annual visit with key decision makers responsible for resource decisions. The meetings should be replete with data that substantiate any new requests for resources.

3. Special invitations to attend events (for example, opening night for a play, Women's Studies Symposium day, an art gallery reception) remind administrators about the public relations contributions special programs can make, regardless of whether the dean or provost is able to attend. Similarly, student-written notes of appreciation for decisions that had a positive impact on program quality can foster strong positive feelings even among jaded administrators.

Faculty Characteristics and Program Climate

Undeveloped programs run a particular risk in allowing standards of faculty performance to either evolve willy-nilly or not be established at all. In such circumstances, program climate will suffer. Crucial decisions may be made based on faculty charisma rather than on any actual data. When faculty cannot trust that their own performances will be equitably reviewed, the program climate may exacerbate normal tensions and generate turmoil down to the level that even students will perceive. Investing time in improved accountability in this arena can have far-reaching, positive impacts.

How High Is the Bar?

Determining what type or number of achievements demonstrate solid quality in the faculty members in special programs is a bit more vexing and open to variation than in most traditional disciplines. English, history, and philosophy, for example, rely on the time-honored standards of monograph, book, or refereed journal article production and regional or national presentations at professional meetings. But in the arts, reliance on the old bromide of "publish or perish" may fail to engage the core mission of those areas.

In this section, we will emphasize how standards can be developed in the arts, although the principles probably apply to other specialties. In the arts, where the desirable end product is the production of a play, performing in a concert, or creating sculpture, the simplistic approach of counting the number of such activities and proclaiming "Quality!" when the total reaches certain threshold seems untenable. That approach neatly sidesteps the central issue of what constitutes quality, particularly when comparisons across different types or specialties of artistic endeavor may be involved.

Venue quickly becomes a determining factor; most people would recognize that there is a wide gulf between an organ recital at a local church and an appearance as a guest soloist with a major symphony. In art, the same principle applies, as it easier for a faculty member to exhibit at a local annual art show than to have a piece placed in an exhibition at the Art Institute of Chicago. Even though those distinctions seem to be clear-cut, the nature of faculty activity in theatre complicates the issue significantly. Given that nearly all theatre productions require at a minimum a six-week rehearsal schedule (and a much longer production and planning schedule), it can be extremely difficult, if not impossible, for theatre faculty to have access to nonlocal venues (aside from summer recess) because of regular teaching obligations in the academic year.

Clearly drawn and well-articulated benchmarks that speak to those distinctions therefore are themselves bedrock indicators of a quality climate for arts faculty. Item 4 in Appendix C is an example of tenure, promotion, and evaluation language that establishes performance benchmarks. Guidelines must be capacious as well as lucid to accommodate innovation. In the hard sciences especially, breakthrough and discovery are well-recognized and celebrated indicators of preeminence, but in the arts, edginess in technique or content can lead directly to very unpleasant controversy, and a department need not hire or enroll a Robert Mapplethorpe to get embroiled in one.

Community supporters are likely to view college or university arts programs as significantly enriching the quality of life in the community. At the most basic level, attendance data, whether drawn from ticket sales or head counts (as might be needed for, say, an art show opening), reflect the community's value of what is happening; if relatively few community members show up for a University Singers recital but pack the local house for a choral society performance (or vice versa), then that says something about the music department's reputation. Beyond such a crass measure, there should be a continuum of partnerships and interactions that bind the community to the institution, and these can take many forms. At the most formal, there could be extensive agreements that articulate the parameters of partnerships between the institution and local professional companies, such as agreements between the institution and the symphony that spell out the terms of use of rehearsal space or instruments. Moving down the scale, faculty participation on local arts boards should be prevalent and noticeable (the chair of studio art serving on the board of the art museum, for example), as well as mutual assistance pacts that permit the pooling or sharing of costumes, sets, or properties as appropriate. Visibility alone fosters trust and respect (not to mention a potential increase in the recruitment of talented students); therefore the fine and performing arts faculty should at the least be present for local high school and community shows and performances. When all of those activities are consciously and continuously geared toward the end of enhancing educational opportunities for the students at the institution, the result will most likely be community engagement and support that will lead to positive capital campaigns.

The Contribution of Climate

Faculty in undeveloped programs do not typically recognize the value of creating a climate conducive to learning. There may be longstanding tensions, evidenced by corridors of closed doors and whispered innuendo. The individuals the department has recruited may see little value in actively working on palpably positive working conditions.

Recommendations for Climate and Standards

1. The struggle to produce a set of clearly articulated guidelines can be as challenging as the struggle to develop a reliable assessment plan for the curriculum, but will be worth the effort in the long run. If nothing else, evaluation guidelines that integrate both venue estimation and professional external review (that is, juried performances or shows) can go a long way toward countering diva tendencies.

2. Embedding data collection in response to a performance (for example, a survey tucked into a program, an e-mail to season ticket holders) may serve to engage community members as partners in improving program quality.
3. A prominently posted bulletin board that articulates the community relationships developed by the program can serve as a reminder of this crucial obligation and provide readily available evidence of community impact.

STUDENT DEVELOPMENT

In a normal university context, the four years (or more) of a student's college life will unfold and changes will transpire that can be attributed to the talented intervention of faculty. However, undeveloped programs often take student development for granted. In this section we address three dimensions that can have a significant impact on quality of student development: optimizing high-impact opportunities, the role of close mentoring, and the deleterious effects of elitism.

HIGH-IMPACT OPPORTUNITIES

The most fundamental and effective indicator of a program designed to enhance student development in the arts, humanities, and interdisciplinary programs is the presence of high-impact activities. Kuh (2008) described the beneficial effects of high-impact activities on student satisfaction and retention. Although many readers associate undergraduate research with the recent nationwide effort to place undergraduate students alongside the faculty and graduate students doing significant research in the hard science labs, undergraduate research options capture only a portion of the practices that produce enriched experiences for students. One could make the argument that the senior-level capstone projects and performances that have long held sway in the arts are the forerunners of the undergraduate research experiences so prevalent in today's science departments. The arts have always acknowledged what many now seem to be just discovering, thanks to the now widespread reliance on (the new) Bloom's learning hierarchy (Anderson et al., 2000): namely, that creation reflects the highest level of mastery and learning.

Quality programs in the arts and interdisciplinary studies have long cherished the senior capstone project as the culmination of the student's learning experience. There is probably no truer creative experience than the challenge of putting together a BFA exit show or designing the set for, say, a production of Moliere's *The Miser.* Although capstone projects have not been a central component of the curriculum in the humanities traditionally, faculty recognize the value of a capstone project or senior thesis as providing a vehicle for quick and accurate measurement of the coherence and quality of the curriculum.

Close Mentoring

Programs in the arts, humanities, or interdisciplinary studies may foster relationships between the faculty and students that are probably closer than those found in most academic disciplines. Consequently, boundary issues may become a predictable source of potential danger. When students are in their seats and the teacher is up front, a respectful distance naturally occurs. However, when both student and teacher are crowded around the pottery wheel, a chumminess can ensue that can create confusion in the teacher-student relationship. In the worst-case scenario, the student-teacher rapport devolves into a star-groupie dynamic sometimes followed by an inappropriate romantic entanglement. In the former case, legitimate student learning can be diminished in service to an overblown faculty ego. In the latter case, the adverse impact and accusation of sexual harassment can spread beyond the partners to their families and the student's classmates. Administrators recommend following the dictum ''Be friendly, but not familiar'' to create the right distance to foster learning.

The Problem of Elitism

A related concern involves the unfortunate tendency of many faculty to lapse into elitism. In the arts, that inclination can be manifested in the vacuous argument that artists are born, not made. Although there is no doubt a great deal of truth in the observation that some are born with talent and some without, if the faculty are foolish enough to adopt that stance stridently, they are essentially arguing themselves out of a job. If all artists are born, why should we invest in the resources needed to teach art? This stance may thinly disguise an underlying resistance to assessment; it runs counter to the fundamental assumption that a coherent curricular design will promote developmental progress even in those of limited talents. This approach may also mask a more insidious elitism in which some faculty will accept only the best and most talented into their inner circle. Both stances need to be countered vigilantly. Even the best and most talented need to have their skills honed and their horizons broadened through guidance and practice. All endeavors in the academy have at their roots an intellectual component, but a more profound and helpful intellectual outcome might be humility regarding how much is yet to be learned. An elitist approach will not foster the best learning conditions for any apprentice in the arts, humanities, or interdisciplinary studies.

RECOMMENDATIONS FOR STUDENT DEVELOPMENT

1. Programs should monitor student experience to find out which features of the program truly produce high impact. Focus groups of randomly selected students may be able to provide helpful feedback about awareness of opportunities as well as perceptions of obstacles, inclusiveness, and potential favoritism problems.
2. Quality programs will not only have clearly articulated sexual harassment policies, but also actively counsel and work against the creation of too-close mentor-protégé relationships.
3. Challenge behavior that creates artificial divides within the learning community. Students who are imbued with their own sense of specialness potentially end up with baggage that can interfere with achieving the professional outcomes they seek. Faculty should be evenhanded in their treatment, to bring out the collective best performance in their students.

CONCLUSION

The effort to move faculty from resisting assessment activity to accepting and even embracing assessment is not for the weak of spirit. However, the traction that assessment has generated means that no matter how intense the wishing or how prolonged the waiting, assessment will not go away. Instead, it is time for faculty who have been disengaged to recognize assessment for what it offers: a set of tools that can provide the best array of strategies to assist the program to achieve a variety of honorable ends, most notably gains in student learning and achievement. Whether benchmarking transpires to lay claim to distinction, to avoid going on the program chopping block, or any goal in between, benchmarking practice offers new opportunities for faculty to revitalize their work.

Chapter Eleven

Special Issues in Benchmarking in the Natural Sciences

Natural science and assessment have a lot in common. Both involve problem-solving processes, rely on measurement, and thrive on discovery. Both enterprises are founded on firm theoretical bases. In the case of natural science, the specific disciplines provide the foundation. In the case of assessment, pedagogical theory provides the infrastructure. Academic programs embark on assessment with the ultimate goal of improving learning experiences for students. In a similar vein, scientific knowledge is often applied to improve human health and well-being or to solve problems.

In many ways, then, it seems that there would be a natural fit between science programs and assessment activities. Both enterprises center on the collection of evidence to support claims and to advance understanding. However, despite these similarities, natural science programs and assessment practices may not always happily coexist on campuses. One possible reason is that, on many campuses, assessment has long been considered the purview of the administration, something not to be embraced by scholars in search of new and exciting advances in science. Scientific research is about discovery. Discovery is a process that engages critical thinkers and will undoubtedly bring students into the academy. Why should scientists consider diluting their scholarly efforts with activities that do not directly contribute to discovery of knowledge? Is it not enough to engage students in the discovery process? Student involvement is at the heart of learning and is evidence of quality undergraduate education.

In some respects, the argument that engagement of students in the scientific enterprise is evidence enough of student learning is correct. Student engagement is one component of a quality undergraduate program. However, single achievements, ergo an outstanding student paper, provide only preliminary evidence of discovery. True scientific discoveries rely on an accumulation of evidence; therefore, to assess student learning fully, a larger set of indicators of program success is necessary. A host of interrelated factors contribute to student achievement or learning. Thus, evidence must be garnered from a broad set of quality indicators (for example, curriculum, resources). Gathering evidence of learning in ways that parallel the methods used in the natural sciences is difficult because measuring knowledge is latent and evidence is indirect. Chemists, biologists, and physicists rely on clear empirical measures (for example, number of molecules), using techniques that have been well validated in the discipline. Evidence of learning cannot be measured as directly, but latent measures do provide some insight into the efficacy of a program.

In this chapter we revisit several dimensions of program quality that we discussed in Chapter Ten (curriculum, assessment and student learning outcomes, program resources and administrative support, faculty characteristics and climate, and student development). This time, we examine these dimensions from the perspective of natural science programs. Programs in science, technology, engineering, and mathematics (STEM) face specific challenges, such as the need for expensive laboratory equipment, that set them apart from other programs that are not as resource intensive. Despite these challenges, there are common principles that can be used to distinguish outstanding programs. Curriculum in the sciences is highly susceptible to pressures from limited fiscal and space resources, so we consider the threats that fiscal constraints may impose on curricular dimensions in the sciences. We also consider the challenges of assessing student learning outcomes in the scientific domain. We conclude by offering guidance on how the climate is influential in shaping the unique challenges facing faculty in the sciences.

CURRICULUM DEVELOPMENT

The challenges of creating a well-designed curriculum in the natural sciences differ from those in the social sciences and humanities. For one thing, the method for validating knowledge in the natural sciences is more structured than is the case for some other disciplines (Donald, 1995, 2002). Not only are the methods of investigation well prescribed, but so too are the courses that are considered to be the foundations of the discipline. For example, an undergraduate program in chemistry must offer a specific set of courses in order for it to be approved by the American Chemical Society (ACS, 2009). When evaluating the curriculum of a chemistry department, a distinguished program would offer core courses following a well-defined sequence specified by ACS. Chemistry, as a discipline, is highly prescriptive in its core curriculum requirements. Although curricula in biology and physics (American Association of Physics Teachers, 2002, 2005) are slightly less fixed, the natural sciences, as a whole, require basic coursework in chemistry, biology, mathematics, and often statistics. This lack of degrees of freedom in terms of curriculum design in STEM disciplines means that opportunities for curricular diversity are limited (Huber, 2006). A distinguished program in the natural sciences must balance innovative courses with simultaneously offering the essential courses required in the discipline.

CHALLENGES EXPLICIT TO STEM

The natural sciences may also face challenges in trying to address issues that are not regarded as central to the core knowledge of the discipline (for example, ethics, cultural diversity, international perspectives). How should programs in the natural sciences be evaluated relative to addressing ethics in the curriculum? A distinguished program will be innovative. For instance, the biological sciences may address ethical issues by systematically incorporating ethical dilemmas into courses at different points in the curriculum, or students may take a course in bioethics (see Johansen & Harris, 2000; Bryant & Baggott la Velle, 2003). Students might be challenged to consider the ethical dilemmas associated with nonhuman animal research, or chemistry students might learn about conflicts of interest that may be created when pharmaceutical companies fund drug research. Advanced coursework may focus on ethical decision making that students may face as they enter the workforce or go on to graduate work.

A particular challenge for STEM disciplines is the recruitment of a diverse student body. The curriculum for scientific disciplines necessarily contains a large complement of mathematics and laboratory courses and the pipeline of diverse students is often limited because young women and students of color have opted out of the prerequisite courses for science, math, and engineering. Although fully capable of managing these courses, women are frequently socialized in ways that reduce their interest in math and science. Women have made significant gains in many of the sciences; however, women remain underrepresented in computer science and engineering (National Science Foundation, 2006). Similarly, students of color are also underrepresented and often opt not to pursue science and math—in part because role models are limited.

The STEM disciplines are rife with opportunities to infuse service learning systematically into the curriculum. Serving the local community through undergraduate research may be attractive for chemists, geographers, physicists, and biologists. Although the STEM disciplines are not typically considered as primary players in the service learning movement, they are particularly well positioned to respond to community needs. The Building Engineering and Science Talent (BEST) program targets minority applicants for entry into scientific disciplines; in particular, they recommend new and innovative strategies, such as enriched learning experiences, or internships, as a mechanism for attracting minority students (National Academies of Sciences, 2007). Innovative programs such as the Canisius College community health-based internship program are successful in attracting minority students to research in the sciences and in meeting community needs through this service learning program (Dehn, 2009). The American Association for Higher Education (AAHE) has produced discipline-specific handbooks for service learning in several science disciplines, including biology (Brubaker & Ostroff, 2006), engineering (Tsang, 2000), and environmental studies (Ward, 2006).

Recommendations for Curriculum Development

STEM disciplines face unique challenges in that the epistemology is pragmatic, well structured, and more limited in content than the arts and humanities (Donald, 2002). Therefore curricular offerings are more restricted, and the systematic structure of the curriculum may serve as a distinguishing factor for a program. Because the natural sciences derive from a more prototypical approach, there are fewer opportunities to offer coursework in ethics, diversity, or international dimensions. Programs that are distinguished in the curricular dimension may simply be more structured than programs in the humanities. Exceptional programs retain the necessary rigor of the discipline, yet provide multiple points of access to ensure a diversity of students.

Departments that are underdeveloped will want to consider the following recommendations for moving the curriculum forward:

1. Carefully review curriculum recommendations promulgated by disciplinary associations and adopt the recommendations to the extent possible. Programs should also consider innovative offerings that are consistent with the mission of both the department and institution.
2. Because the STEM disciplines face challenges with recruiting a diversity of students, departments should consider developing curriculum that attracts a diversity of students to the major. For example, the curriculum should ensure that contributions to the discipline from women and people of color receive appropriate attention.

Student Learning Outcomes and Assessment

Faculty in STEM disciplines rigorously evaluate student learning through traditional assessment measures (that is, exams, problem sets) and laboratory experiences (including research reports), yet assessment of student learning outcomes is sometimes conducted at the individual course level with little attention to a broader assessment plan. Distinguished programs embrace a broad assessment plan that provides clear evidence of student learning across the curriculum. In this section we recommend capitalizing on the assessment practices that are common in STEM disciplines and building on these practices to develop a coherent assessment plan.

Authentic Assessment

Authentic assessments use real-world tasks to measure student learning (Halonen, Bosack, Clay, & McCarthy, 2003). One of the many advantages of authentic assessment is that it allows for an evaluation of a set of skills and higher cognitive level skills rather than just discrete components of knowledge (Wiggins, 1990). STEM disciplines have long used authentic assessments to measure student learning. For example, biology students may be required to identify the primary structures of a cell in a general biology lab exam, or a chemistry student may be required to produce a chemical reaction. In both instances students are performing a task that is integral to the discipline, and the task reflects competency or learning. Both activities could culminate in conventional reports that simulate the real work of scientists. As such, the natural sciences have some advantages in the rich opportunities available for students to produce science in authentic assessments.

Professional Standards

Some STEM disciplines provide specific curricular guidance for core courses that the major comprises. The American Chemical Society (ACS), through its program approval process, offers specific suggestions for courses. ACS also publishes the entry-level text used by all students majoring in chemistry. The explicit requirements related to space concerns in ACS can often be used by department chairs to lobby successfully for remodeling or equipment funding. Similarly, the Accreditation Board for Engineering and Technology (ABET) lays out explicit expectations for what constitutes professional preparation.

The American Chemical Society (ACS Committee on Professional Training, 2008), in its program approval process, specifies content that must be included in courses for an undergraduate degree in chemistry. ACS goes further to identify student skills (such as problem solving, literacy, communication, safety, team skills, ethics) or learning outcomes that must be developed in programs that are approved by the society. The approval mechanism available to chemistry programs provides departments with useful guidance for creating student learning outcomes. Biology programs require specific courses and are therefore less specific in identifying student learning outcomes (National Association of Biology Teachers, 2009). STEM disciplines vary in the amount of explicit guidance provided for student learning outcomes, and very few disciplines offer an approval or accreditation process that validates the undergraduate program.

Recommendations for Student Learning Outcomes and Assessment

Although STEM disciplines are at the forefront of authentic assessment of student learning outcomes, results may not be used to inform departmental practice. Measuring student performance in individual courses is important. Faculty can assess whether students have acquired the necessary skills to understand scientific taxonomies, processes, and theories. We offer the following suggestions to enhance the department's reliance on and benefit from the use of outcome assessments:

1. Convene departmental conversations about what skills sets the curriculum should foster. One important source of the outcomes deemed most critical by the department is comparing letters of recommendation for graduates. Typically, recommenders focus on the skills and abilities demonstrated by the best students in these tributes. The collected observations can serve as the foundation of what should be accomplished by students as a result of training in the program.
2. Once the department identifies the central outcomes, students will benefit from exposure to the ideas. Outcomes should be printed on informational brochures, displayed in the website, and featured in the department syllabi. Regular exposure will assist students in developing their metacognitive skills.

3. Authentic assessment, particularly with the large number of undergraduate research opportunities, offers the potential for evaluating the broader undergraduate experience in the discipline. Distinguished programs in the sciences will systematically incorporate authentic assessment results into the planning and refinement of the curriculum.

Program Resources and Administrative Support

STEM disciplines are faced with a double-edged sword when it comes to program resources. On the one hand, laboratories, supplies, and equipment are expensive but necessary requirements for the natural sciences. On the other hand, available funding sources, beyond the resources typically provided by the host institution, are more plentiful. National funding agencies, corporate foundations, and private donors offer multiple opportunities for funding. Programs in the STEM disciplines pride themselves on their ability to recruit and use tangible resources. Program quality then is not just evaluating the quality of resources (for example, laboratories and equipment). Distinguished programs clearly exceed minimal standards for laboratories and supplies. They achieve these standards through planning for efficient use of resources and tapping into available funding streams. In this section we provide recommendations for how STEM programs can demonstrate areas of distinction based on planning for physical resources derived from multiple revenue streams.

Physical Resources

Science and engineering are particularly susceptible to financial exigency factors as these disciplines require a significant investment in laboratory space and highly specialized equipment. For example, increasingly sophisticated microscopes in biology and similar scanning devices in chemistry and physics render basic equipment obsolete in a relatively short span of time. The STEM disciplines must access multiple revenue streams to meet the minimal standards for the discipline. Programs that wish to be characterized as distinguished must not only remain current with regard to obtaining equipment but also maintain a basic infrastructure to house the equipment and secure funds for ongoing maintenance needs of complex technologies. A truly exceptional program engages in planning that includes a systematic set of steps for accessing external funding as well as thinking about the long-range needs related to securing targeted equipment.

Although programs need to obtain external funding to be distinguished, funding streams for the sciences are commensurate with the needs of the discipline. The National Science Foundation provides significant opportunities for funding of equipment, including many new opportunities designed to address the needs of smaller undergraduate programs under the REU program. Additional sources of funding are typically available through partnership efforts with private industry (for example, pharmaceuticals, agriculture, chemical companies). Distinguished science programs nourish relationships with local science-based firms, as they may be able to realize donations of cast-off equipment that will still meet academic needs. The sciences can benefit beyond mere financial support when leveraging outside funding. Partnerships can generate positive publicity for both the company and the program.

Recommendations for Physical Resources and Funding

Distinguished programs must engage in strategic planning to anticipate the rapid advances of science and technology. It is essential that STEM disciplines remain current with the technology of the discipline. Therefore, departments must be poised to take advantage of any opportunities to expand laboratories and research space.

1. Project Kaleidoscope (PKAL) provides excellent guidance on how to create spaces that serve the institutional mission and the needs of students and that allow departments to remain current with contemporary science (PKAL, 2008b). Departments only rarely have the opportunity to design new space for their programs, so we recommend that any redesign of space be conducted using the resources provided by PKAL. Departments must also balance the need for research space with that of providing space for students to congregate.

2. Although opportunities to secure brand-new space are quite rare, occasionally science units may find themselves with a funding opportunity that calls for maximum creativity. Requesting substantially more space than currently required will facilitate room for growth. If science buildings have a life-span of thirty to forty years, then anticipated enrollments must be factored into any building proposal.
3. Department chairs need to maintain a close relationship with campus development officials. Chairs should always maintain a current list of equipment that will enhance their work. University donors can suddenly appear on the scene, looking for the right kind of project to underwrite. When development officials feel pressed to find the right project, the well-prepared chair who has already established a relationship will come to mind more quickly.
4. Interdisciplinary requests for big-ticket equipment can sometimes succeed where individual department requests fail. Typically, deans or other budget gatekeepers view collaborative requests as a way to discharge obligations for funding support efficiently while simultaneously supporting conversations that reduce rigid boundaries between disciplines.

FACULTY CHARACTERISTICS AND PROGRAM CLIMATE

The intensive emphasis on research in the STEM disciplines creates a culture that is highly competitive and potentially contentious. Agencies are concerned with funding research that will make a significant contribution to the advancement of science. Therefore institutions are attentive to their respective ranking or tier in their pursuit of external funding. Some institutions are in the process of elevating the visibility of their institution, and in so doing they create faculty positions that will attract high-profile researchers. On the one hand, a high-profile researcher gives the department visibility that will increase the likelihood of external funding. However, bringing a high-profile researcher into a department may create inequities where resources for other colleagues are concerned.

Regardless of whether a department resides in the upper tier of research intensive programs, the vast majority of faculty in the sciences are researchers and research mentors. There are many ways of engaging students in research. In some departments faculty independently recruit students to participate in their labs. Alternatively, some departments pool the available student researchers and attempt to create equity in their assignments across faculty. Each of these models has advantages and disadvantages. However, it is essential that the department engage in some attempt to distribute resources and students equitably.

Faculty Recruitment

In addition to recruiting a diverse group of students, recruiting diverse faculty is a challenge for programs in the STEM disciplines. Although this goal is both difficult and essential, departments must work toward recruiting and maintaining diversity in faculty ranks. There are very few resources addressing diversity of faculty in the STEM disciplines; however, the Disciplinary Society and Education Alliance (DSEA, 2009) is making progress in addressing this critical issue. Capitalizing on prior work of Project Kaleidoscope, the collaborative is identifying successful practices for recruiting and retaining diverse faculty.

Recent legal rulings have complicated the process of recruiting diversity in both faculty and student ranks. The American Association for the Advancement of Science (AAAS), in its publication *Standing Our Ground*, provides guidance for addressing the complicated issues of recruitment of a diverse student body (Malcom, Chubin, & Jesse, 2004). The availability of role models and mentors is of paramount importance. Yet programs may well have to adapt, because such individuals are in short supply.

Workload calculations in the STEM disciplines can be particularly problematic. With increasing financial pressures to increase student access, universities must examine all expenditures. Traditionally, faculty load in the STEM disciplines has been calculated to account for the additional time associated with laboratory courses; however, the metric varies across programs. For example, a three-hour lab may count as only one hour toward faculty load, as the nature of the teaching is more supervisory than in a non-lab-based classroom. On other campuses, faculty members may get the full contact hour credit for conducting their labs. Departments in the STEM disciplines may need to be prepared to justify the workload associated with undergraduate laboratories and undergraduate research supervision particularly in challenging economic times.

RECOMMENDATIONS FOR FACULTY CHARACTERISTICS AND PROGRAM CLIMATE

Research is critical to the STEM disciplines, and funding streams are essential for advancing programs. Therefore it is essential that departments are united in their mission and vision. A strong sense of community will enable departments to engage in open communication that will promote healthy growth. Here are a few more suggestions:

1. Departments need to audit the interests and capabilities of faculty members to ensure that the broad range of work can be done by people operating from their strengths. For example, if a department wishes to enhance its visibility by hiring a high-profile researcher, then a candid discussion of the advantages and disadvantages of such actions should be undertaken early in the process. Other faculty members may be needed to take up the slack (for example, advising, orientation duties, and committee service) to allow the high-profile researcher to make the contributions that will enhance the department's visibility without sacrificing essential duties at the university.
2. A strong department will actively build a diverse community by encouraging faculty members who differ in seniority, ethnic background, gender, and specialization. A program that has rich membership can become even richer by fostering research collaborations among its members as well as reaching out to other related disciplines on campus.
3. Programs that are small should consider developing depth in particular areas of a science rather than giving in to the impulse to keep adding faculty with new specializations. By concentrating on people with related interests, costs can be

contained and synergies among faculty can lead to enhanced grant pursuits.

Student Development

Earlier we discussed theories of student development and the importance of cocurricular experiences in the intellectual development of students. Students majoring in STEM disciplines can benefit from the larger student affairs experiences. However, the activities that distinguish students in STEM are related to intense research experiences that extend for long periods in a laboratory setting. Distinguished departments are particularly sensitive to the rigors of intensive work in laboratories, and they ensure that students are provided with appropriate support. For example, in addition to ensuring the basic safety of students who may enter laboratories unusually late during off hours, departments provide students with comfortable working conditions (for example, refrigerators and collaboration space) that encourage a sense of community.

Undergraduate Research

The STEM disciplines uniformly provide students with undergraduate research experiences (see Chapter Six). Traditionally, some faculty conduct research during summer sessions, when laboratories are more available and students can work intensively on a single project. However, for students to participate in these experiences, programs must provide students with stipends that allow them to work consistently on a project. Funding streams for student support can be secured by successful grant capture through agencies and corporations.

As challenging as research can be for students, the intensive experience can also give them an opportunity to build strong professional relationships (see Seymour, Hunter, Laursen, & Deantoni, 2004). An intensive research experience is a mechanism for building community. Undergraduate research experiences provide exactly the type of cocurricular opportunities that allow students to develop a sense of autonomy, competency, and cognitive complexity. Outstanding programs offer innovative opportunities for students to develop a breadth of skills in the undergraduate research experience.

For example, Bradley University in Peoria, Illinois, offers an innovative program that engages undergraduates as leaders for a research team (Morris, McConnaughay, & Wolffe, 2009). Through Research Experiences for Undergraduates (REU) funding, a grant competition offered by the National Science Foundation, the university created a program to help educators engage in authentic science or undergraduate research during a summer research program.

Although externally funded, high-profile undergraduate research programs are the ideal for programs that wish to distinguish themselves, equally creative means for compelling undergraduate research experiences are also viable. For example, biologists may wish to provide students with an integrated research experience (for example, botany, invertebrate zoology, ichthyology). Ensign (in a personal communication October 28, 2009) and colleagues offer an inquiry-based field experience in which students engage in study of the related biological areas both in the lab and during weekend outings. The Council on Undergraduate Research (CUR) provides numerous resources for faculty interesting in incorporating undergraduate research experiences in their courses and curricula.

Recommendations for Student Development

Distinguished programs in the STEM disciplines must attend to the ancillary support of students in the research enterprise. They must ensure that students have the necessary financial, personal, and intellectual support to engage in undergraduate research experiences. Innovative approaches to undergraduate research experiences will advance the development of students in all areas.

1. We recommend that programs pursue mission-consistent funding (such as REU funds) to advance undergraduate research opportunities. Such approaches provide for in-depth research experiences that can facilitate student identification with the role of the scientist.
2. Faculty may need professional development experiences (for example, CUR, Project Kaleidoscope) to enhance the undergraduate research experience. These national movements regularly feature best practices related to ways to recruit and engage student participation.

3. Departments may need to make special steps to make the discipline inviting to underrepresented groups. Special mentoring programs or projects that highlight contributions of individuals with whom students can readily identify as role models may help produce a welcoming atmosphere.
4. Departments need to create welcoming spaces that encourage collaboration and nurture the intellectual development of all students. Setting aside dedicated space for students signals the department's interest in having students engaged in departmental activities.

Conclusions

Programs in the sciences pose particular problems in achieving distinction. STEM programs generally attract fewer students while simultaneously requiring a larger number of resources to meet the minimum requirement for delivering the curriculum. Because the STEM disciplines are generally considered more intellectually challenging, recruitment of students into the disciplines is difficult, and achieving diversity among both students and faculty is particularly challenging. As departments engage in self-evaluation, they will need to consider innovative approaches for balancing the unique financial challenges of recruiting students and delivering a rigorous curriculum.

Despite the difficulties, the sciences also have some unique advantages in the quest for distinction. Safety issues dictate that space and equipment needs in the sciences often must take priority over the funding of other discipline requests. The sciences are often the most successful in getting funding for building construction or renovation. Many disciplinary societies offer explicit guidelines on the nature of preparation at the undergraduate level. The hands-on nature of training in the sciences offers a perfect vehicle for authentic assessment. The outcome of successful scientific endeavors makes good copy; accordingly, science programs are well positioned to generate positive publicity about the nature of their training to enhance the reputation. Finally, high-quality science endeavors are supported by the Council of Undergraduate Research and Project Kaleidoscope, which can provide ongoing support for departments striving to be the best.

CHAPTER TWELVE

CONDUCTING A SELF-STUDY

Colleges and universities conduct program reviews for a variety of reasons. Some institutions follow a regular schedule, requiring departments and programs to undertake a review at some specified interval (such as every five years). Reviews also can be part of an accreditation process. In contrast, the department or program itself may initiate a review in response to particular questions or circumstances, or it can be mandated by an administration to address perceived problems or inequities. In any case, program reviews provide the perfect context to demonstrate the value of quality benchmarks in the evaluation of undergraduate education.

This chapter ties together the frameworks presented in the earlier chapters by providing concrete guidance on effectively conducting an internal program review (self-study) and inviting and hosting an external reviewer or team. We also address applications of this model to small departments and community college divisions. We provide recommended timelines and suggest what information should appear in evaluation reports. Guiding questions conclude the chapter.

WHY DO A PROGRAM REVIEW?

Whether a department is housed at a college or a university, a two-year school or a four-year school, all programs benefit from regular review (Kells, 1980; Shavelson & Huang, 2003). Higher education's recent focus on assessment encourages ongoing, internal program review, coupled with periodic visits by external experts. To paraphrase the poet Robert Burns, program reviews help us to see ourselves through the eyes of outside experts—warts and all. Where undergraduate education is concerned, a program review can help faculty and administrators determine whether the curriculum and facilities achieve their expressed expectations and goals and those of current and prospective students.

What other reasons promote program reviews?

External reviews necessitate internal reviews. Before asking for outside guidance, program members need to undertake a careful examination about what is already happening in the program in the spirit of *know thyself.* As argued throughout this book, such insider benchmarking can identify distinguished or effective areas as well as those needing attention.

Program reviews track change. A solid program review will point to areas of growth, decline, and opportunity. The responsibilities of teaching, advising, and scholarship rarely allow the members of any department or program to evaluate objectively the broad educational experience that they are giving to undergraduates; it's tough to see the larger academic forest for all those tress.

Program reviews promote future planning and development. Departments and programs must not become static settings or they risk becoming intellectually stale. Periodic reviews encourage program leaders and members to be aspirational and sometimes entrepreneurial; that is, to seek new ways to improve the undergraduate education students receive.

Program reviews anticipate accountability pressures constructively. Instead of being put on the defensive by being asked to demonstrate whether a program is achieving its touted goals, why not take a proactive rather than a reactive stance? Learn about a program's strengths and weaknesses so that the latter can be dealt with constructively on the inside before pressures mandate required change from the outside.

Program reviews rely on formative assessment, not summative assessment. Quality program reviews shift personnel efforts for the future. The assessment of teaching and learning should be used to improve the efforts of teacher-scholars in a program, not selectively reward or punish those activities. Individuals will be more open to suggestions and to make improvements to the program if a formative rather than a summative approach is used (see Black, Harrison, Lee, Marshall, & Wiliam, 2003; Butler & Winnie, 1995; Sadler, 1998).

Program reviews foster collegiality, community, and camaraderie. Departments and programs are busy places during the academic year. So much must be done on semester or quarterly timetables that colleagues have precious little time to talk to one another about pedagogy, let alone program issues. A program review encourages colleagues to reflect on and to appreciate the community they have crafted and maintain; it can motivate them to make changes for the greater good of the program and the wider institution.

Where to Begin?

To begin a program review, revisit the department or program's mission statement and goals for student learning within the existing undergraduate curriculum. Presumably, the faculty in the program have previously discussed and agreed upon this set of goals (for example, a list indicating what content and skill sets a history major graduating from the department should have after completing the curriculum). If not, then a meeting should be convened where colleagues can identify, discuss, and then agree upon the program's main goals. As Walvoord (2004) notes, the focus must be on the sorts of skills, information, and habits of mind that students acquire during their time in the program and not on any actions or activities performed by the program itself. Consequently, learning goals should be stated concretely; as, for instance, "Based on their learning experiences in this program, students will develop skills, including . . . " or "After completing this nine-course major, students will be able to . . . " Learning goals are represented in the program curriculum but they are not the curriculum per se. Thus they should not be presented as lists of courses that are completed in a particular order; however, careful consideration of the desired skill sets may influence course sequence decisions. Faculty will benefit from designing courses developmentally to achieve the outcomes that validate their efforts (see Chapter Four).

WRITING A SELF-STUDY

The most important part of any self-study is producing a document that summarizes the observations, findings, implications, and, of great importance, questions for the future. Your self-study should be open, candid, and focused on portraying your department or program in its current state. Those areas that are distinguished or effective must be clearly identified; so must any developing or undeveloped dimensions. Remember, your department or program can make the greatest gains by presenting your accomplishments in a straightforward manner. The subsequent program review, especially if you invite an external reviewer to campus, will be much better if you and your colleagues are honest from the beginning. Indeed, the benchmarking approaches we advocate in this book will do little good if problems are overlooked or forgotten, or if relatively good parts of a program are unduly touted as "marks of excellence" (we have all read college or university reports containing such hyperbole). The watchwords for your work should be "informed candor." As a result, your initial efforts at benchmarking will produce true baselines of performance. Subsequent reviews that demonstrate substantial progress on the undeveloped areas can produce significant public relations gains for the program.

Before turning to the issues surrounding internal reviews and their content, a brief word about writing style is called for here. Too many academic reports are heavily detailed and ponderous; the writing style is stilted or jargon-laden. Avoid writing that type of report. Focus instead on writing a clear and carefully paced narrative, one that is organized and captures the appropriate level of detail—not too broad and certainly not lost in arcane minutiae. Include supporting documentation when appropriate. Appendix B contains potential sources for documenting evidence in each area. A strong self-study should be written so that any colleague in any department or any administrator at virtually any level can quickly digest its meaning and main points. To that end, we urge you to take your (reasonable) time to write multiple drafts of the self-study and rely on timeworn writing wisdom espoused by O'Conner (1999), Strunk and White (1972), and Zinsser (1990), among other worthy writing resources. And one more suggestion: remember, you are not writing for disciplinary colleagues who speak your special language; rather, you want to write in the vernacular so that everyone can understand what's been happening lately in your department or program.

TYPICAL ORGANIZATION FOR A SELF-STUDY REPORT

What sort of information should be included in a self-study report? How should the report be organized? Most reports will have three kinds of information: the actual text constituting the report, supporting tables and figures, and appendices.

Text. Table 12.1 lists the sections typically found in a self-study report. This narrative portion of the self-study should contain an *introductory* or *overview* statement explaining the genesis of the report. For example, many programs conduct self-studies as a rotating exercise, so that a given department at a college or university

TABLE 12.1 TYPICAL TABLE OF CONTENTS FOR A SELF-STUDY

Section	*Approximate Length*
Introduction	One or two pages
Background and History Mission statement (including program goals and objectives) Student/faculty ratio for the department	One to five pages
Current State of the Program or Department Curriculum Assessment issues Student learning outcomes Program resources Student development Faculty characteristics Program climate Administrative support Special considerations or issues (add as many additional sections as necessary)	Ten to fifteen pages
Issues of Concern, Questions, and Future Directions (that is, the reviewer's charge)	One to three pages

is evaluated every five years or so. Alternatively, there may be some event or even a crisis that prompted a self-study (for example, multiple new faculty hires, sudden departure of several tenured or untenured colleagues, a precipitous drop in enrollment, fewer student majors, or even combinations of these or other matters for concern). Clarity and brevity in this section is important, as your readers should clearly understand the impetus for the self-study before they read the full narrative. Thus the reasons for the self-study should be clearly articulated here at the beginning of the report.

The *background* or *history* section of the self-study is the place to conduct a brief review of the findings from the immediate past review (a copy of the previous report should be included as an appendix to the current one; see later discussion), including past concerns and any actions taken to correct them. Ideally, each past concern and its resolution can be presented in a few paragraphs. If any prior problems are yet to be addressed, rest assured that the visiting reviewer or team will want to know why there has been no change in the situation. Any important and recent changes to the program's curriculum, for example, as well as the arrival or departure of faculty members should be discussed here, too. As noted in Table 12.1, the program's mission statement, its goals and objectives, and the student/faculty ratio in the department should be provided. Finally, any noteworthy accomplishments of the program (for example, donor gifts, curricular developments, media coverage) or its members (teaching or scholarly awards, publications, research or travel grants, new courses), funded grants (internal, local, or national; disciplinary or transdisciplinary), major equipment acquisitions, space or laboratory enhancements, and the like also should be noted here.

Following the two opening sections, the current state of the program should be presented. Minimally, we recommend that this section of the self-study should be focused on the eight domains of program review concerning undergraduate education: assessment issues, curriculum, student learning outcomes, program resources, student development, faculty characteristics, program climate, and administrative support. Based on the discussion and directions presented in Chapters Two through Nine, quality benchmarks related to each domain should be drawn up and used to characterize current efforts in the program along the dimensions ranging from undeveloped to distinguished. Each domain merits at least a few paragraphs in the self-study, if not a page or two. Certainly, if particular issues have arisen about one or more of these domains, then greater depth—and report space—should be dedicated to their careful review.

Besides the eight domains, an additional section or sections can be added in which special considerations or issues pertaining to the program can be discussed (see Table 12.1). Earlier in this book we discussed some of the particular concerns that often arise when program reviews need to deal with special issues connected with the arts, humanities, and the natural sciences (see Chapters Ten and Eleven). Some of these issues might merit their own section. For example, suppose unprofessional behavior has emerged as a serious enough problem during juried performances in art that reviewers may want to make recommendations for attending to this problem a central feature of their report. Other issues may be more easily dispatched within the text dedicated to one or more of the eight domains, such as the current status of external resource acquisition. Other issues may not fit this scheme but still deserve attention. For example, a program in which student retention was a nascent issue would warrant a more detailed review in a subsequent section.

The last section of the self-study report is apt to be the most important one because it sets the agenda for the next step in the program review. The section dedicated to *issues of concern, questions, and future directions* is the place where the authors of the self-study reflect on what they have learned by engaging in the benchmarking process. In other words, undeveloped and developing areas of the program discerned during the review should be listed. Suggested courses of action based on discussion within the department or program should appear in this section. If the administration or an external reviewer will be reading the self-study (especially the latter), then questions targeting the issues would be appropriately raised here.

If student retention were a matter of concern, a section of the self-study might explore possible program-based explanations for the decline in returning majors, as well as seeking advice from readers on what to do in response. The list of questions need not be exhaustive; however, they should frame the problem so that readers of the self-study understand its scope and program impact to date. Reviewers can then generate ideas, formulate answers, or suggest where answers might be found prior to a campus visit or afterward, when preparing a report.

As discussed in Chapter Thirteen, one role of an external reviewer is to offer ideas or another perspective on whatever problem is at issue. The more candid a program review is about its own concerns, whether curricular or collegial, the more helpful the external reviewer can usually be. If the program has clear plans for the future—especially if program faculty design their plans to address issues of concern based in the self-study—these should close the text of the report.

One final comment about the text section of the self-study: there is nothing wrong with acknowledging—indeed, even celebrating—departmental strengths (that is, effective and distinguished areas) in print. All too often, academics seem drawn to the negative, to problems rather than prospects; rarely, if ever, are exemplary aspects of a program highlighted. We are not advocating an all-out love fest about the good things found in a program, of course, but some recognition—even a reasonable expression of pride for a job well done—is appropriate.

Supporting Tables and Figures

The self-study's text will need supporting and illustrative information in the form of tables and figures. In general, tables contain numbers, whereas figures illustrate trends across some period of time using line or bar graphs. There are exceptions to these rules; as when, for example, a table contains a list (such as peer departments or programs at other institutions). One rule is immutable: tables and figures must be as simple to read as possible. Complex or "busy" data summaries have no place in a self-study. The goal is to inform readers, not to confuse them or to obfuscate the issues raised by the data. In the ideal case, a reviewer should be able to read the title of a given table or figure and then glance at its contents to gain understanding and meaning quickly. Good discussions of how to present data clearly are available in Nicol and Pexman (1999, 2003) and in the inspiring work of Edward Tufte (2001; see also 1990, 1997).

Thus the role of supporting tables or figures in a self-study is to present easy-to-understand data summaries for reviewers and administrators. We have chosen the word "support" carefully; numbers and graphs should provide additional detail to the narrative, but are not substitutes for the written word. Tables and figures add essential detail; however, the self-study itself must draw attention to what is important. As with any research or technical writing, the author's responsibility is to explain the importance of issues, patterns, findings, and the like to the reader. Reviewers should not be expected to search or sift through pages of charts and graphs themselves; rather, the main issues summarized therein should be highlighted for them in the text of the report. Having tables and figures available will give reviewers the opportunity to make a quick confirmation of issues raised by the self-study. As other related issues occur to them based on what they read, reviewers can pursue any data of interest by consulting the additional tables and figures provided in the self-study. Naturally, if a reviewer requests information that is not currently available in the self-study portfolio, members of the program must be ready to obtain the needed information as quickly and efficiently as possible.

What supporting tables and figures should or could be included in a self-study? Exhibit 12.1 lists some of the more common tables and figures included in self-studies. Please note that Exhibit 12.1 does not include all possible data sources, nor should any given report necessarily include all those noted here. The authors of any self-study should make available those tables and figures that reveal a relatively comprehensive view of the department or program. A good place to begin drawing up a list for inclusion is by culling data from any departmental or program reports that are submitted annually (the full text of such reports might be included in the self-study's appendices, which are discussed below). Alternatively, annual reports generated by a dean's or provost's office, as well as the institution's office of admissions, regarding profiles of admitted and current students, number of undergraduate applicants, financial aid, student retention and graduation rates, grade inflation, and other similar information can be added to the self-study as needed.

Exhibit 12.1 Suggested Supporting Tables and Figures for Department or Program Self-Studies

Undergraduate catalog

Faculty handbook (including procedures for tenure and promotion)

Departmental or program bylaws

List of department or program committees

Data on teaching loads and student/faculty ratios across departments and programs at the institution

Data on teaching evaluations for program faculty (with norms for the program and the institution)

Course enrollments (introductory, intermediate, advanced, capstone)—note service courses

Majors by gender and year in program

List of community internships and sites

Lists of honors and independent study students with project titles

Student and faculty-student conference presentations

Student and faculty-student publications

List of student study abroad programs and sites

List of majors' post-graduate employment

List of majors' graduate school programs

List of four-year transfer programs for two-year college students

Number of majors as percentage of total student enrollment at institution

Ranking of majors and/or programs by student enrollment at institution

Number of adjunct faculty by course and year

List of peer departments and programs

List of grants (funded and unfunded) by purpose, title, source, and amount

Note: Whenever possible, tables and figures should provide data for the last five years or the period since the last self-study.

Appendices

Following supporting tables and figures are appendices to the self-study. These serve as an archive or repository for in-depth data related to the program or the larger institution. The content of the self-study narrative often prompts readers to seek more detail about an issue (for example, the equipment budget for the program), which should be readily found in one of the appendices. Exhibit 12.2 lists some typical appendices found in a self-study portfolio; others may be appropriate, based on your program's needs or circumstance.

Exhibit 12.2 Typical Appendices Found in Self-Study Portfolios

Appendix A—Undergraduate course descriptions

Appendix B—Curriculum flow chart for majors indicating required and optional courses

Appendix C—Sample course evaluation forms

Program form

Institutional form

Appendix D—Course syllabi for most recent academic year

Appendix E—Program handouts

Course selection directions for majors

Information for minors

Program newsletter

Appendix F—Budget report

Appendix G—Current curriculum vitae from program faculty, including adjuncts

Appendix H—Annual reports or minutes from department or program meetings

Appendix I—Technology resources (for example, schedule of updating of computers, classroom equipment)

Appendix J—Library resources report, including relevant journal subscriptions

Appendix K—Most recent self-study

Appendix L—Most recent external review

Length of the Report

How long should the self-study report be? It may seem like a flip response, but the answer is, "As long as necessary." Keep in mind, however, that the document is supposed to be used for some purpose; for example, to inform the institution's administration or a designee (for example, an external reviewer) about a program's current state, including problems and prospects for the future. Thus the report should be thorough but not encyclopedic; readers should get a clear view of the program while being able to focus on their particular task (for example, evaluating the curriculum, recommending profiles for future department hires). A detailed self-study should probably be no more than twenty-five pages of text (see the approximate page lengths suggested in the right column of Table 12.1). Naturally, supporting materials—such as course enrollment data, grade distributions, faculty vitae, course syllabi, and the like—can lengthen the document considerably. A typical self-study portfolio can run between one hundred and two hundred or so pages, if not more. No one expects either administrators or visiting reviewers to read all of the materials contained in a portfolio, but they should be able to find any information or the answers to their questions quickly (for example, "What percentage of graduating seniors attend graduate school immediately?" or "What percentage attend five years after they graduate from the institution?").

INVOLVING COLLEAGUES, ALUMNI, AND STUDENTS

Before you begin the task of writing, you should consider whom to involve in the project. Our experience, as well as the philosophy behind the benchmarking process, informs us that the best self-studies emerge from a group effort.

Colleagues

Involve as many colleagues as possible to gather information and to draft sections of the report. If your department or program is a small one (fewer than ten full-time colleagues), you may be able to capitalize on the natural camaraderie. If not, it's entirely legitimate for you to explain that the document is too important to be left to one person to write, and that everyone should have a say in the writing and revision process. The involvement of many people will also distribute the labor of tracking down facts and figures. If the department or program is a medium to large one (between ten and twenty people or more), then you can look for volunteers or recruit a number of individuals who will not view pulling together files or writing as an onerous task. It is not unreasonable to ascertain whether there could be additional compensation for the work rendered.

We believe that you should begin by explaining the benchmarking process to the group of colleagues who will be taking part in the self-study. Explain the concepts outlined earlier in this book and ask them to read particular chapters. Depending on the number of volunteers available, an ideal approach is to form subcommittees assigned the task of doing benchmarking on the eight benchmarking domains and any special areas of interest (see Table 12.1). The chair, head, or program director should prepare the introductory section (see Table 12.1), sharing drafts widely and frequently, asking for concrete feedback and constructive criticism along the way. The chair might also write the background or history section; however, there may be a senior colleague or colleagues whose long view of departmental or program doings could inform this section (again, see Table 12.1).

The final section of the self-study narrative, which deals with concerns and future directions (see Table 12.1), should be written once the earlier text is completed. The whole committee should be encouraged to suggest material for inclusion in these few pages; however, one person—perhaps the chair—or a separate subcommittee should have the actual task of writing this section. A draft should be shared with the committee for comments before the final draft of the self-study is prepared for department or program review.

We suggest that one or two weeks be allotted for all colleagues to read and comment on the self-study. At the end of the review period, the chair should make appropriate revisions to the document. Naturally, the self-study is unlikely to please all department or program citizens, but a reasonable attempt should be made to do so; indeed, reasonable disagreements can inform the process and should be included in the final version of the self-study before it is sent out.

Alumni Input

Graduates of your program can provide the self-study with a perspective on how time and their subsequent educational and professional experiences encourage them to look back at the institution. Did their undergraduate experience adequately prepare them for graduate study, professional school, or the world of work? We need not add that any contact with alumni can often benefit a program. Many graduates are delighted, even honored, to be asked to comment on their student days and to offer suggestions regarding how best to prepare future majors. Some alumni may want to help the program in more material ways following this opportunity to reconnect with the program.

Student Comments

Ultimately, the program reviews we advocate are about the quality of education that undergraduate students enjoy in a particular department. It is only fitting, then, that current students should have a participatory role in the process of composing the self-study report. To that end, their opinions should be solicited, assessed, and shared.

Venues for gathering student opinion are not hard to come by. If your department requires a capstone course, for example, a portion of class could be dedicated to a discussion or completion of a brief survey. Similarly, if your program does any sort of senior exit interview prior to graduation, those results should be included in the report. Alternatively, during the early stage of the self-study, some simple focus groups (composed of majors and non-majors) could be organized; offering refreshments works wonders when it comes to encouraging students to share their experiences. Again, a summary of such comments can be included in the self-study.

A PRACTICAL MATTER: TIMING AND TIME FRAME ISSUES

As one of our colleagues is wont to say, "Things always take longer than they do." This sentiment is especially apt when trying to conduct a thorough program review from beginning to end and to write the accompanying self-study. Time is a precious commodity for department chairs, program directors, and faculty members. How much time will it take to accomplish all that needs to be done before any external reviewer sets foot on campus? We believe that you should resolve to create and to follow a timeline outlining necessary duties and when each one should be performed.

Exhibit 12.3 sets out a reasonable timeline for doing a self-study. As you can see, four months serve as preparation time for the external review. Much of that time is set aside for fact finding, gathering materials for the self-study portfolio, and drafting sections of the report. Obviously, if colleagues from the department or program volunteer to draft sections of the report, things should go smoothly and end on time. One person—it need not be the chair or program director—should be designated as editor and organizer of the self-study. He or she should have editorial control, making certain that the narrative is written to have "one voice" rather than many disparate ones. In the same way, this individual should organize the final sections and content of the self-study, double check them before they are printed, and see that copies of the portfolio are appropriately distributed to key people on campus as well as any external reviewers.

Special Issues for Small Departments and Community College Programs

Unlike larger departments or programs, small departments and community college programs tend to have less material resources available for reviews, fewer program members, and smaller facilities. The combination of these factors can mean that fewer people will share the burden for organizing and executing a review.. Therefore, building and maintaining good will throughout the self-study becomes even more important than is generally the case, because the work of every faculty or staff member in the program is integral to effectively completing the report. Insofar as possible, old rivalries, disagreements, and professional differences must be put aside so that necessary work can be completed in the available time.

Exhibit 12.3 A Timeline for Drafting a Self-Study

Month 1—Organization

Form self-study committee (appointed or elected).

Select committee chair (if not department or program director, then appoint or elect someone).

Hold one open meeting in which faculty colleagues can offer ideas about what issues should be included in the self-study; the benchmarking process should also be introduced during this meeting.

Hold weekly committee meetings to discuss the benchmarking process (one to two hours each).

Month 2—Data Gathering

Create subcommittees and put them to work.

Each subcommittee develops appropriate benchmarks for one or more domains, as well as for any areas of special concern.

Chair collects and collates materials for appendices (see Exhibit 12.2).

Month 3—Preliminary Benchmarking Results and Section Drafts

Weeks 1 and 2: Sections are drafted by designated author(s).

Week 3: Drafts are circulated to committee for editorial comments, additions, deletions, and other revisions.

Week 4: Appointed organizer edits revised sections, blending them into a coherent narrative with one "voice."

The self-study report is read by the committee; final changes are sent to the organizer, who prepares the penultimate draft for circulation within the program.

Month 4—Sharing the Report

Weeks 1 and 2: Share the self-study report draft with program colleagues; allow two weeks for it to be read.

Week 3: Host an open meeting in which program colleagues can share reactions and discuss the self-study.

Week 4: Host a final committee meeting in which revisions are made to the final self-study portfolio.

One Month Before External Review

Distribute copies of self-study report to relevant administrative offices.

Mail copy to designated external reviewers.

Smaller programs and community (two-year) colleges may choose to give a review focus on what they do well, as well as one or more areas targeted for future development. Small departments in a liberal arts college, for example, might seek external advice on curricular trends in the wider discipline or guidance on searching for a new faculty member to hire. In some small departments, the area of need—such as faculty specialization or expertise within the discipline—is obvious; for example, a history department might be missing a twentieth-century American historian. In other departments, student enrollment demands drive the need independent of specialization. A savvy external reviewer can suggest the sort of faculty member with training in a given area or areas who can satisfy course demands while also providing the expertise that the department was heretofore lacking.

A community college may want to expand its nontraditional offerings by moving toward more of an online and distance learning presence. Recruiting experienced faculty members who can advance these goals is a key issue. A sympathetic and knowledgeable external reviewer can help a program craft cogent arguments for increasing the faculty complement while also seeking additional technical resources to launch the online initiatives successfully. The most adept external reviewer will keep the two-year institution's community mission in clear focus throughout the review process.

SELECTING A REVIEWER

In the end, the most important decision a program makes when conducting a review is really the selection of the reviewer. What sort of person should you seek? Benjamin (2008) puts it succinctly: "Ideally, reviewers should have experience in institutions similar to those that they are evaluating. Further, it is typically advantageous to select reviewers who have experience in conducting reviews of a similar nature" (p. 1).

How can a program find reviewers? In the first place, many disciplines actually maintain lists of individuals who routinely serve as program reviewers. Consult the main professional organization in your discipline to learn whether such a list is available. There may be a link on the organization's website so you can view reviewer biographies, areas of expertise, and even their curriculum vitae. Keep in mind that there are some disciplines that do not condone formal program reviews by maintaining a list of reviewers or any related guidelines (for example, American Philosophical Association). If your discipline falls into this category, then you will need to pursue other leads to locate reviewers.

An obvious approach is to rely on your professional networks or those of your program colleagues. This strategy can be accomplished formally or informally. In the former case, you might put out a call for experienced reviewers on a discussion list you belong to, explaining your program's needs and asking for experienced individuals to send their credentials to you via e-mail. Informally, you might e-mail or call colleagues at peer programs to inquire whose services they have used for their program reviews.

We do want to caution you against asking close friends or research collaborators, either your own or a program colleague's. The reasons are obvious: they may lack relevant experience or feel compelled by circumstance and the established relationships to avoid offering critical comments. There is a related problem: by bringing in an acquaintance, you may undermine the confidence of the program faculty and the institution's administrators in the review's veracity. Again, consider Benjamin's (2008) wise counsel: "In selecting reviewers, it is generally advisable to avoid using individuals who may have a conflict of interest with the department in question, or might even be perceived to have the possibility of a conflict of interest" (p. 1). More to the point, you may actually weaken your role as a leader or agent of change by alienating some colleagues who feel you have played favorites to better your standing or to hide the program's problems. Certainly, these sorts of problems are exacerbated if there are already political problems, different faculty camps, and strong personalities in the program. All of these problems can be avoided by inviting a neutral reviewer who has few or preferably no ties to the program.

Prior to selecting a reviewer, administrators sometimes ask programs to provide the credentials of several reviewer candidates—say, three or four. After reviewing the candidates, a dean or provost can make the final selection, whether individual or team. Assuming that the administration is trustworthy, the advantage to such a process is to depoliticize the review at the program level. (Still another alternative is to have the program select one reviewer and to allow the administration to choose another if resources permit.)

Implications of Quality Benchmarks for Self-Study

The quality benchmarks outlined in this book can help a department or program conduct a thoughtful self-study as well as prepare for a thorough external review. A self-study can be a general one, in which case the suggested benchmarks for all eight domains can be considered. Naturally, these are only starting points; some programs will have unique features that are not reflected in either the text or the tables found in this book. When this occurs, the self-study committee and program chair or director are in the happy position of being able to expand the list of characteristics, qualities, or categories found in the left column of the domain's tables as needed. We have also found that convening faculty colleagues and having them use the tables to benchmark the program is a great way to begin the self-study and to think about the department or program's future directions.

What happens when a self-study is more circumscribed—that is, focused on a salient issue or set of issues? The self-study committee will want to focus discussion on the one or two key dimensions (and their accompanying benchmarks) to identify the program's strengths and areas for development within these selected dimensions. Again, the categories found in the far left column of each table of benchmarks should be expanded as needed to reflect local conditions, traditions, and needs. That being said, we do not recommend ignoring the other areas of evaluation. Whenever possible, departments and programs should adopt a broad view of what they do: even a cursory review of the remaining dimensions can identify areas of excellence or academic issues that need to added, addressed, or somehow remediated.

Hosting an External Review

Following the hard work of the self-study, department faculty have a few more decisions to make to get their work across the finish line. These include electing team members and making arrangements to optimize the impact of their visit.

Inviting an Individual or a Team

The decision whether to invite one or more reviewers will be based on the size of the program, the result of the self-study benchmarking process, and the resources available. Smaller departments are likely to need only one reviewer; however, larger programs—those with more than twenty faculty members and several degree programs, for example—can benefit from two or more reviewers. The choice of reviewers can be based on their professional standing, review experience, and how their skills can be used to best comment on the existing program, future directions, and, of course, the issues raised by the self-study.

If only two reviewers can be invited to campus, some programs use a model whereby they invite one reviewer from a primarily undergraduate institution (PUI) and the other from a graduate program related to the program's mission (for example, a biologist from a Ph.D.-granting institution). The former can focus on the program's curricular issues and undergraduate experience, whereas the latter can offer counsel on helping program graduates gain admission to graduate or post-baccalaureate professional programs. More reviewers can be added when new degree programs are being considered or accreditation issues must be addressed. If an institution can afford to bring in a team of external reviewers, it might be advisable to include other voices who can give perspective to the study; for example, an employer who frequently hires graduates of the program.

Naturally, the availability and amount of resources for the program review will dictate its scope. Before any planning begins in earnest or any reviewers receive invitations, a program director or department chair should review the available budget and perhaps speak to the relevant administrative office to learn whether supplemental funds are available. Resource constraints need not compromise the quality of a review; however, they will require a program to plan the review and visit very carefully.

PLANNING AND EXECUTING THE VISIT

What happens during an external review? Exhibit 12.4 shows the outline of events for a typical program review visit of two days (actual times would be added to the list shown here once the visit is finalized). As you can see, the reviewer or team receives the self-study a month before the two-day visit. The visit itself consists of a variety of meetings with the program director, faculty members (group and individual gatherings), students, support staff, and key administrators. These interview sessions are broken up by tours of the program and institution's facilities, the campus, meals, and breaks. All appointments with faculty, staff, and administrators should be arranged well in advance, and the final hour by hour schedule should be shared with the reviewer(s) or team when they arrive on campus. Faculty members or students should serve as tour guides for the reviewer(s), shuttling them from meeting to meeting or place to place as needed. Ideally, some free time for the reviewer or team to begin outlining the report should be built into the schedule. (If the host institution plans an exit interview with the program director, faculty, or the administration, such time is essential to organize ideas and highlight the most crucial points to be made.)

THE EXIT REVIEW

As a campus visit draws to a close, a reviewer or team may be asked to meet with the self-study committee, the program head or department chair, the dean or provost, or some combination thereof. During this meeting, the reviewers will give an oral report in response to the self-study report and the visit to campus. This final meeting gives the program a sense of the content of the forthcoming written review and enables the reviewers a last chance to ask questions, gather more data, address misconceptions, or to seek clarification on matters related to the report. For members of the program, this closing meeting should provide

Exhibit 12.4 A Typical Schedule for an External Review

One Month Prior to External Review

Reviewer or team receives self-study portfolio

Day Before Review

Arrival afternoon or evening before external review begins

Dinner with program colleagues or self-study committee

Team meeting to outline roles (optional)

Day One

Breakfast meeting—team alone or with program members

Early morning meeting with program director or self-study chair or both (forty-five minutes to one hour)

Tour of facilities—for example, classrooms, labs, offices, department library, common areas, performance or rehearsal spaces, studios, computer labs (one to two hours)

Break

Start of individual interviews with members of the department or program (thirty to forty-five minutes each)

Lunch meeting with department colleagues or working lunch with team (one hour)

Afternoon meeting with dean, provost, or CAO (this meeting may be held earlier in the day or previous day; forty-five minutes to one hour)

Continuation of individual interviews with department or program members (thirty to forty-five minutes each)

Break

Dinner with department or program colleagues or working dinner with team

Day Two

Breakfast meeting for team to discuss initial observations

Completion of individual interviews (thirty to forty-five minutes)

Group interview with self-study committee (thirty minutes to one hour)

Group meeting with non-program faculty (thirty minutes to one hour)

Lunch meeting with undergraduate student majors (one hour)

Group meeting with non-major students (thirty minutes to one hour)

Group meeting with graduate students (thirty minutes to one hour)

Group meeting with secretarial, clerical, lab, and other support staff related to program needs and services (thirty minutes to one hour)

(*continued*)

EXHIBIT 12.4 (CONTINUED)

Break to prepare oral report (thirty minutes)

Oral report presentation to self-study committee and program faculty (thirty to forty-five minutes)

Exit interview and oral report to dean, provost, or CAO (thirty to forty-five minutes)

Two Weeks Later

Transmittal of written report to designated parties at host institution

Some Time Later

Program response to the external review (usually written and shared with administration and external reviewer)

Implementation of reviewer recommendations

ample time for discussion, questions, and comments before the reviewers head home.

TRAVEL EXPENSES AND HONORARIA

The host institution is expected to reimburse external reviewers for any travel expenses incurred, including airfare, cab fare, rental car expenses, meals, and reasonable incidentals. Host institutions normally make hotel reservations for visitors, paying for them in advance (if Internet access is available at the hotel, as a courtesy to reviewers it should be included as part of the room fee). Many institutions maintain rooms or apartments on campus for visitors, making a hotel stay unnecessary. Reviewers must retain and submit receipts for any and all expenses, submitting them shortly after the campus visit. In turn, the host institution pledges to send a reimbursement check quickly. Some institutions prefer to handle all travel arrangements for visitors, including flight reservations; others trust reviewers to seek reasonably priced flights during reasonable hours of the day. Whatever the financial arrangements, host institutions should reimburse a reviewer's travel expenses as soon as possible after the review occurs.

As noted in the preceding discussion of serving as an external reviewer, the amount of a reviewer's honorarium should be based on the nature of the review and discussed up front. So should the schedule of payment for the service. Some institutions send the honorarium check to a reviewer once the final report is submitted. This practice is entirely reasonable and a way to encourage a reviewer to complete the review in a timely manner. Other institutions give the reviewer half the honorarium at the end of the campus visit, sending the remaining amount once the final report is received. Either practice is fine as long as both parties agree to the one selected.

LAST WORDS ON PROGRAM REVIEWS

When viewed from a proper perspective, program reviews are opportunities for renewal, not onerous obligations to be dispatched with as quickly as possible. Regardless of the outcome of the review, programs should view the process as a chance to improve the educational experience they provide to undergraduate students. They should also view the reviewer's visit as a chance to spread the good word about their program beyond campus.

GUIDING QUESTIONS

1. When was the department or program mission statement last reviewed? Should you revisit and possibly revise the mission statement in light of any recent department changes?
2. What changes and improvements did the last self-study (and external review) bring to the program?
3. How can the availability of quality benchmarks inform the program's self-study?
4. How can you involve department colleagues in writing the self-study report? Which colleagues will contribute to which sections of the report?
5. What will the timeline for your program's self-study look like?
6. Will your program invite a single external reviewer or a team? How will you select the reviewer or team?
7. How can you help an external reviewer understand the culture of your campus?

Chapter Thirteen

Serving Our Students and Our Institutions

In the opening chapter of this book, we began by acknowledging that assessment, in the form of program review, is not a new phenomenon (see Berquist & Armstrong, 1986; Bogue & Saunders, 1992; Boyer, 1987; Haworth & Conrad, 1997), and that the review process is continuing to gain traction among stakeholders. Accrediting bodies, federal and state legislatures, and the most important constituency—students—should have the assurance that a completed undergraduate degree reflects a basic level of academic skill. Ensuring quality undergraduate education is in the best interest of not only constituents but also the academy itself. An educated populace is essential for global advancement. We believe that using benchmarks to ensure quality undergraduate education will not only improve the undergraduate experience, but that benchmarking will strengthen undergraduate programs overall and advance university research programs.

Although assessment has been slowly working its way into our practice, the relative absence of large-scale assessment efforts is surprising (Burke, 1999). Assessment has largely and appropriately been focused on measuring the outcomes of student learning (Allen, 2004; Angelo & Cross, 1993; Ewell, 2008). By comparison, systematic evaluation of the broader undergraduate experience has been slow to emerge, in part because there are a limited number of resources to guide the process. Student learning is at the heart of the academy, yet it is not determined by curriculum alone. As evidenced in our earlier chapters, experiences beyond the classroom (for example, undergraduate research, learning communities) play a significant role in student learning, yet systematic evaluation of the comprehensive collegiate experience remains limited (see Winter, McClelland, & Stewart, 1981). Many efforts to evaluate programs have been conducted at the behest of accreditation agencies—such as the Association to Advance Collegiate Schools of Business (AACSB), the Accreditation Board for Engineering & Technology (ABET), the Commission on Collegiate Nursing Education (CCNE), the Council on Education for Public Health (CEPH), and the National Council for Accreditation of Teacher Education NCATE)—and often by virtue of university system governing boards. Given the relative lack of emphasis on systematic department evaluation, it is therefore not surprising that few resources have emerged to guide the systematic evaluation of undergraduate programs. Early efforts to guide the process were undertaken by the American Council on Education (Kells, 1980), which produced a guide for the self-study process. A limited set of resources has since been published (Berquist & Armstrong, 1986; Bogue & Saunders, 1992; Haworth & Conrad, 1997; Wergin, 2003), yet until recently no comprehensive set of department specific criteria had been clearly articulated (Dunn, McCarthy, Baker, Halonen, & Hill, 2007).

Expansion of assessment to include the academic unit began occurring in the late 1990s with support by the Carnegie Foundation and the Pew Charitable Trusts. In their analysis, Wergin and Swingen (2000) deemed the state of department assessment as dismal at best. They contend that one reason comprehensive department assessment has been lacking is that the process is not vibrant because it has not been linked to the important activities of the academy. Further, these researchers suggest that we are not really obtaining accurate measures of unit effectiveness, and they decry the reliance on some easier metrics (such as number of publications or FTEs) that may not necessarily guarantee high quality. In essence, in this volume we provide a comprehensive approach to assessing unit effectiveness.

Wergin (2002) found that prerequisites for successful evaluation are strong leadership, engaged departments, a culture of evidence gathering, peer collaboration and review, respect for differences, and a link to resource allocation. When these conditions are present, an academic unit can engage in a self-study process, or the first step in a comprehensive program review, that will focus the collective efforts of the departments. As most programs that have survived the academic program review process are surprised to discover, the processes of reviewing and creating the self-study document are typically more valuable than the feedback that results from an external review.

In the benchmarks model of program evaluation we identified criteria that can be used to evaluate the whole of an academic unit by expanding the traditional quantitative evaluation process to include essential quality indicators that have not been used traditionally (Wergin, 2002; Wergin & Swingen, 2000). The domains—*curriculum, assessment, student learning outcomes, program resources, student development, faculty characteristics, program climate,* and *administrative support*—collectively offer evidence of department quality that can be used to systematically evaluate academic units and improve program quality.

Why use the benchmarks to engage in a self-study and external review? Explicitly using the benchmarks allows academic units to identify areas that may be in need of development along with areas or elements of the program that merit distinction. These eight quality dimensions should be used when evaluating an undergraduate program (naturally, dimensions unique to a given program or campus can be added as needed). Each of these dimensions is composed of multiple components that can individually provide evidence of distinction or point to a need for improvement. Not only can the benchmarks provide guidance for improving a program, but when elements of distinction are identified, they can also be used to highlight the accomplishments of a program. Addressing undeveloped areas of the program, along with highlighting elements of distinction, will only serve to move programs forward.

Despite long-standing resistance to assessment (Clarke, Ellett, Bateman, & Rugutt, 1996), we believe that creating a positive assessment climate will help units move toward a culture of evidence that will sustain assessment, improve student learning, and strengthen scholarship. Attention to each of the eight benchmark domains helps to make the assessment process manageable.

Although the process of evaluation is made easier by considering the individual components, the final step in the evaluation process is to integrate the performance indicators so that departments can obtain a comprehensive picture of their overall quality.

In addition to providing a new framework for program review in the form of comprehensive benchmarks, we provide a comprehensive plan for the review process (see Chapter Twelve). We want to emphasize the importance of using the benchmarks to create a living, guiding resource, one that is ongoing rather than sporadic. Without a commitment to continued use of the review and continuing assessment practices, the evaluation efforts will be wasted. In other words, although a full-scale review may occur on a five-year cycle, progress should be assessed annually (Wergin, 2002), and emphasis should be placed on continually moving programs forward. Recommendations for change, coupled with opportunities for discussion and consensus building, almost assuredly offer more utility for planning than program ratings that can be used punitively.

Some Caveats Regarding Benchmarking

We want to offer a few caveats for using the benchmarks to conduct a program review. As your campus moves forward with implementation of program assessment, it is important to remain realistic about potential challenges. As with any implementation of a new process, several potential problems can be anticipated, such as faculty resistance, lack of faculty participation, the Lake Wobegon effect, counterproductive competition, inappropriate use of assessment, rigid application of criteria, and the perils of sporadic assessment. However, we also believe that strategic implementation of the program review process can overcome these challenges.

Don't Make Us Go There

Generally, faculty members are deeply committed to each area of academic life—chiefly, of course, teaching, service, and scholarship. Faculty feel genuinely proud and validated when they discover that their teaching has enriched the lives of their students. Still, faculty members rarely embrace assessment mandates with enthusiasm, particularly those that are imposed by administrators. The antagonism may arise in part from a shared lack of appreciation for the obligations of both faculty and the administration, so it is paramount to build a shared sense of purpose: namely, to accurately assess the educational experience. Most important, incentives should be provided to engage faculty in the assessment work, in the form of either release time or financial compensation.

We are realistic. Not everyone will embrace the academic review process, and some will resist using the benchmarks as a set of criteria to identify programs of distinction. We hope that faculty and administrators will be willing to engage in the evaluative process for the altruistic purpose of providing quality undergraduate education. Realistically, we anticipate that some of the elements of the benchmarks will be attractive because evidence of quality can help departments advance their programs. For example, physical space is at a premium on most campuses, so if the benchmarks can be used as a vehicle for obtaining additional space or maximally using existing rooms, then that success will indirectly increase support for the assessment process. Similarly, if the benchmarks can be used to leverage additional release time for creating a course that will improve students' ability to write effectively, then the evaluation process is useful.

Administrators need to think carefully about how to facilitate the evaluation process. Making program grants available to fund retreats can sometimes stimulate the types of conversations that will lay a foundation for good assessment efforts. Prioritizing assessment activities by providing release time for faculty to engage in assessment or providing summer funding for a committee to conduct an assessment project can also produce effective results. Recognizing high-quality assessment initiatives with campus awards and featuring successful practices in a campus-wide forum can also reinforce the larger assessment process.

The Career-Limiting Responsibility

Some faculty members may discover that they have been drafted to serve as the program's resident assessment "expert." They may also decry their fate and wonder how such a task befell them. For this reason and others, framing assessment as one person's responsibility is not a good idea. Although one person may be charged with leading and organizing the overall effort, assessment activities must be a collective responsibility across program members. If the department discovers that results of the assessment are less than satisfactory, then a collective effort to implement change will be more productive than relying on a single faculty member. Similarly, if the assessment results are positive, a collective celebration is in order. In any event, we wish to point out that when done well, assessment can serve as an inexpensive form of faculty development that benefits everyone in a department or program. In other words, sharing in the collective effort to evaluate program effectiveness provides all faculty with assessment experience.

THE LAKE WOBEGON ILLUSION

In author and humorist Garrison Keillor's mythical community of Lake Wobegon, "all the women are strong, all the men are good-looking, and all the children are above average." When faculty engage in self-assessment, they may inadvertently fall prey to the desire to be strong, good-looking, and above average on all dimensions—that is, to rely on some self-serving biases. It is important to note that departments are unlikely to be distinguished in all areas, but may be effective on many measures, and perhaps still developing on only a few dimensions. Therefore, performing benchmarking during a program review of one's own department should be undertaken with care. For example, if the results of such self-assessment will be used to make budget-cutting decisions, the odds of inflated ratings increase. In fact, assessment expert K. Pat Cross (1977) highlights this phenomenon in a shrewd observation: "In what may as well be starkly labeled smug satisfaction, an amazing 94% [of college instructors] rate themselves as above average teachers, and 68% rank themselves in the top quarter of teaching performances" (p. 1).

To provide objective evaluations, it is helpful to employ multiple independent judges and to produce some type of composite measure so that multiple perspectives can counterbalance inflated ratings. Above all, the purpose of a program review is to provide a department with feedback that will help guide future planning and development.

Avoid the Admissions Arms Race

Assessment activities and the benchmarking process are meant to improve the teaching and learning that take place in an academic department or program (and, by broader application, an institution). We note that although the results of the program review process can be used to tout program strengths (for example, in admissions or alumni materials), the findings (notably areas found to be *distinguished*) should not simply be used to bolster the institution's standing in the game of college rankings. In other words, the benchmarking process and its assessment activities should not be fodder for the annual college admissions "arms race" of institutional standing. To be sure, gaining notoriety for what a department does well is one thing—and we believe that programs should be acknowledged and rewarded for their contributions. However, the results of benchmarking are best used for improving a program's (ongoing) educational activities rather than simply calling attention to its successes. The ultimate goal of program review reverts back to the initial purpose: improving the education of the students earning an undergraduate degree.

Assessment as a Lethal Weapon

It is possible to misuse the evaluation process to take punitive action against faculty or to eliminate an entire program. However, using assessment as a means to impose negative actions is less than productive. Faculty will be more likely to enter into the assessment process if they can confidently assume that the results will be used productively. In other words, identification of a weakness should serve as a basis for planning improvement rather than a cause for punitive action (for example, funding changes, reallocation of faculty lines). The assessment process can be successful only if administrators are willing to endorse the critical importance of candid assessment and the collection of baseline data that reflect reality, while simultaneously ensuring that the results of the assessment will not be used to sanction a program or any faculty member in it. So, too, faculty must be convinced that those aspects of a program that register in the lower evaluative ranges can nonetheless, with subsequent work and planning, show promise for positive growth. One of our administrative colleagues emphasizes that the results of assessment should never be used for punishment; however, failure to *perform* assessment, in an accountability-driven environment, is tantamount to performing ineffectively.

THE ONE-SIZE-FITS-ALL PITFALL

Unwavering and rigid application of the benchmarks to generate a program review can be detrimental to the health of a program. When using the benchmarks to generate a program review, open-mindedness and flexibility are critical. For example, our development of the benchmarks was predicated on some assumptions about dimensions that capture effective functioning in programs that may or may not correspond with the values of the institution wishing to adopt this method of assessment. We recommend that potential users carefully weigh whether the eight dimensions suit their purposes. A department should feel free to drop dimensions that may not be of substantial value and to add other dimensions that our model does not address. After the stakeholders agree on a benchmarking protocol that will appropriately capture their work, they should perform some pilot measurements. Once the pilot data are in, these stakeholders can return to the protocol and make adjustments until everyone can live with the metrics that will be used in the evaluative process.

THE LOCUST PROBLEM

Institutions that have not developed a true culture of assessment may discover that they are ill prepared for accreditation visits. Assessment activities are often likened to the systematic return of locusts. On a cyclical schedule, locusts infest and preoccupy the environment. When the invasion is over, the memory of the overwhelming presence of the locusts recedes. Similarly, as the accreditation or periodic program review fades from the collective memory of the department, systematic assessment efforts may not receive adequate attention. Administrators, by virtue of their positions, cannot afford to allow assessment activities to go dormant. If the review process has been successful, then faculty too should remain invested in the assessment process, if for no other reason than to realize the generative results of their efforts. As programs conclude the formal review process, they should create mechanisms for maintaining the ongoing assessment of program goals. Annual reports that summarize ongoing efforts to reach these goals (assuming that they are read, discussed, and used for subsequent planning and decision making) may be one such mechanism for promoting a more vibrant assessment culture.

What Trumps What?

Contexts matter: the students, the faculty, the department, the college, and the university all play a role in determining quality. For example, a department that carefully designs a program that is central to the mission of the university may perform in many distinguished ways but not fare well on more traditional evaluation measures (for example, student credit hour production). Engineering programs often fall into this category of offering pedagogically sound programs, but when evaluated using standard metrics, they may fall short of university goals for student credit hour production. Institutions should be able to apply differential weights to elements of a program that are important, but may simply be more costly, when decisions are being made about resource allocation. In other words, program quality, evaluated using benchmarks of quality, may yield data (that is, quantitative as well as qualitative) that highlight the important contributions of a program that may not produce large numbers of students yet nonetheless offers students an extraordinary learning opportunity. Balancing the constituents within the university will remain challenging, and fiscal realities may ultimately play a more significant role than we might hope. Nevertheless, it is essential to recognize that competing forces are always present when trying to provide students with a distinguished undergraduate experience.

FINAL THOUGHTS

Although eight separate dimensions, or benchmarks, make up the framework for evaluating undergraduate programs, we want to offer some final cautionary notes for using the model. Rigid application of the benchmarks may only serve to obfuscate opportunities for program improvement. After reviewing the individual components of a program, it is important to consider how the program is functioning in sum. If even one area of the program is seriously flawed, it is possible that the single problem will reduce all aspects of program function. For example, if a program is composed of individual faculty members who each are producing great scholarship, the program can be classified as distinguished in the area of scholarship. However, this scholarship alone will not distinguish a program in total. Multiple dimensions (for example, leadership, administrative support, physical resources) must also be present for a program to fully realize an overall level of distinction. Thus an overall examination of the program review will help to identify opportunities for program development. Similarly, an exceedingly outstanding dimension may serve to carry a program forward, despite many smaller, less effective components. However, this level of productivity is limited, and an overall evaluation of the program will help to improve the less effective elements before the program begins flagging.

We are confident that our benchmarking model provides a mechanism for improving undergraduate education and moves the national conversation about program quality forward. For the first time we offer a comprehensive framework for systematically evaluating undergraduate programs in all disciplines across the university. At a minimum, the use of benchmarks as specific criteria offers departments guidance for evaluating effectiveness and continuously improving the undergraduate learning experience. We hope that administrators will employ these criteria in a way that fosters overall positive growth and development of programs. We are optimistic that faculty will embrace the benchmarks as a mechanism for engaging in program evaluation to advance the strength of individual departments. Our hope is that the benchmarking strategies we have outlined can become part of the strategies that faculty will consider when deciding the best ways to invest their energy and creativity in answering their own questions about educational quality. We look forward to the ongoing national conversation about delivery of quality undergraduate programs, and we are optimistic that reflective program review will serve only to strengthen the undergraduate experience.

Appendix A

Using Benchmarking to Serve as an External Reviewer

You are probably reading this appendix because you wish to serve as an external reviewer at some point in the future or you have been invited to do so. In either case, you are to be congratulated, because you are clearly interested in performing an essential collegial service on behalf of your discipline. If you have been invited, you should be flattered to have the opportunity to comment on and make recommendations regarding a department or program at another institution.

The fit between a reviewer and the host institution matters a great deal. Before you agree to serve in this capacity, keep the issue of fit in mind. Compare your institution with the host institution on criteria like the following (adapted from Pusateri, Poe, Addison, & Goedel, 2004):

- Institution type (public, private, religious; liberal arts, comprehensive, research-oriented)
- Program mission
- Faculty complement
- Teaching load
- Enrollment size and selectivity
- Student body (traditional, nontraditional, commuter, online)
- Similarity of degrees offered by program (baccalaureate only, master's, doctoral)

- Same or similar regional accrediting body
- Geographical or cultural similarities

If your institution and the host campus are similar to one another on several of these criteria, then you are likely to be able to offer constructive advice based on your own experiences. If there is a fair degree of disparity between the institutions, you should have a candid discussion with the department or program chair, expressing appropriate reservations about your ability to provide useful and helpful feedback.

This appendix is briefer and more focused than the chapters appearing earlier in this book. Herein we discuss the practical matters of being a reviewer, including appreciating the culture found on another campus, meeting with a dean or provost, using performance benchmarks prior to and during your visit, writing the actual review, and dealing with the matter of compensation.

Let's begin by assuming that the fit between you and your host site is a good one.

SERVING AS AN EXTERNAL REVIEWER

What is entailed in being an external reviewer? What do you need to know and do? First, as already noted, realize that being asked to serve as an external reviewer is a great honor. Your hosts invited you because you possess particular expertise or have relevant professional experiences, and they believe that you are appropriate for the role. Second, if you accept, you are taking on an important professional obligation. As a reviewer, you are responsible for taking time out of your professional life to (1) read a detailed report about an academic program somehow related to your skills or interests, (2) visit the program and its campus, (3) interview the program's members and students as well as select administrators, and (4) write a critical but constructive program evaluation—your own detailed report—based on your observations and the benchmarking process we advocate. You may be working alone, as the member of a team (usually two or three, but possibly more, colleagues whose areas of expertise reflect those present in or sought by the program), or even as a team leader. Third, you are rendering an important service to your discipline and higher education in general. Program improvement does not always occur from within; outside opinions can validate belief and sanction previous supposition. Finally, you are also helping yourself by being an active, committed professional and by keeping your skills as an outside evaluator fresh.

What will a program want from you initially? Once you accept the invitation, they will want to identify dates for your visit. They no doubt have some dates in mind but will understand your need to work with, if not around, your teaching and personal schedules. Besides carving out time needed for the visit (usually two or three days), be sure to view your schedule in terms of time after the visit. How much time will you need and have available to write your external review report? (As we will suggest later, you should complete and submit this document within two weeks.) You may be asked to make your own travel arrangements, or the host program may make them for you. Your contact at the host program will probably need a copy of your curriculum vitae, so be sure that it is up to date before you send it along. If your service will be remunerated, for tax purposes you will also need to communicate your social security number, preferably over a phone line, to facilitate preparation of the fee.

In addition to finalizing these logistical matters, you will need to read the self-study report before your visit. This step is crucial, of course, as that document will prepare you for the many meetings with program members and students during your campus visit. You may also want to visit the institution's website, as well as the one maintained by the program or department. In addition, if there are disciplinary standards (such as accreditation standards for music) that pertain to your judgment, refamiliarize yourself with what the disciplines claim is best practice. Be sure to work from the most recent revisions of any pertinent standards documents.

Listening and Understanding a Particular Campus Culture

What happens during your visit to another campus and program? For the most part, you will spend your time asking questions that emerge from the self-study report. Indeed, the self-study should provide you with the starting list of questions. You will think of many others to ask as you hear people offer answers and speak to you about their feelings, opinions, and experiences in the program. As they do, you will need to listen carefully to their comments. Taking notes can be useful, but after a few meetings with individuals, you are apt to see a pattern emerge. The same set of issues, whether they are concerns, problems, or opportunities for the program, will be mentioned. You should attend to these ''presenting'' items because they are obviously at the forefront of the program members' thoughts. Bear in mind that the students and the administrators may raise other matters, although they too may echo the program faculty.

As a reviewer, your role is to reflect on what you hear with what you read in the self-study. How closely are they linked? Have any new issues been raised? Is there consensus about the main issues the program faces? If there is consensus, then you can focus on developing suggestions, ideas, and alternatives for the program to consider. We chose the word ''consider'' here with care. Only the program can decide how to proceed. Your role is to make recommendations—ultimately, however, the constituents of the program must choose whether to follow your lead. They may choose not to, for whatever reason, if that is their prerogative. More than likely, however, they will heed your counsel carefully, either following it or tailoring it in a manner that works given local constraints, institutional folkways, and resources.

What if you do not sense much consensus regarding the issues raised in the self-study? First, try to keep track of what you do hear so that you can appropriately characterize it later in your review. Second, in subsequent discussions, try to discern the possible reasons for a lack of consensus so that they, too, can be reported and probed to determine possible recommendations for a profitable course of action. Remember that you are not an arbitrator (unless you have been explicitly brought to campus for that purpose), but an objective reporter with expertise related to the program. You will be doing a good service for the program if your report faithfully what you observe and hear, as well as your interpretation of what both mean in light of the self-study.

Aside from advising would-be reviewers to ask critical questions and listen intently, the best advice we can offer is that you try to learn about the host program's culture; that is, try to understand the program's customs, folkways, and traditions that the faculty and students (for whatever reasons) have embraced. Avoid being judgmental or too quick to suggest changes. Immersing yourself for a day or two in a program different from your own will make you appreciate some things about your own institution while also helping you to identify things that should be revisited at the host institution. You may also take away some new ideas for your home program based on your program review. You may not agree with how some things are done at your host program, but before you point out a ''better way,'' make certain that your suggested change is necessary or even warranted. Be especially careful not to superimpose the features of your own program on the program to be reviewed; different cultures give rise to very different traditions, and simply importing a practice you know works well in your environment is no guarantee that the transplant will take. Happily, as frequent program reviewers each of us typically completes a review by taking home one or two new ways of doing or thinking about some aspect of our own teaching or the departments or programs where we work.

MEETING WITH THE CHIEF ACADEMIC OFFICER

As part of many program reviews, the chief academic officer (CAO) who oversees the host program—usually a dean or a provost—will want to meet with you. Sometimes the meeting is simply a pro forma welcome and thank-you for visiting the campus. Very often, however, the CAO has a sincere interest in learning your views on how the program you are reviewing is doing where undergraduate education and the use of disciplinary best practices are concerned. When you meet with the CAO can vary as well. On some campuses the meeting will occur early in the review, in others toward or at the end (in fact, the meeting with the CAO may be the exit portion of the review). Once in a while an institution will have a reviewer meet with the CAO at the start of the review—some charge from the dean, for example, may be involved—and then once more at the end of review for a debriefing of sorts.

Sometimes a dean or provost will begin a review discussion by asking "is this a closed or open door meeting?"—this means he or she is asking if there are potentially serious problems with the program being reviewed. We suggest that candor is always the best way to begin. If all is well, say so immediately. If not, identify the problems you see, clearly and without emotion. Explain why you believe the problems exist and what, if anything, you believe can be done to address them constructively. Most of the time, of course, the nature of the review will fall between these two extremes, so that you can identify areas for improvement as well as areas of strength or even excellence.

USING PERFORMANCE BENCHMARKS AS A VISITOR

An invited reviewer will want to follow a program's lead when it comes to performing a program review. Whether specific or general, the reviewer will want to fulfill the department's mandate. That being said, the availability of quality performance benchmarks like those articulated in this book can be used to exemplify best practices found in academic programs of all types. A reviewer can use the quality benchmarks found throughout the chapters in this book as a way to guide his or her review—they can form a template for questions on campus as well as a guide for drafting sections of the final report. At the same time, an external reviewer can rely on the benchmarks as a way to raise the academic consciousness of the program faculty, department chair, and dean or provost regarding important aspects of quality undergraduate programs. Again, as a visitor, you will need to respect local conditions and traditions on the host campus, but there is a compelling case for using best practices for undergraduate academic program review.

One option we recommend is to invite the host program to perform a pre-review benchmarking exercise that can inform both the program's self-study document as well as your review. To do so, you, as the invited reviewer will need to define and describe the use of quality benchmarks for evaluating the eight dimensions discussed in this book, as well as the meaning of the four levels of program development (undeveloped, developing, effective, distinguished). You might prepare a brief questionnaire or a chart or two based on the contents of this book, encouraging the program members to rate how they believe their undergraduate program fares on the relevant qualities and dimensions. The results of this exercise can help you to think about, structure, and begin to draft the review document. Once you arrive on campus, you can compare the colleagues' perceptions with your own, which will also inform the program review you write.

Writing a Program Review

What information goes into a program review document? In general, a program review authored by an external reviewer or team should respond to the questions, issues, and "charge" made by the program itself. Responses to these matters will form the bulk of the review. Naturally, when a reviewer or team notices other topics, whether problems or prospects, these, too, should be discussed in some detail.

Here are some tips for writing a solid program review:

- *Style.* The tone of a review should be professional and constructive. Critical comments may need to be made, but these should not be framed as criticisms. The most helpful reviews are those that candidly point to undeveloped or developing areas in the program while also offering options for addressing them. Areas that are already distinguished or effective should also be acknowledged. The best program reviews are comprehensive, not exclusively focused on problem areas.
- *Recommendations.* The last section of the review should list a set of concrete recommendations. The bulk of these recommendations should be directly linked to the charge issued by the program itself. However, as already noted, during the course of a review we often notice other areas—most minor, others major—that also warrant attention. These additional recommendations should be added to the list. In well-run programs, your recommendations will serve as the baseline for the next academic program review; therefore, the recommendations need to be achievable in relation to the

resources and energies available to implement the changes you think are important.

- *Divide and conquer.* If you are working on a review team, divide up the writing responsibilities for the first draft of the review; that is, assign each member of the team writing responsibilities for different sections of the review. Because of his or her expertise or review experience, the host program will usually appoint one member of the team to serve as the lead reviewer; this individual should merge all of the first drafts together into a penultimate draft. The penultimate draft can then be shared with the team via e-mail for final substantive and editorial changes before it is sent to the host program.
- *Length.* Although the best answer is ''as long as it needs to be,'' our experience suggests that most reviews will fall somewhere between ten and fifteen single-spaced pages, including references. Some reviews will be much shorter or longer depending upon the program's original request and reviewer observations.
- *Turnaround time.* How quickly should an external review be written by an individual or team and then submitted to the host program? Our experiences suggest that the ideal time frame is the sooner, the better—or no more than two weeks. The reasons are simple: (1) the reviewer(s), who may be charged with a final responsibility of writing an official response to your comments, need to complete their obligation and return to their normal routines, and (2) the host program will want to capitalize on the institutional interest created by the visit.
- *A word on resource implications of recommendations.* Change is important, but it also comes with a price tag. As a reviewer, you must be conscious of the potential cost for the suggestions you make; there are no unlimited budgets. In fact, most deans have come to expect that nearly every program reviewer will conclude there are insufficient resources and faculty lines. To make your case compelling, you will need to focus your arguments on the real promise of delivering distinguished programming or avoiding dire outcomes, such as litigation. We are not suggesting that you forgo making the best (that is, often the most costly) recommendations, but we do encourage

you to offer additional workable alternatives. What improvements can be made that don't require financial investment? If the "best" outcome cannot be achieved in the immediate future, perhaps you can suggest a doable or satisfactory alternative for the near term.

Exhibit A.1 presents a typical outline for an external review report. Naturally, the precise sections of a review will depend on its scope based on the host institution's charge. General reviews are broader, of course, and targeted reviews will highlight specifics. Whatever the nature of the review, try to provide a list of concrete and doable recommendations toward the end of the review. No program will address all of the suggestions you offer, but you will help the program chair and colleagues by giving a road map of possible future changes or directions to consider.

One last suggestion: Be sure to inform the program director or chair that you will be pleased to correct any inadvertent errors appearing in the review (such as spelling or course numbering

Exhibit A.1 Typical Outline for an External Review Report

Overview of review charge (for example, general or targeted to address particular issue)

Background paragraph regarding reviewer's background, institution, teaching load, administrative responsibilities and experiences, prior review experiences

Observations gleaned from self-study document and onsite visit

Option: Invite the host program to benchmark itself using the eight dimensions of evaluation before the onsite visit; evaluate the results in this part of the report

Specific needs expressed by the host program

Reviewer responses or suggestions

Additional questions or issues that emerged during the visit

Reviewer responses or suggestions

List of numbered recommendations (with supporting details as needed) for host program

Conclusions (optional)

errors or factual mistakes) or to go into more detail on any issues as needed. Given the amount of time, energy, and effort a program expends to host an external review, your openness and flexibility will be greatly appreciated.

THE MATTER OF COMPENSATION

Typically, a host institution will offer a modest honorarium to a reviewer as compensation for time dedicated to reading the self-study, visiting the campus, and then writing a report after the return home. The amounts of such honoraria vary depending on the time involved, the expectations for the level of detail in the report, and the host institution's resources. Remuneration can range from several hundred dollars to a few thousand depending on the nature and depth of the consultation. In general, compensation for a standard program review will be less than for one in which special issues or problems must be tackled or multiple external reviewers are involved in the process.

Unless you are consulting under the auspices of some professional organization that explicitly forbids reviewers from accepting honoraria (such as the Middle States Commission on Higher Education), you should expect to receive some modest compensation for your time. The amount of the compensation should always be determined in advance of the review and agreed upon by both parties. If your host institution asks your fee and you have not ever done a review, defer naming one until you can speak to a colleague who is used to doing similar professional reviews. Ask your colleague what a reasonable honorarium would be, given the nature of the review.

One important point: devoting your professional time and energy to doing an external review is an important service. Unless you have some special tie with the host institution (in which case you might consider how objective you will be before accepting), you should not do a program review gratis, just as you should not expect to become rich by writing reviews. Seek a middle path where compensation is concerned. If you are offered an honorarium that you believe is too modest for the amount of work involved, be candid about this fact with the institution; this will give them the opportunity to reconsider the remuneration or to search for another reviewer who fits better with their real budget constraints.

Guiding Questions

1. Why do you want to serve as an external reviewer? What strengths or skills do you believe you bring to this task?
2. Is there a good fit between your background and the profile of the host institution? If not, why not? Can the difference be overcome or should you decline to serve?
3. What can you learn about the host program by visiting its website? What was the most useful information found in the self-study report? What additional information do you still need to do the review?
4. What specific questions will you address during the site visit? Can you draft a portion of the external review before you visit the host program?
5. Without being mercenary, what level of compensation or honorarium will be reasonable for you to accept the commitment to do an external review?

Appendix B

Sources of Data

Sources of Data to Document Administrative Support

Mission	Documents should include the university mission, college mission, and department mission, vision, and goals. Additional documents may include disciplinary guides.
Bylaws and Procedures	A copy of department governance documents.
Evaluation System	All materials associated with faculty evaluation. Documents should include an example evaluation and department tenure and promotion criteria.
Teaching Assignments	A five-year analysis of teaching assignments could be included. Other documents, including specifications that clarify how reassigned time is granted, could also be included.
Scholarship Support	Funding streams for supporting scholarship identified across the university.
Recognition System	Discipline-specific recognitions and university, college, and department mechanisms for acknowledging support should be included; for example, teaching awards or systematic mechanisms for highlighting scholarship, teaching, and service.

SOURCES OF CURRICULUM DATA

Curricular Structure and Sequence	Curriculum planning guides from each of the major concentrations and university catalog
Course Variety	Course offerings for the past five years
Disciplinary Perspective Breadth	Course offerings compared to disciplinary recommendations
Curricular Ethics	Courses and syllabi
Curricular Cultural Diversity	Courses and syllabi
Service Learning	Internship materials

SOURCES OF ASSESSMENT DATA

Assessment Planning	Assessment reports for five years, with corresponding data
Data Gathering	Summary of data that are routinely collected (such as outcomes assessments), alumni surveys
Program Improvement	Reports summarizing iterative change as a result of assessments
Program Promotion	Program brochures that reference data about the program

SOURCES OF STUDENT LEARNING OUTCOMES DATA

Writing Skills	Sample papers, syllabi, capstone course description
Speaking Skills	Sample papers, syllabi, capstone course description
Research Skills	Evidence of student requirements both inside and outside the classroom
Collaborative Skills	Sample papers, syllabi, capstone course description
Information Literacy and Technology Skills	Sample papers, syllabi, capstone course description

SOURCES OF STUDENT DEVELOPMENT DATA

Student Advising	Advisement policy and procedures
Advising Materials	Materials distributed to students
Engagement Beyond the Classroom	Summaries of students engaged in service learning, research, and other activities
Student Organizations	Awards and documentation of student organizations
Participation in Department Decisions	Minutes from faculty meetings that document student participation

SOURCES OF FACULTY DATA

Teaching Orientation	Summary of student evaluations
Scholarship Orientation	Summary of publications and presentations: faculty vitae
Resource Development	Summary of grants and contracts
Professional Involvement	Compilation of faculty memberships and leadership positions in professional organizations
Community Orientation	Summary of community service
Accessibility to Students	Summary of online and office hours policies
Faculty Ethics	Policies addressing faculty ethics

SOURCES OF PROGRAM RESOURCES DATA

Institutional Administrative Climate	Materials from the president's office, including rankings from *U.S. News and World Report*
Physical Facilities	Listing of classrooms, faculty offices, and other spaces; discipline-specific reports on space
Administrative Support	Listing of support staff

Extramural Funding	Listing of revenue streams
Departmental Website	Link to website
Technology	Technology inventory
Alumni Connection	Alumni data

SOURCES OF ADMINISTRATIVE SUPPORT DATA

Mission	Copy of mission, vision, goals, and strategic plan
Bylaws and Procedures	Copy of department governance document
Evaluation System	Copy of tenure and promotion guidelines for the department, copy of guidelines for faculty evaluation, links to the university faculty handbook
Teaching Assignments	Matrix detailing faculty teaching assignments
Scholarship Support	Narrative describing support for faculty scholarship
Recognition System	Listing of awards available for department, college, university, and nationally

SOURCES OF PROGRAM CLIMATE DATA

Program Ethics	Copy of disciplinary ethics code and university ethics codes
Program Leadership	If appropriate, publicly available evaluation data (such as an administrator's evaluation)
Relationship with University Community	Spreadsheet of university-wide committee appointments, interdisciplinary course listings
Greater Community Involvement by Program	Highlights from community-based projects
Collegiality	Assessment by site visitors
Respect for Individual and Cultural Differences	Assessment by site visitors

APPENDIX C

ASSESSMENT MATERIALS FOR THE ARTS

ITEM 1: MUSICAL THEATRE VOICE PERFORMANCE RUBRIC*

Tone Quality

4—Consistently focused and clear, open, warm, and mature

3—Usually clear, focused, somewhat warm

2—Somewhat unfocused, thin

1—Very unfocused and strident, detracts from performance

Rhythm

4—Beat is secure, rhythms accurate

3—Beat is secure, rhythms mostly accurate

2—Beat erratic, frequent or repeated duration errors detract from overall performance

1—Erratic beat and rhythms detract significantly from performance

Note and Pitch

4—Virtually no errors; pitch is accurate

**Source:* The San Diego School of Creative and Performing Arts (SCPA) High School Audition Guidelines, http://www.scpa.sandi.net/ADMISSIONS/Audition%20Procedures/Audition%20Requirements.pdf

3—Occasional isolated error, most of the time pitch is accurate and secure

2—Very few accurate or secure pitches

1—Pitch of voice has no relation to pitch of accompaniment

Dynamics

4—Dynamic levels are obvious, consistent, and match the style of music

3—Dynamic levels are obvious and consistent but do not match style of music

2—Dynamic levels fluctuate but can be discerned

1—No attention given to dynamics

Expression and Style

4—Performs with creative nuance and style appropriate to the music

3—Sometimes performs with creative nuance and style appropriate to the music

2—Very little demonstration of style or expressive nuance

1—No demonstration of style or expressive nuance

Ability to take direction

4—Performed all requested changes correctly

3—Performed most of the requested changes correctly

2—Performed few of the requested changes correctly

1—Unable to make any requested changes

ITEM 2: HOLISTIC WRITING RUBRIC*

*Adapted from Barbara Walvoord, Winthrop University, Virginia Community College System, University of Washington. D.C., as cited in Mary Allen, ''Developing and Using Rubrics for Assessing, Grading, and Improving Student Writing'' (mallen@csub.edu), Humboldt State University, http://www.humboldt.edu/~ugst/downloads/Complete%20Writing%20Rubric%20Packet%20by%20Mary%20Allen.doc.

Quality Criteria	*No/Limited Proficiency*	*Some Proficiency*	*Proficiency*	*High Proficiency*
1. Thesis or Focus: (a) Originality	Thesis is missing.	Thesis may be obvious or unimaginative.	Thesis is somewhat original.	Develops fresh insight that challenges the reader's thinking.
2. Thesis or Focus: (b) Clarity	Reader cannot determine thesis and purpose *or* thesis has no relation to the writing task.	Thesis and purpose are somewhat vague or only loosely related to the writing task.	Thesis and purpose are fairly clear and match the writing task.	Thesis and purpose are clear to the reader and closely match the writing task.
3. Organization	Unclear organization *or* organizational plan is inappropriate to thesis; no transitions.	Some signs of logical organization. May have abrupt or illogical shifts and ineffective flow of ideas.	Organization supports thesis and purpose. Transitions are mostly appropriate. Sequence of ideas could be improved.	Fully and imaginatively supports thesis and purpose. Sequence of ideas and transitions are effective.
4. Support or Reasoning (a) Ideas (b) Details	Offers simplistic, undeveloped, or cryptic support for the ideas. Inappropriate or off-topic generalizations, faulty assumptions, errors of fact.	Offers somewhat obvious support that may be too broad. Details are too general, not interpreted, irrelevant to thesis, or inappropriately repetitive.	Offers solid but less original reasoning. Assumptions are not always recognized or made explicit. Contains some appropriate details or examples.	Substantial, logical, and concrete development of ideas. Assumptions are made explicit. Details are germane, original, and convincingly interpreted.
5. Use of sources and documentation	Neglects important sources. Overuse of quotations or paraphrase in place of writer's own ideas. May use source	Uses relevant sources but lacks in variety of sources and/ or the skillful combination of sources. Quotations and	Uses sources to support, extend, and inform, but not substitute writer's own development of idea.	Uses sources to support, extend, and inform, but not substitute writer's own development of idea.

Quality Criteria	*No/Limited Proficiency*	*Some Proficiency*	*Proficiency*	*High Proficiency*
	material without acknowledgment.	paraphrases may be too long and/or inconsistently referenced.	Doesn't overuse quotes, but may not always conform to required style manual.	Combines material from a variety of sources, including personal observation, scientific data, authoritative testimony. Doesn't overuse quotes.

ITEM 3: INTERDISCIPLINARY SOCIAL SCIENCES ASSESSMENT PLAN

Mission Statement

The field of interdisciplinary studies is dedicated to providing excellence in education, personal growth, civic awareness, and unique learning experiences by offering cutting-edge programs. Designed for students desiring a focused yet broad exposure to these complex and interconnected issues, the interdisciplinary studies programs provide student-centered learning opportunities for explaining phenomena, solving problems, creating new knowledge, and raising new questions in ways that would have been unlikely through single disciplinary focus.

Student Learning Outcomes

Students graduating with a degree in interdisciplinary social sciences should be able to demonstrate the following skills:

Content

- Appraise the knowledge, concepts, techniques, and methodology appropriate to the cross- or multidisciplinary nature of the capstone project.

- Identify major issues, debates, or approaches appropriate to the cross- or multidisciplinary nature of the capstone project.
- Synthesize complex information appropriate to the cross- or multidisciplinary nature of the capstone project.
- Develop an argument or project and defend or present it appropriately in accordance with the methods of the cross- or multidisciplinary nature of the capstone project.

Critical Thinking

- Exhibit cross- or multidiscipline-based higher-order thinking skills.
- Distinguish the essential features and underlying issues of a significant problem appropriate to the cross- or multidisciplinary stream.
- Select and organize credible evidence to support converging arguments.
- Solve cross- or multidiscipline-based problems using strategies appropriate to the subject of the capstone project.

Communication

- Communicate effectively in one-on-one or group contexts.
- Present a complex body of information appropriate to the cross- or multidisciplinary stream in written and oral formats clearly and concisely.
- Employ writing conventions suitable to the research method and/or creative process of the subject of the capstone project.

Integrity and Values

- Practice appropriate standards related to respect for intellectual property.
- Practice appropriate professional standards of behavior.
- Contribute materially to the social needs appropriate to the cross- or multidisciplinary stream in an honest, responsible, and respectful manner.

Project Management

- Exhibit disciplined work habits as an individual.

- Apply cross- or multidiscipline-based knowledge to design a problem-solving strategy.
- Conceive, plan, and execute a high-quality research or creative capstone project appropriate to the cross- or multidisciplinary context.

Assessment of Student Learning Outcomes

Students pursuing a baccalaureate degree in interdisciplinary social sciences will be assessed through their performance in the interdisciplinary social sciences core classes and the capstone project. In the core classes, focused exercises and projects will be used to assess progress in the domains of content, critical thinking, communication, and integrity and values. The capstone project, a demanding and stream-specific culminating learning experience, will be used to assess overall achievement in all five domains.

Item 4: Statement on Scholarly and Creative Activity from Music

As a required category for all levels of tenure and promotion, it is essential to define, within the confines of a regional comprehensive university, not only the types of creative and scholarly activity but also the quality of activity. For performance faculty, this category can contain performances by invitation at venues with a local, regional, national, or international reputation; recordings and broadcasts; compositions or arrangements published through reputable outlets; and scholarly publishing activities. Reviews of performances or recordings, when available from respected independent sources, provide important additional evidence of excellence or distinction in this category. It must be noted, however, that such reviews are not regularly available and their absence should not be taken in a negative vein. For performers, invitations to perform with recognized orchestras and ensembles, or to give solo recitals in important venues, in many ways play the role of the pre-publication peer adjudication used by other disciplines. An invitation to perform at a national or international venue or with a performing organization with such a reputation can be taken as a strong indication of excellence or distinction in the performing field. Typically, and by way of illustration only, some American orchestras (such as those of Atlanta, Houston, Naples, and Jacksonville) have a national reputation, whereas others (such as the Cleveland Orchestra and the New York Philharmonic) have an international reputation. Similar interpretations could be placed on invitations to perform recitals in various locations. To allow for the large variety of performance locations and venues, in individual tenure and promotion cases, artistic work and like contributions will be clearly assessed by the chair as falling into a local, regional, national, or international category.

The following is an attempt to define local, regional, national, and international activities—not comprehensive but rather representative—understanding that not all presented activities will fall neatly into a specific quality indicator and that regional, national, or international activities may all occur within the local environment.

Local

- Faculty recitals on campus or within the region that are not part of a sponsored concert series independent of the university.
- Collaborative solo or ensemble performances presented in conjunction with faculty recitals as just described or within major ensemble performances.
- Lectures, presentations, clinician, adjudicator to local organizations, such as a music study club, local opera, or musical interest group.
- Conducting, directing, or producing concerts or events in the community serving a local audience base or organization; this may include additional performances of major ensembles beyond the basic curriculum standard of the ensemble course.
- Commissions, compositions, arrangements completed for local or university solo or ensemble performances that are not part of a regional or national conference or performing arts series.

Regional

- Guest solo or collaborative recitals on concerts series or guest artist series in the region.

- Collaborative solo or ensemble performance presented with a regional professional orchestra, band, chorus, opera, concert series, or recital series.
- Lectures, presentations, clinician, adjudicator to regional organizations, such as Florida Music Teachers Association, state, or regional National Association of Teachers of Singing conferences; all-county or all-state, district, and regional Metropolitan Opera competitions.
- Conducting, directing, or producing concerts or events within the region serving a regional audience base or organization, professional or academic (this may include additional performances of major ensembles beyond the basic curriculum standard of the ensemble course as a guest concert series performance or tour).
- Commissions, compositions, arrangements completed for regional, professional, or university solo or ensemble performances that are part of a regional conference, dedication, or performing arts series.

National and International

- Guest solo or collaborative recitals on concerts series or guest artist series with a national or international reputation, such as Carnegie Hall, Kennedy Center, Tanglewood Festival, or Aspen Festival.
- Collaborative solo or ensemble performance presented with a national professional orchestra, band, chorus, opera, concert series, and/or recital series.
- Lectures, presentations, clinician, adjudicator to national organizations, such as the Music Teachers National Association (MTNA) conferences or competitions, National Association of Teachers of Singing (NATS) conferences or competitions, National Federation of Music Clubs conferences or competitions, national MET competitions, or international conferences.
- Conducting, directing, or producing concerts or events serving a national or international audience base or organization, professional or academic; this may include additional performances of major ensembles beyond the basic curriculum

standard of the ensemble course in a national or international guest concert series performance or tour.

- Commissions, compositions, arrangements completed for national or international, professional, or university solo or ensemble performances that are part of a national or international conference, dedication, or performing arts series.

Appendix D

Disciplinary Accrediting Organizations for Bachelor's Degree Programs

The following organizations are currently recognized by the Council for Higher Education Accreditation (CHEA):

AACSB International—The Association to Advance Collegiate Schools of Business (AACSB)

Accreditation Board for Engineering and Technology, Inc. (ABET)

Accreditation Council for Occupational Therapy Education (ACOTE)

Accrediting Council on Education in Journalism and Mass Communications (ACEJMC)

American Association of Family and Consumer Sciences (AAFCS) Council for Accreditation

American Board of Funeral Service Education (ABFSE) Committee on Accreditation

American Council for Construction Education (ACCE)

American Dietetic Association Commission on Accreditation for Dietetics Education (CADE-ADA)

American Occupational Therapy Association (AOTA)

American Society of Landscape Architects (ASLA) Landscape Architectural Accreditation Board (LAAB)

Association of Collegiate Business Schools and Programs (ACBSP)

Association of Technology, Management, and Applied Engineering (ATMAE) (formerly National Association of Industrial Technology)

Aviation Accreditation Board International (AABI) (formerly Council on Aviation Accreditation)

Commission on Accreditation of Allied Health Education Programs (CAAHEP)

Commission on Accreditation of Healthcare Management Education (CAHME)

Commission on Collegiate Nursing Education (CCNE)

Council on Social Work Education (CSWE) Commission on Accreditation

Joint Review Committee on Education Programs in Radiologic Technology (JRCERT)

National Accrediting Agency for Clinical Laboratory Sciences (NAACLS)

National Association of Schools of Art and Design (NASAD) Commission on Accreditation

National Association of Schools of Dance (NASD) Commission on Accreditation

National Association of Schools of Music (NASM) Commission on Accreditation

National Association of Schools of Theatre (NAST) Commission on Accreditation

National Council for Accreditation of Teacher Education (NCATE)

National League for Nursing Accrediting Commission, Inc. (NLNAC)

National Recreation & Park Association (NRPA/COA) Council on Accreditation

Planning Accreditation Board (PAB)

Society of American Foresters (SAF)

Teacher Education Accreditation Council, Inc. (TEAC)

References

Allen, I. E., & Seaman, J. (2007). *Online nation: Five years of growth in online learning.* Needham, MA: The Sloan Consortium.

Allen, M. J. (2004). *Assessing academic programs in higher education.* Bolton, MA: Anker.

Altman, H. B. (2000). Strengthening the departmental voice in the faculty reward system. In A. F. Lucas (Ed.), *Leading academic change* (pp. 138–157). San Francisco: Jossey-Bass.

American Association for Higher Education. (1992). *Nine principles of good practice for assessing student learning.* Washington, DC: American Association for Higher Education.

American Association of Physics Teachers. (2002). *Guidelines for two-year college physics programs.* College Park, MD: American Association of Physics Teachers. aapt.org

American Association of Physics Teachers. (2005). *Guidelines for self-study and external evaluation of undergraduate physics programs.* College Park, MD: American Association of Physics Teachers. aapt .org

American Association of University Professors. (1990). 1940 *Statement of principles on academic freedom and tenure.* Retrieved from http://www.aaup.org/AAUP/pubsres/policydocs/contents/1940statement.htm

American Chemical Society. (2009). *Ethics code.* Retrieved from http://portal.acs.org/portal/acs/corg/content?_nfpb=true&_pageLabel=PP_TRANSITIONMAIN&node_id=1095&use_sec=false&sec_url_var=region1&__uuid=de6051ff-215f-4c3f-82cf-9a1c8853130d

American Chemical Society Committee on Professional Training. (2008). *Undergraduate professional education in chemistry: ACS guidelines and evaluation procedures for bachelor's degree programs.* Washington, DC: American Chemical Society Committee on Professional Training. Retrieved from http://portal.acs.org/portal/Public WebSite/about/governance/committees/training/acsapproved/degreeprogram/WPCP_008491

American Council of Education. (1937). *The student personnel point-of-view, 1937.* Retrieved from http://www.bgsu.edu/colleges/library/cac/sahp/word/THE%20STUDENT%20PERSONNEL.pdf

American Council of Education. (1949). *The student personnel point-of-view, 1949.* Retrieved from http://74.125.47.132/search?q=cache:XC3LJiD53zYJ:www.naspa.org/pubs/files/StudAff_1949.pdf+student+personnel+point+of+view&cd= 1&hl=en&ct=clnk&gl=us&client=safari

American Historical Association. (2007). *Liberal learning and the history major.* Retrieved from http://www.historians.org/pubs/Free/LiberalLearning.htm

American Psychological Association. (2007). *APA guidelines for the undergraduate psychology major.* Washington, DC: Author. Retrieved from www.apa.org/ed/resources.html

American Psychological Association. (2008). *Teaching, learning, and assessing in a developmentally coherent curriculum.* Washington, DC: Author. Retrieved from http://www.apa.org/ed/pcue/bea_coherent.pdf

Ancis, J. R., Sedlacek, W. E., & Mohr, J. J. (2000). Student perception of the campus cultural climate by race. *Journal of Counseling and Development, 78*(2), 180–185.

Anderson, L. W., Krathwohl, D. R., Airasian, P. W., Cruikshank, K. A., Mayerm, R. E., Pintrich, P. R., Raths, J., & Wittrock, M. C. (2000). *A taxonomy for learning, teaching, and assessing: A revision of Bloom's taxonomy of educational objectives.* Boston: Allyn & Bacon.

Angelo, T. A. (1993). A "teacher's dozen": Fourteen general, research-based principles for improving higher learning in our classrooms. *AAHE Bulletin, 45,* 3–13.

Angelo, T. A., & Cross, K. P. (1993). *Classroom assessment techniques: A handbook for college teachers* (2nd ed.). San Francisco: Jossey-Bass.

Appleby, D. C. (2010). Advising in the classroom: A career exploration class for psychology majors. In D. S. Dunn, B. C. Beins, M. A. McCarthy, & G. W. Hill, IV (Eds.), *Best practices for teaching beginnings and endings in the psychology major: Research, cases, and recommendations* (pp. 31–48). New York: Oxford.

Arreola, R. A. (2007). *Developing a comprehensive faculty evaluation system: A guide to designing, building, and operating large-scale faculty evaluation systems.* Bolton, MA: Anker.

Association of American Colleges and Universities. (2002). *Greater expectations: A new version for learning as America goes to college.* Retrieved from http://www.greaterexpectations.org

Association of American Colleges and Universities. (2009). *VALUE: Valid assessment of learning in undergraduate education.* Retrieved from http://www.aacu.org/value/rubrics/index.cfm

Association of College and Research Libraries. (2001). *Objectives for information literacy instruction: A model statement for academic librarians.* Chicago, IL: Author. Retrieved from http://www.ala.org/ala/mgrps/divs/acrl/standards/objectivesinformation.cfm

Astin, A. W. (1993a). *Assessment for excellence: The philosophy and practice of assessment and evaluation in higher education.* New York: Macmillan.

Astin, A. W. (1993b). *What matters in college? Four critical years revisited.* San Francisco: Jossey-Bass.

Astin, A. W. (1996). *Involvement in learning* revisited: Lessons we have learned. *Journal of College Student Development, 37,* 123–134.

Badura, A. S., Millard, M., Johnson, C., Stewart, A., & Bartolomei, S. (2003). Positive outcomes of volunteering as a peer educator. (ED473426)

Bain, K. (2004). *What the best college teachers do.* Cambridge, MA: Harvard University Press.

Banta, T. W. (1997). Moving assessment forward: Enabling conditions and stumbling blocks. *New Directions for Higher Education, 100,* 79–91.

Banta, T. W., & Lefebvre, L. A. (2006). Leading change through assessment. *Effective practices for academic leaders, 1*(4), 1–16.

Banta, T. W., Lund, J. P., Black, K. E., & Oblander, F. W. (1996). *Assessment in practice: Putting principles to work on college campuses.* San Francisco: Jossey-Bass.

Barkley, E. F., Cross, K. P., & Major, C. H. (2004). *Collaborative learning techniques: A handbook for college faculty.* San Francisco: Jossey-Bass.

Barr, R. B., & Tagg, J. (1995). From teaching to learning: A new paradigm for undergraduate education. *Change,* 27(6), pp. 12, 14.

Bates, A. W., & Poole, G. (2003). *Effective teaching with technology in higher education: Foundations for success.* San Francisco: Jossey-Bass.

Baxter Magolda, M. B. (2001). *Making their own way: Narratives for transforming higher education to promote self-development.* Sterling, VA: Stylus.

Bean, J. C. (1996). *Engaging ideas: The professor's guide to integrating writing, critical thinking, and active learning in the classroom.* San Francisco: Jossey-Bass.

Belenky, M. E., Clinchy, B. M., Goldberger, N. R., & Tarule, J. M. (1986). *Women's ways of knowing: The development of self, voice, and mind.* New York: Basic Books.

Benjamin, L. T., Jr. (2008). External departmental reviews. Unpublished manuscript, Department of Psychology, Texas A&M University, College Station, TX.

Berquist, W. H., & Armstrong, J. L. (1986). *Planning effectively for educational quality: An outcomes-based approach for colleges committed to excellence.* San Francisco: Jossey-Bass.

Biemiller, L. (2008, July). To college employees, the work environment is all-important. *Chronicle of Higher Education, 54*(45), pB1.

Black, P., Harrison, C., Lee, C., Marshall, B., & Wiliam, D. (2003). *Assessment for Learning: Putting it into practice.* Berkshire, England: Open University Press.

Bland, C. J., Weber-Main, A. M., Lund, S. M., & Finstad, D. A. (2005). *The research productive department: Strategies from departments that excel.* Bolton, MA: Anker.

Bogue, E. G., & Hall, K. B. (2003). *Quality and accountability in higher education: Improving policy, enhancing performance.* Westport, CT: Praeger.

Bogue, E. G., & Saunders, R. L. (1992). *The evidence of quality: Strengthening the tests of academic and administrative effectiveness.* San Francisco: Jossey-Bass.

Boice, R. (1996). *First order principles for college teachers: Ten basic ways to improve the teaching process.* Bolton, MA: Anker.

Boice, R. (2000). *Advice for new faculty members: Nihil nimus.* Boston: Allyn & Bacon.

Bonk, C. J., & Zhang, K. (2008). *Empowering online learning: 100+ activities for reading, reflecting, displaying, and doing.* San Francisco: Jossey-Bass.

Bowles, T. J., McCoy, A. C., & Bates, S. (2008). The effect of supplemental instruction on timely graduation. *College Student Journal, 42,* 853–859.

Boyer, E. L. (1987). *College: The undergraduate experience in America.* New York: Harper & Row.

Boyer, E. L. (1990). *Scholarship reconsidered: Priorities of the professoriate.* Princeton, NJ: Carnegie Foundation for the Advancement of Teaching.

Boyer, E. L. (1997). *Scholarship reconsidered: Priorities of the professoriate* (2nd ed.). San Francisco: Jossey-Bass.

Bracken, S.J., Allen, J. K., Dean, D. R. & Austin, A. E. (2006). *The balancing act: Gendered perspectives in faculty roles and work lives.* Sterling, VA: Stylus.

Branche, J., Mullennix, J., & Cohn, E. R. (Eds.). (2007). *Diversity across the curriculum: A guide for faculty in higher education.* San Francisco: Jossey-Bass.

Braskamp, L. A., Trautvetter, L. C., & Ward, K. (2006). *Putting students first: How colleges develop students purposefully.* San Francisco: Jossey-Bass.

Brewer, C. L., Hopkins, J. R., Kimble, G. A., Matlin, M. W., McCann, L. I., McNeil, O. V., et al. (1993). Curriculum. In T. V. McGovern (Ed.), *Handbook for enhancing undergraduate education in psychology* (pp. 161–182). Washington, DC: American Psychological Association.

Brown-Glaude, W. R. (Ed.). (2009). *Doing diversity in higher education: Faculty leaders share challenges and strategies.* Piscataway, NJ: Rutgers University Press.

Brubaker, D. C., & Ostroff, J. H. (Eds.). (2006). *Life, learning, and community: Concepts and models for service-learning in biology.* Sterling, VA: Stylus.

Bruff, D. (2009). *Teaching with classroom response systems: Creating active learning environments.* San Francisco: Jossey-Bass.

Bryant, J., & Baggott la Velle, L. (2003). A bioethics course for biology and science education students. *Journal of Biological Education, 37*(2), 91–95.

Bueschel, A. C. (2008). *Listening to students about learning.* Report from the Carnegie Foundation for the Advancement of Teaching, Strengthening Pre-Collegiate Education in Community Colleges. Stanford, CA: The Carnegie Foundation for the Advancement of Teaching.

Buller, J. L. (2006). *The essential department chair: A practical guide to college administration.* Boston: Anker.

Burke, J. C. (1999, July/August). The assessment anomaly: If everyone's doing it why isn't more getting done? *Assessment Update, 11*(4), 4.

Burke, J. C. (2004). *Achieving accountability in higher education: Balancing public, academic, and market demands.* San Francisco: Jossey-Bass.

Buskist, W., & Irons, J. G. (2008). Simple strategies for teaching our students to think critically. In D. S. Dunn, J. S. Halonen, and R. A. Smith (Eds.), *Teaching critical thinking in psychology: A handbook of best practices* (pp. 49–57). Malden, MA: Wiley-Blackwell.

Buskist, W., Keeley, J., & Irons, J. (2006). Evaluating and improving your teaching. *APS Observer, 19*(4), 27–30.

Butler, D. L., & Winnie, P. H. (1995). Feedback and self-regulated learning: A theoretical synthesis. *Review of Educational Research, 65*(3), 245–281.

Calefati, J. (2009, August 5). Budget cuts hit California campuses. *Paper Trail, U.S. News & World Report.* Retrieved from http://www.usnews.com/blogs/paper-trail/2009/08/05/budget-cuts-hit-california-campuses.html

Center for Teaching, Learning, and Assessment. (2005). *9 Principles of good practice for assessing student learning.* Retrieved from http://www.iuk.edu/~koctla/assessment/9principles.shtml

Centra, J. A. (1993). *Reflective faculty evaluation: Enhancing teaching and determining faculty effectiveness.* San Francisco: Jossey-Bass.

Chea, T. (2009, August 25). Will budget cuts cripple California campuses? *USA Today*. Retrieved from http://www.usatoday.com/news/education/2009–08–05-california-colleges_N.htm

Chickering, A. W. (1969). *Education and identity.* San Francisco: Jossey-Bass.

Chickering, A. W., & Ehrmann, S. C. (1996). Implementing the seven principles: Technology as lever. *AAHE Bulletin, 49*(2), 3–6.

Chickering, A. W., & Gamson, Z. F. (1987). Seven principles for good practice in undergraduate education. *AAHE Bulletin, 39*(7), 3–7.

Chickering, A. W., & Reisser, L. (1993). *Education and identity* (2nd ed.). San Francisco: Jossey-Bass.

Clarke, J. S., Ellett, C. D., Bateman, M., & Rugutt, J. K. (1996). Faculty receptivity to change, personal and organizational efficacy decision deprivation and effectiveness in research I universities. ASHE Annual Meeting Paper. (ED402846)

Cohen, J. (2008, Summer). Social, ethical, and academic education: Creating a climate for learning, participation in democracy, and well-being. *Harvard Educational Review, 76*(2), 201–237.

Cooper, D. L., Healy, M. A., & Simpson, J. (1994). Student development through involvement: Specific changes over time. *Journal of College Student Development, 35,* 98–102.

Copenheaver, C. A., Duncan, D. W., Leslie, L. D., & McGehee, N. G. (2004). An exploration of cross-disciplinary peer education in natural resources. *Journal of Natural Resources Life Science Education, 33,* 124–130.

Council for Higher Education Accreditation. (2008). *New leadership for student learning and accountability.* Retrieved from http://www.chea.org/pdf/2008.01.30_New_Leadership_ Statement.pdf

Crimson Staff. (2006, March 30). Harvard: Free tuition for families earning under $60K. *The Harvard Crimson*. Retrieved from http://www.thecrimson.com/article.aspx?ref=512382

Cross, K. P. (1977). Not can, but will college teaching be improved? *New Directions for Higher Education, 17,* 1–15.

Cross, K. P., & Steadman, M. H. (1996). *Classroom research: Implementing the scholarship of teaching.* San Francisco: Jossey-Bass.

Damast, A. (2008, February 3). Tuition assistance for the middle class. *BusinessWeek*. Retrieved from http://www.busi nessweek.com/bschools/content/feb2008/bs2008023_374181.htm

Dehn, P. F. (2009). Community health-based internships as an entry into research. In M. K. Boyd & J. L. Wesemann (Eds.), *Broadening participation in undergraduate research: Fostering excellence and enhancing impact* (pp. 334–336). Washington, DC: The Council on Undergraduate Research.

Diamond, R. M. (1995). *Preparing for promotion and tenure review: A faculty guide.* Bolton, MA: Anker.

Diamond, R. M. (2000). The department statement on promotion and tenure: A key to successful leadership. In A. F. Lucas (Ed.), *Leading academic change* (pp. 95–106). San Francisco: Jossey-Bass.

Diamond, R. M. (2002). *Serving on promotion, tenure, and faculty review committees: A faculty guide* (2nd ed.). San Francisco: Jossey-Bass.

Diamond, R. M. (2004). *Preparing for promotion, tenure, and annual review* (2nd ed.). San Francisco: Jossey-Bass.

Diamond, R. M. (2008). *Designing and assessing courses and curricula: A practical guide* (3rd ed.). San Francisco: Jossey-Bass.

Dicroce, D. M. (2006, September 1). Both lamp and mirror. *Chronicle of Higher Education*, B7–8.

Disciplinary Society and Education Alliance. (2009). *What works, what matters, what lasts: Disciplinary Society and Education Alliance.* Retrieved from http://www.pkal.org/documents/DSEA.cfm

Dittoe, W. (2002). The importance of physical space in learning. *New Directions for Teaching and Learning, 92*, 81–90.

Donald, J. G. (1995). Disciplinary differences in knowledge validation. *New Directions for Teaching and Learning, 64*, 7–17.

Donald, J. G. (2002). *Learning to think: Disciplinary perspectives.* New York: Jossey-Bass.

Dunn, D. S. (2006, January). *Teaching writing: Exercises and assessment methods for use across the psychology curriculum.* Presentation at the 28th Annual Meeting of the National Institute of the Teaching of Psychology, St. Petersburg Beach, FL.

Dunn, D. S., Brewer, C. L., Cautin, R. L., Gurung, R. A., Keith, K. D., McGregor, L. N., Nida, S. A., et al. (2010). The undergraduate psychology curriculum: Call for a core. In D. F. Halpern (Ed.), *Undergraduate education in psychology: A blueprint for the future of the discipline* (pp. 47–61). Washington, DC: American Psychological Association.

Dunn, D. S., McCarthy, M., Baker, S., Halonen, J. S., & Hill, G. W., IV. (2007). Quality benchmarks in undergraduate psychology programs. *American Psychologist, 62*, 650–670.

Dunn, D. S., Mehrotra, C., & Halonen, J. S. (Eds.). (2004). *Measuring up: Educational assessment challenges and practices for psychology.* Washington, DC: American Psychological Association.

Dunn, D. S., Wilson, J. C., Freeman, J., & Stowell, J. R. (Eds.). (In press). *Getting connected: Best practices for technology-enhanced teaching and learning in psychology.* New York: Oxford University Press.

Dunn, D. S., & Zaremba, S. B. (1997). Thriving at liberal arts colleges: The more "Compleat Academic." *Teaching of Psychology, 24,* 8–14.

Eaton, J. S. (2008a, July/August). Attending to student learning. *Change, 40*(4), 22–29.

Eaton, J. S. (2008b, December). Accreditation after the 2008 reauthorization of the Higher Education Act. General Session address at the annual meeting of the Commission on Colleges, Southern Association of Colleges and Schools (SACS), San Antonio, TX.

Ender, S. C., & Newton, F. B. (2000). *Students helping students: A guide for peer educators on college campuses.* San Francisco: Jossey-Bass.

Evans, N. J., Forney, D. S., Guido, F. M., Patton, L. D., & Renn, K. A. (2010). *Student development in college: Theory, research, and practice* (2nd ed.). San Francisco: Jossey-Bass.

Ewell, P. T. (2007). Accreditation in the hot seat [From the States column]. *Assessment Update, 19,* 11–13.

Ewell, P. T. (2008). Assessment and accountability in America today: Background and context. *New Directions for Institutional Research, S1,* 7–17.

Eyler, J., & Giles, D. E. (1999). *Where's the learning in service learning?* San Francisco: Jossey-Bass.

Facione, P. A. (2009, Summer). Adaptive budgeting: Thirty-four suggestions for raising revenues, cutting costs, retaining students, and saving jobs in hard times. *Liberal Education, 95*(3), 24–31.

Falconer, J., & Holcomb, D. (2008). Understanding undergraduate research experiences from the student perspective: A phenomenological study of a summer student research program. *College Student Journal, 42,* 869–878.

Finder, A. (2007, June 20). Some colleges to drop out of rankings by magazine. *New York Times,* A13.

Fink, L. D. (2003). *Creating significant learning experiences: An integrated approach to designing college courses.* San Francisco: Jossey-Bass.

Fitzgerald, C., & Kirby, L.K. (1997). *Developing leaders: Research and applications in psychological type and leadership development.* Palo Alto, CA: Davies-Black Publishing.

Foubert, J. D., & Cowell, E. A. (2004). Perceptions of a rape prevention program by fraternity men and male student athletes: Powerful effects and implications for changing behavior. *NASPA Journal, 42,* 1–20.

Foubert, J. D., & Grainger, L. U. (2006). Effects of involvement in clubs and organizations on the psychosocial development of first-year and senior college students. *NASPA Journal, 43*(1), 166–182.

Francis, P. L., & Steven, D. A. (2003). The SUNY assessment initiative: Initial campus and system perspectives. *Assessment & Evaluation in Higher Education, 28,* 333–349.

Friedman, T. L. (2007). *The world is flat 3.0: A brief history of the twenty-first century.* New York: Picador.

Fritschler, A. L., Weissburg, P., & Magness, P. (2008, Fall). Growing government demands for accountability vs. independence in the university. *Liberal Education, 94,* 40–47.

Gabelnick, F., MacGregor, J., Matthews, R. S., & Smith, B. L. (1990). *Learning communities: Creating connections among students, faculty, and disciplines.* San Francisco: Jossey-Bass.

Garrison, D. R., & Vaughan, N. D. (2008). *Blended learning in higher education: Framework, principles, and guidelines.* San Francisco: Jossey-Bass.

Germaine, M., & Scandura, T. A. (2005). Grade inflation and student individual differences as systematic bias in faculty evaluations. *Journal of Instructional Psychology, 32,* 58–67.

Gifford, R. (2002). Making a difference: Some ways environmental psychology has improved the world. In R. B. Bechtel & A. Churchman, (Eds.), *Handbook of environmental psychology* (pp. 323–334). New York: Wiley.

Gillespie, K. H., Hilsen, L. R., & Wadsworth, E. C. (Eds.). (2002). *A guide to faculty development: Practical advice, examples, and resources.* Bolton, MA: Anker.

Gilligan, C. (1982). *In a different voice: Psychological theory and women's development.* Cambridge, MA: Harvard University Press.

Glassick, C. E., Huber, M. T., & Maeroff, G. I. (1997). *Scholarship assessed: Evaluation of the professoriate.* San Francisco: Jossey-Bass.

Gordon, V. N., Habley, W. R., Grites, T. J., & Associates. (2008). *Academic advising: A comprehensive handbook* (2nd ed.). San Francisco: Jossey-Bass.

Graff, G., & Birkenstein, C. (2008, May-June). A progressive case for educational standardization. *Academe: Bulletin of the American Association of University Professors, 94*(3), 16–18.

Grappa, J. M., Austin, A. E., & Trice, A. G. (2007). *Rethinking faculty work: Higher education's strategic imperative.* San Francisco: Jossey-Bass.

Grasmuck, S., & Hyatt, S. (2003). Sequencing writing across liberal arts majors. *Peer Review, 6,* 18–20.

Green, M. F., & Shoenberg, R. (2006). *Where faculty live: Internationalizing the disciplines.* Washington, DC: American Council on Education.

Gurung, R. A. R., & Prieto, L. R. (2009). *Getting culture: Incorporating diversity across the curriculum.* Sterling, VA: Stylus.

Habley, W. R. (2003). Faculty advising: Practice and promise. In G. L. Kramer (Ed.), *Faculty advising examined: Enhancing the potential of college faculty as advisors* (pp. 23–37). Bolton, MA: Anker.

Habley, W. R., & Bloom, J. L. (2007). Giving advice that makes a difference. In G. L. Kramer and Associates (Eds.), *Fostering student success in the campus community* (pp. 171–192). San Francisco: Jossey-Bass.

Halonen, J. S., Bosack, T., Clay, S., & McCarthy, M. (with Dunn, D. S., Hill, G. W., IV, McEntarfer, R., Mehrotra, C., Nesmith, R., Weaver, K., & Whitlock, K.). (2003). A rubric for learning, teaching, and assessing scientific inquiry in psychology. *Teaching of Psychology, 30,* 196–208.

Halonen, J. S., & Ellenberg, G. B. (2006). Teaching evaluation follies: Misperception and misbehavior in student evaluations of teachers. In P. Seldin (Ed.), *Evaluating faculty performance: A practical guide* (pp. 150–165). San Francisco: Anker Publishing.

Halpern, D. F. (2004). Outcomes assessment 101. In D. S. Dunn, C. M. Mehrotra, & J. S. Halonen (Eds.), *Measuring up: Educational assessment challenges and practices for psychology* (pp. 11–26). Washington, DC: American Psychological Association.

Halpern, D. F., Smothergill, D. W., Allen, M., Baker, S., Baum, C., Best, D., et al. (1998). Scholarship in psychology: A paradigm for the twenty-first century. *American Psychologist*, 53, 1292–1297.

Harkavy, I., & Donovan, B. M. (Eds.). (2005). *Connecting past and present: Concepts and models for service learning in history.* Sterling, VA: Stylus.

Haworth, J. G., & Conrad, C. F. (1997). *Emblems of quality in higher education: Developing and sustaining high-quality programs.* Boston: Allyn and Bacon.

Henderson, B. B. (2007). *Teaching at the people's university.* Bolton, MA: Anker.

Hernandez, K., Hogan, S., Hathaway, C., & Lovell, C. D. (1999). Analysis of the literature on the impact of student involvement on student development and learning: More questions than answers? *NASPA Journal, 36,* 184–197.

Hersh, R. H., & Merrow, J. (Eds.). (2005). *Declining by degrees: Higher education at risk.* New York: Palgrave Macmillan.

Heubner, A. M., & Garrod, A. C. (1993). Moral reasoning among Tibetan monks: A study of Buddhist adolescents and young adults in Nepal. *Journal of Cross-Cultural Psychology,* 24, 167–185.

Hillard, V., and Harris, J. (2003). Making writing visible at Duke University. *Peer Review, 6*(1), 15–17.

Hu, S., Scheuch, K., Schwartz, R., Gayles, J. G., & Li, S. (Eds.). (2008). Reinventing undergraduate education: Engaging college students in research and creative activities [Special issue]. *ASHE Higher Education Report, 33*(4), 1–103.

Huber, M. T. (2006). Disciplines, pedagogy, and inquiry-based learning about teaching. *New Directions for Teaching and Learning, 107,* 69–77.

Huber, R. M. (1992). *How professors play the cat guarding the cream: Why we're paying more and getting less in higher education.* Fairfax, VA: George Mason University Press.

Hurd, S. N. (2004). *Building and sustaining learning communities: The Syracuse experience.* San Francisco: Jossey-Bass.

Hutchings, P. (1990, June 30). *Assessment and the way we work.* Closing plenary, 5th American Association of Higher Education Conference on Assessment, Washington, DC.

Jacoby, B., & Associates. (1996). *Service-learning in higher education.* San Francisco: Jossey-Bass.

Jamieson, P. (2003). Designing more effective on-campus teaching and learning spaces: A role for academic developers. *International Journal for Academic Development, 8,* 119–33.

Jamieson, P., Fisher, K., Gilding, T., Taylor, P., & Trevitt, A. (2000). Place and space in the design of new learning environments. *Higher Education Research and Development, 19,* 221–236.

Jaschik, S. (2009, January 15). Rejecting the academic fast track. *Inside Higher Ed.* Retrieved from http://insidehighered.com:80/news/2009/01/15/family

Johansen, C. K., & Harris, D. E. (2000). Teaching the ethics of biology. *American Biology Teacher, 62*(5), 352–358.

Katsinas, S. G., & Tollefson, T. A. (2009). *Funding and access issues in public higher education: A community college perspective. Findings from the 2009 survey of the national council of state directors of community colleges.* Education Policy Center, University of Alabama.

Kegan, R. (1994). *In over our heads: The mental demands of modern life.* Cambridge, MA: Harvard University Press.

Kells, H. R. (1980). *Self study processes: A guide for postsecondary institutions.* Washington, DC: American Council on Education.

Kershaw, T., Lazarus, F., Minier, J., & Associates. (2009). *Partnerships for service learning: Impacts on communities and students.* San Francisco: Jossey-Bass.

King, P. M., & Kitchener, K. S. (1994). *Developing reflective judgment: Understanding and promoting intellectual growth and critical thinking in adolescents and adults.* San Francisco: Jossey-Bass.

Kinzie, J., & Kuh, G. (2004). Going DEEP: Learning from campuses that share responsibility for student success. *About Campus, 9*(5), 2–8.

Knefelkamp, L. L. (1999). Introduction. In W. G. Perry, Jr., *Forms of ethical and intellectual development in the college years: A scheme.* San Francisco: Jossey-Bass.

Kohlberg, L. (1969). Stage and sequence: The cognitive developmental approach to socialization. In D. A. Goslin (Ed.), *Handbook of socialization theory and research* (pp. 347–480). Skokie, IL: Rand McNally.

Kohlberg, L. (1976). Moral stages and moralization: The cognitive-developmental approach. In T. Lickona (Ed.), *Moral development and behavior: Theory, research, and social issues.* New York: Holt.

Kolb, D. A. (1984). *Experiential learning: Experience as the source of learning and development.* Upper Saddle River, NJ: Prentice Hall.

Kramer, G. L. (Ed.). (2003). *Faculty advising examined: Enhancing the potential of college faculty as advisors.* Bolton, MA: Anker.

Kreber, C. (2002). Teaching excellence, teaching expertise, and the scholarship of teaching. *Innovative Higher Education, 27,* 5–23.

Kuh, G. D. (2008). *High-impact educational practices: What they are, who has access to them, and why they matter.* Washington, DC: AAC&U Press.

Kuh, G. D., Kinzie, J., Schuh, J. H., & Whitt, E. J. (2005, July/August). Never let it rest: Lessons about student success from high-performing colleges and universities. *Change, 37*(4), 44–51.

Kuh, G. D., Kinzie, J., Schuh, J. H., Whitt, E. J., & Associates. (2005). *Student success in college: Creating conditions that matter.* San Francisco: Jossey-Bass.

Laird, T. F., & Kuh, G. D. (2005). Student experiences with information technology and their relationship to other aspects of student engagement. *Research in Higher Education, 46,* 211–233.

Landrum, R. E., & Nelsen, L. R. (2002). The undergraduate research assistantship: An analysis of the benefits. *Teaching of Psychology, 29,* 15–19.

Lang, J. M. (2005). *Life on the tenure track: Lessons from the first year.* Baltimore: Johns Hopkins University Press.

Lattuca, L. R., & Stark, J. S. (2009). *Shaping the college curriculum: Academic plans in context.* San Francisco: Jossey-Bass.

Laufgraben, J. L., Shapiro, N. S., & Associates. (2004). *Sustaining and improving learning communities.* San Francisco: Jossey-Bass.

Leaming, D. R. (1998). *Academic leadership: A practical guide to chairing the department.* Bolton, MA: Anker.

Leiter, M. P., & Maslach, C. (2000). *Preventing burnout and building engagement: A complete program for organizational renewal.* San Francisco: Jossey-Bass.

Leiter, M. P., & Maslach, C. (2005). *Banishing burnout: Six strategies for improving your relationship with work.* San Francisco: Jossey-Bass.

Levy, J., Burton, G., Mickler, S., & Vigorito, M. (1999). A curriculum matrix for psychology program review. *Teaching of Psychology, 26,* 291–294.

Licata, C. M. (1986). *Post-tenure faculty evaluation: Threat or opportunity?* (ASHE-ERIC Higher Education Report No. 1). Washington, DC: Association for the Study of Higher Education. (ED270009)

Licata, C. M., & Morreale, J. C. (2006). *Post-tenure faculty review and renewal III: Outcomes and impact.* Bolton, MA: Anker.

Lisman, C. D., & Harvey, I. E. (Eds.). (2006). *Beyond the tower: Concepts and models for service learning in philosophy.* Sterling, VA: Stylus.

Lockie, N. M., & Van Lanen, R. J. (2008). Impact of supplemental instruction experience on science SI leaders. *Journal of Developmental Education, 31*(3), 2–14.

Logan, R., Snarey, J., & Schrader, D. (1990). Autonomous versus heteronomous moral judgment types. *Journal of Cross-Cultural Psychology, 21,* 71–89.

Loher, B. T., & Landrum, R. E. (2010). Building a psychology orientation course: Common themes and exercises. In D. S. Dunn, B. C. Beins, M. A. McCarthy, & G. W. Hill IV (Eds.), *Best practices for teaching beginnings and endings in the psychology major: Research, cases, and recommendations* (pp. 49–68). New York: Oxford.

Lopatto, D. (2007). Undergraduate research experiences support science career decisions and active learning. *CBE-Life Sciences Education,* 6, 297–306. DOI: 10.1187/cbe.07–06–0038.

Lopez, C. L. (2000, April). Assessing student learning: Using the Commission's Levels of Implementation. Paper presented at the meeting of the North Central Association of Colleges and Schools Commission on Institutions of Higher Education, Chicago, IL.

Lyall, K. C., & Sell, K. R. (2006). *The true genius of America at risk: Are we losing our public universities to de facto privatization?* American

Council on Education/Praeger series on higher education. Westport, CT: Praeger.

Maki, P. L. (2001). From standardized tests to alternative methods: Some current resources on methods to assess learning in general education. *Change, 33*(2), 29–31.

Maki, P. L. (2004). *Assessing for learning: Building a sustainable commitment across the institution.* Sterling, VA: Stylus.

Maki, R. H., & Maki, W. S. (2007). Online courses. In F. T. Durso, S. Dumais, S. Lewandowsky, & T. J. Perfect (Eds.), *Handbook of applied cognition* (pp. 527–552). West Sussex, England: Wiley.

Malcom, S. M., Chubin, D. E., & Jesse, J. K. (2004). *Standing our ground: A guidebook for STEM educators in a post-Michigan era.* Washington, DC: American Association for the Advancement of Science.

Marcia, J. E. (1966). Development and validation of ego-identity status. *Journal of Personality and Social Psychology, 3,* 551–558.

Martin, L. M. (2000). The relationship of college experiences to psychosocial outcomes in students. *Journal of College Student Development, 41,* 294–303.

Maryland Higher Education Commission (2004). *2004 Student learning outcomes assessment reports.* Retrieved from http://www.mhec.state.md.us/publications/research/2004Studies/2004SLOAR.pdf

Maslach, C., Schaufeli, W. B., & Leiter, M. P. (2001). Job burnout. *Annual Review of Psychology, 52,* 397–422.

Mason, M. A., Goulden, M., & Frasch, K. (2009, January-February). Why graduate students reject the fast track: A study of thousands of doctoral students shows that they want balanced lives. *Academe Online.* Washington, DC: American Association of University Professors. Retrieved from http://www.aaup.org/AAUP/pubsres/academe/2009/JF/Feat/maso.htm

Massy, W. F., Graham, S. W., & Short, P. M. (2007). *Academic quality work: A handbook for improvement.* Bolton, MA; Anker.

Matchett, N. J. (2008). Ethics across the curriculum. *New Directions for Higher Education, 142,* 25–38.

McCoy, J. M. (2002). Work environments. In R. B. Bechtel & A. Churchman (Eds.), *Handbook of environmental psychology,* (pp. 443–460). New York: Wiley.

McGuinness, A. C. (1996). A model for successful restructuring. In T. L. MacTaggart & C. L. Crist (Eds.), *Restructuring in higher education: What works and what doesn't in reorganizing governing systems* (pp. 203–229). San Francisco: Jossey-Bass.

McKeachie, W. J. (1997). Student ratings: The validity of use. *American Psychologist, 52,* 1218–1225.

McKeachie, W. J. (2002). *McKeachie's teaching tips: Strategies, research, and theory for college and university teachers* (11th ed.). Boston: Houghton Mifflin.

McKeachie, W., & Svinicki, M. (2005). *McKeachie's teaching tips: Strategies, research, and theory for college and university teachers* (12th ed.). Belmont, CA: Wadsworth.

McKinney, K. (2004). The scholarship of teaching and learning: Past lessons, current challenges, and future visions. *To Improve the Academy, 22*, 3–19.

McKinney, K. (2007). *Enhancing learning through the scholarship of teaching and learning.* Bolton, MA: Anker.

Mentkowski, M., Rogers, G., Doherty, A., Loacker, G., Hart, J. R., Richards, W., et al. (2000). *Learning that lasts: Integrating learning, development, and performance in college and beyond.* San Francisco: Jossey-Bass.

Middaugh, M. F. (2001). *Understanding faculty productivity: Standards and benchmarks for colleges and universities.* San Francisco: Jossey-Bass.

Miller, M. (2006, September 22). The legitimacy of assessment. *Chronicle of Higher Education*, B24.

Millett, C. M., Stickler, L. M., Payne, D. G., & Dwyer, C. A. (2007). *A culture of evidence: Critical features of assessment for postsecondary student learning.* Princeton, NJ: Educational Testing Service. Retrieved from http://www.ets.org/Media/Resources_For/Higher_Education/pdf/4418_COEII.pdf

Monroe, J. (2003, Fall). Writing and the disciplines. *Peer Review, 6*(1), 4–7.

Moos, M. S. (2002). 2001 invited address: The mystery of human context and coping: An unraveling of clues. *American Journal of Community Psychology, 30*, 67–88.

Morrill, R. L. (2007). *Integrating strategy and leadership in colleges and universities.* Washington, DC: American Council on Education.

Morris, S. J., McConnaughay, K. D., & Wolffe, R. J. (2009). Empowering undergraduates to lead teams of researchers with different levels of experience and perspectives. In M. K. Boyd & J. L. Wesemann (Eds.), *Broadening participation in undergraduate research: Fostering excellence and enhancing impact* (pp. 179–190). Washington, DC: The Council on Undergraduate Research.

Morrison, S. D., & Talbott, L. L. (2005). TRUCE for advocacy and peer education in tobacco prevention. *Journal of American College Health, 54*, 193–195.

Moses, Y. T. (2002) *Diversity, globalism, and democracy: Higher education's imperative.* Retrieved from http://www.salzburgseminar.org/reports/AAHE_Diversity.pdf

Myers, D. G., & Waller, J. E. (1999). Reflections on scholarship from the liberal arts academy. *American Psychologist, 54*, 358–361.

Myers, I. B., & McCaulley, M. H. (1985). *Manual: A guide to the development and use of the Myers-Briggs Type Indicator.* Palo Alto, CA: Consulting Psychologists Press.

National Academic Advising Association (NACADA). (2005). *NACADA statement of core values of academic advising.* Retrieved from http://www.nacada.ksu.edu/Clearinghouse/AdvisingIssues/Core-Values.htm

National Academies of Sciences. (2007). *Rising above the storm: Energizing and employing America for a brighter economic future.* Retrieved from http://www.nap.edu/catalog/11462.html

National Association of Biology Teachers. (2009). *Guidelines for evaluation of four-year undergraduate biology.* Retrieved from http://www.nabt.org/websites/institution/index.php?p=118

National Science Foundation. (2006). *National Center for Education Statistics, Integrated Postsecondary Education Data System, Completions Survey, 1997–2006.* Retrieved from http://www.nsf.gov/statistics/wmpd/pdf/tabc-4.pdf

National Survey of Student Engagement. (2009). *Benchmarks of effective educational practice.* Retrieved from http://nsse.iub.edu/pdf/nsse_benchmarks.pdf

Nelson, C.E. (2007). Student diversity requires different approaches to college teaching, even in math and science. In *Volume IV: What works, what matters, what lasts.* Retrieved from Project Kaleidoscope website: http://www.pkal.org/documents/Student%20Diversity%20Requires%20Different%20Approaches%20to%20College%20Teaching.pdf

Nicol, A.A.M., & Pexman, P. M. (1999). *Presenting your findings: A practical guide for creating tables.* Washington, DC: American Psychological Association.

Nicol, A.A.M., & Pexman, P. M. (2003). *Displaying your findings: A practical guide for creating figures, posters, and presentations.* Washington, DC: American Psychological Association.

O'Brien, J. G., Millis, B. J., & Cohen, M. W. (2008). *The course syllabus: A learning-centered approach* (2nd ed.). San Francisco: Jossey-Bass.

O'Conner, P. T. (1999). *Words fail me: What everyone who writes should know about writing.* New York: Harcourt Brace.

Olson, C. L., Green, M. F., & Hill, B. A. (2005). *Building a strategic framework for comprehensive internationalization.* Washington, DC: American Council on Education.

O'Meara, K. A. (2005). Encouraging multiple forms of scholarship in faculty reward systems: Does it make a difference? *Research in Higher Education, 46,* 479–510.

O'Meara, K., & Rice, R. E. (Eds.). (2005). *Faculty priorities reconsidered: Rewarding multiple forms of scholarship.* San Francisco: Jossey-Bass.

Osborn, J. M., & Karukstis, K. K. (2009). The benefits of undergraduate research, scholarship, and creative activity. In M. K. Boyd & J. L. Wesemann (Eds.), *Broadening participation in undergraduate research: Fostering excellence and enhancing impact* (pp. 41–53). Washington, DC: The Council on Undergraduate Research.

Ozar, D. T. (2001). An outcomes centered approach to teaching ethics. *Teaching Ethics, 2,* 1–29.

Palloff, R. M., & Pratt, K. (2005). *Collaborating online: Learning together in community.* San Francisco: Jossey-Bass.

Palloff, R. M., & Pratt, K. (2007). *Building online learning communities: Effective strategies for the virtual classroom.* San Francisco: Jossey-Bass.

Palloff, R. M., & Pratt, K. (2009). *Assessing the online learner: Resources and strategies for faculty.* San Francisco: Jossey-Bass.

Paris, S. G., & Ayres, L. R. (1994). *Becoming reflective students and teachers with portfolios and authentic assessment.* Washington, DC: American Psychological Association.

Pascarella, E. T., & Terenzini, P. T. (2005). *How college affects students: A third decade of research.* San Francisco: Jossey-Bass.

Payette, P., & Shaw, A. (2008, October 24). Risks and rewards of being an organizational change agent. Paper presented at Professional Organizational Development/NCSPOD 2008 Joint Conference Reno, NV.

Perry, W. G., Jr. (1968). *Forms of ethical and intellectual development in the college years: A scheme.* New York: Holt, Rinehart, & Winston.

Perry, W. G., Jr. (1981). Cognitive and ethical growth: The making of meaning. In A. W. Chickering & Associates (Eds.), *The modern American college: Responding to the new realities of diverse students and a changing society* (pp. 76–116). San Francisco: Jossey-Bass.

Perry, W. G., Jr. (1999). *Forms of ethical and intellectual development in the college years: A scheme.* San Francisco: Jossey-Bass.

Philipsen, M. I. (2008). *Challenges of the faculty career for women: Success and sacrifice.* New York: Anker.

Pittenger, D. (1993, November). Measuring the MBTI . . . and coming up short. *Journal of Career Planning and Employment, 54,* 48–52.

Project Kaleidoscope. (1998). *What difference do improved facilities make? A report of the Project Kaleidoscope Committee of Visitors.* Washington, DC: Project Kaleidoscope.

Project Kaleidoscope. (2008a). *Follow-up report: Characteristics of the ideal department.* http://www.pkal.org/documents/FollowUp Report-TheIdealDepartment.cfm

Project Kaleidoscope (2008b). *Volume IV: What works, what matters, what lasts: Characteristics of ideal spaces for science.* Retrieved from http://www.pkal.org/documents/Vol4CharacteristicsOfIdealSpaces.cfm

Pusateri, T. P., Poe, R. E., Addison, W. E., & Goedel, G. D. (2004). Designing and implementing psychology program reviews. In D. S. Dunn, C. M. Mehrotra, & J. S. Halonen (Eds.), *Measuring up: Educational assessment challenges and practices for psychology* (pp. 65–89). Washington, DC: American Psychological Association.

Rama, D. V. (Ed.). (1998). *Learning by doing: Concepts and models for service learning in accounting.* Washington, DC: American Association for Higher Education.

Rossman, J. E., & El-Khawas, E. (1987). *Thinking about assessment: Perspectives for presidents and chief academic officers.* Washington, DC: American Council on Education and the American Association for Higher Education.

Rowley, D. J. (2001). *From strategy to change: Implementing the plan in higher education.* San Francisco: Jossey-Bass.

Sadler, D. R. (1998). Formative assessment: revisiting the territory. *Assessment in Education, 5*(1), 77–84.

Salen, K. (Ed.). (2008). *The ecology of games: Connecting youth, games, and learning.* Cambridge, MA: MIT Press.

Saroyan, A., & Amundsen, C. L. (Eds.). (2004). *Rethinking teaching in higher education: From a course design workshop to a faculty development framework.* Sterling, VA: Stylus.

Schneider, C. G., & Schoenberg, R. (1998). *The academy in transition: Contemporary understandings of liberal education.* Washington, DC: American Association of Colleges and Universities.

Seldin, P. (1984). *Changing practices in faculty evaluation: A critical assessment and recommendations for improvement.* San Francisco: Jossey-Bass.

Seldin, P. (2004). *The teaching portfolio: A practical guide to improved performance and promotion/tenure decisions* (3rd ed.). San Francisco: Anker.

Seldin, P., & Higgerson, M. L. (2002). *The administrative portfolio: A practical guide to improved administrative performance and personnel decisions.* Bolton, MA: Anker.

Seldin, P., & Miller, J. E. (2009). *The academic portfolio: A practical guide to documenting teaching, research, and service.* San Francisco: Jossey-Bass.

Seymour, E., Hunter, A. B., Laursen, S. L., & Deantoni, T. (2004). Establishing the benefits of research experiences in the sciences: First findings from a three year study. *Science Education, 88,* 493–534. DOI: 10.1002/sce.10131.

Shapiro, N. S., & Levine, J. H. (1999). *Creating learning communities: A practical guide to winning support, organizing for change, and implementing programs.* San Francisco: Jossey-Bass.

Shavelson, R. J., & Huang, L. (2003, January/February). Responding responsibly to the frenzy to assess learning in higher education. *Change, 35,* 11–19.

Slattery, P. (2006). *Curriculum development in the postmodern era* (2nd ed.). New York: Routledge.

Smith, B. L., MacGregor, J., Matthews, R. S., & Gabelnick, F. (2004). *Learning communities: Reforming undergraduate education.* San Francisco: Jossey-Bass.

Smith, C. (2008). Building effectiveness in teaching through targeted evaluation and response: Connecting evaluation to teaching improvement in higher education. *Assessment & Evaluation in Higher Education, 33,* 517–533.

Springer, L., Stanne, M. E., & Donovan, S. S. (1999). Effects of small-group learning on undergraduates in science, mathematics, engineering, and technology: A meta-analysis. *Review of Educational Research, 69,* 21–51.

Stanley, C. A. (2006). *Faculty of color: Teaching in predominantly white colleges and universities.* New York: Anker.

Stevens, D. D., & Levi, A. J. (2004). *Introduction to rubrics: An assessment tool to save grading time, convey effective feedback and promote student learning.* Sterling, VA: Stylus.

Stevens, K. E., Kruck, S. E., Hawkins, J., & Baker, S. C. (in press). Second Life as a tool for engaging students across the curriculum. In P. Zemliansky & D. M. Wilcox (Eds.), *Design and implementation of educational games: Theoretical and practical perspectives.* Hershey, PA: Information Science Publishing.

Stone, M. E., & Jacobs, G. (Eds.). (2006). *Editors' notes. New Directions for Teaching and Learning, 106,* 1–2.

Stout, M. L., & McDaniel, A. J. (2006). Benefits to supplemental instruction leaders. *New Directions for Teaching and Learning, 106,* 55–62. DOI: 10.1002/tl.233.

Strange, C., & Banning, J. (2001). *Educating by design: Creating campus learning environments that work.* San Francisco: Jossey-Bass.

Strunk, W., Jr., & White, E. B. (1972). *The elements of style.* New York: Macmillan.

Studer, Q. (2004). *Hardwiring excellence: Purpose, worthwhile work, making a difference.* Gulf Breeze, FL: Fire Starter Publishing.

Sullivan, W. M., & Rosin, M. S. (2008). *A new agenda for higher education: Shaping a life of the mind for practice.* San Francisco: Jossey-Bass.

Suskie, L. (2004). *Assessing student learning: A common sense guide.* Bolton, MA: Anker.

Suskie, L. (2009). *Assessing student learning: A common sense guide* (2nd ed.). San Francisco: Jossey-Bass.

Tchudi, S., & Lafer, S. (1996). *The interdisciplinary teacher's handbook: Integrated teaching across the curriculum.* Portsmouth, NH: Heinemann.

Temple, P. (2008). Learning spaces in higher education: An under-researched topic. *London Review of Education, 6,* 229–241.

Terenzini, P. T., Pascarella, E. T., & Blimling, G. S. (1996). Students' out-of-class experiences and their influence on learning and cognitive development: A literature review. *Journal of College Student Development, 37,* 149–162.

Theall, M. (2002). Leadership in faculty evaluation. In R. M. Diamond & B. Adam (Eds.), *Field guide to academic leadership* (pp. 257–270). San Francisco: Jossey-Bass.

Thompson, W. B., Vermette, P. J., & Wisniewski, S. A. (2004). Ten cooperative learning activities for the cognitive psychology course. *Teaching of Psychology, 31,* 134–136.

Tierney, W. G. (2002). Mission and vision statements: An essential first step. In R. M. Diamond & B. Adam (Eds.), *Field guide to academic leadership* (pp. 49–58). San Francisco: Jossey-Bass.

Traxler, J. (2007, March). Advising without walls: An introduction to Facebook as an advising tool. *Academic Advising Today,* 30(1). Retrieved from http://www.nacada.ksu.edu/AAT/NW30_1.htm#10

Tsang, E. (Ed.). (2000). *Projects that matter: Concepts and models for service-learning in engineering.* Washington, DC: American Association for Higher Education.

Tucker, A. (1993). *Chairing the academic department.* Phoenix, AZ: Oryx Press.

Tufte, E. R. (1990). *Envisioning information.* Cheshire, CT: Graphics Press.

Tufte, E. R. (1997). *Visual explanations: Images and quantities, evidence and narrative.* Cheshire, CT: Graphics Press.

Tufte, E. R. (2001). *The visual display of quantitative information.* Cheshire, CT: Graphics Press.

Twale, D. J., & De Luca, B. M. (2008). *Faculty incivility: The rise of the academic bully culture and what to do about it.* San Francisco: Jossey-Bass.

Umbach, P. D., & Porter, S. R. (2002). How do academic departments impact student satisfaction? Understanding the contextual effects of departments. *Research in Higher Education, 43,* 209–234.

Umbach, P. D., & Wawrynski, M. R. (2005). Faculty do matter: The role of college faculty in student learning and engagement. *Research in Higher Education, 46,* 153–184.

van den Berg, I., Admiraal, W., & Pilot, A. (2006). Peer assessment in university teaching: Evaluating seven course designs. *Assessment and Evaluation in Higher Education, 31,* 19–36.

Walvoord, B. E. (2004). *Assessment clear and simple: A practical guide for institutions, departments, and general education.* San Francisco: Jossey-Bass.

Walvoord, B. E., & Anderson, V. J. (2009). *Effective grading: A tool for learning and assessment in college* (2nd ed.). San Francisco: Jossey-Bass.

Ward, H. (Ed.). (2006). *Acting locally: Concepts and models for service-learning in environmental studies.* Sterling, VA: Stylus.

Webb, K. M., Schaller, M. A., & Hunley, S. A. (2008). Measuring library space use and preferences: Charting a path toward increased engagement. *Portal: Libraries and the Academy, 8,* 407–422.

Weimer, M. (2006). *Enhancing scholarly work on teaching and learning: Professional literature that makes a difference.* San Francisco: Jossey-Bass.

Werder, C., & Otis, M. M. (2009). *Engaging student voices in the study of teaching and learning.* Sterling, VA: Stylus.

Wergin, J. F. (2002). Academic program review. In R. M. Diamond & B. Adam (Eds.), *Field guide to academic leadership* (pp. 241–255). San Francisco: Jossey-Bass.

Wergin, J. F. (2003). *Departments that work: Building and sustaining cultures of excellence in academic programs.* Bolton, MA: Anker.

Wergin, J. F., & Swingen, J. N. (2000). *Departmental assessment: How some colleges are effectively evaluating the collective work of faculty.* Washington, DC: American Association for Higher Education.

West, J. A., & West, M. L. (2009). *Using wikis for online collaboration: The power of the read-write web.* San Francisco: Jossey-Bass.

Wheeler, D. W., Seagren, A. T., Becker, L. W., Kinley, R. R., Mlinek, D. D., & Robson, K. J. (2008). *The academic chair's handbook* (2nd ed.). San Francisco: Jossey-Bass.

Whicker, M. L., Kronenfeld, J. J., & Strickland, R. A. (1993). *Getting tenure.* Newbury Park, CA: Sage.

Wiggins, G. (1990). *The case for authentic assessment.* ERIC Digest. Retrieved from http://ericae.net/edo/ed328611.htm.(ED328611)

Wineberg, S. S., & Grossman, P. L. (2000). *Interdisciplinary curriculum: Challenges to implementation.* New York: Teachers College Press.

Winter, D. G., McClelland, D. L., & Stewart, A. J. (1981). *A new case for the liberal arts: Assessing institutional goals and student development.* San Francisco: Jossey-Bass.

Wolfe, C. R., & Haynes, C. (2003). Interdisciplinary writing assessment profiles. *Issues in Integrative Studies, 21,* 126–170.

Zanna, M. P., Darley, J. M., & Roediger, H. L. (Eds.). (2003). *The compleat academic: A career guide.* Washington, DC: American Psychological Association.

Zinsser, W. (1990). *On writing well: An information guide to writing nonfiction* (4th ed.). New York: Harper.

Zubizarreta, J. (2004). *The learning portfolio: Reflective practice for improving student learning.* Bolton, MA: Anker.

Index